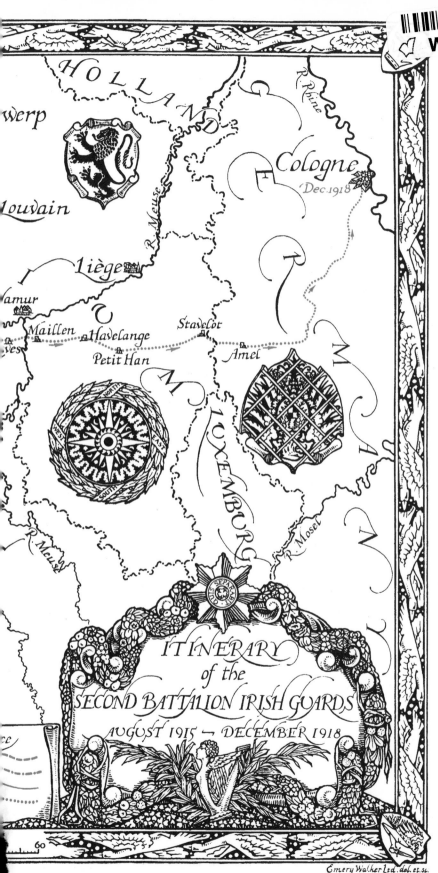

THE
IRISH
GUARDS

SECOND
BATTALION

1915

1916

1917

1918

ITINERARY
of the
SECOND BATTALION IRISH GUARDS
AUGUST 1915 — DECEMBER 1918

Emery Walker Ltd. del. et. sc.

Rudyard Kipling

THE
IRISH
GUARDS
IN THE
GREAT
WAR

THE SECOND BATTALION

Rudyard Kipling

THE IRISH GUARDS IN THE GREAT WAR

THE SECOND BATTALION

EDITED AND COMPILED FROM THEIR
DIARIES AND PAPERS

SARPEDON

New York

Published in the United States by
SARPEDON

Published in the UK in 1997 by
Spellmount Ltd
The Old Rectory, Staplehurst, Kent TN12 0AZ

Library of Congress Cataloging-in-Publication Data available.

ISBN 1-885119-50-X

Set in New Century Schoolbook
Designed and produced by Pardoe Blacker Publishing Limited
Lingfield · Surrey · England

Manufactured in Hong Kong.

10 9 8 7 6 5 4 3 2 1

Contents

PUBLISHER'S NOTE   *page* 6

FOREWORD: LIEUTENANT JOHN KIPLING   7

INTRODUCTION   9

1915   LOOS AND THE FIRST AUTUMN   15
        Loos; The Hohenzollern and Trench Work; A Raid;
        A Rest and Laventie.

1916   THE SALIENT AND THE SOMME   55
        The Salient for the First Time; After Hooge;
        The Raid of the 2nd July; The Somme; Ginchy;
        Mud-fighting on the Somme.

1917   RANCOURT TO BOURLON WOOD   111
        The German Withdrawal; Fatigues on the Somme;
        Third Ypres and Boesinghe; Bourlon Wood.

1918   ARRAS TO THE END   163
        Vieux-Berquin.

COMMANDING OFFICERS: 2ND BATTALION   194

Appendix A: OFFICERS: KILLED IN ACTION OR DIED OF WOUNDS ·   195
              WOUNDED IN ACTION · MISSING · REWARDS

Appendix B: REWARDS TO OFFICERS OF THE FIRST AND SECOND   199
              BATTALIONS: Extracts from the *London Gazette*

Appendix C: W.O.S, N.C.O.S AND MEN KILLED IN ACTION OR DIED   205
              OF WOUNDS OR DISEASE

Appendix D: W.O.S, N.C.O.S AND MEN: FIRST AND SECOND   213
              BATTALIONS · REWARDS

INDEX   217

Publisher's Note

THE PUBLISHERS gratefully acknowledge the permission of A.P. Watt, on behalf of the National Trust, to reproduce the original text for this edition.

The publishers would particularly like to thank Colonel Frank Groves and his colleagues at the RHQ Irish Guards for the invaluable assistance they have given with the production of this edition. Access has been provided to the regimental records and all the photographs used have come from the Irish Guards archives with the exception of the photograph of John Kipling's grave which has been kindly supplied by Mr A. E. Abear. The foreword on John Kipling is also reproduced by kind permission of the Irish Guards. In addition the publishers would like to thank Elizabeth Inglis, the archivist of the Kipling archives at the University of Sussex; David Fox, the administrator at Bateman's and George Webb, the Editor of *The Kipling Journal* who provided valuable information about how this history was commissioned by the Irish Guards.

As far as possible the punctuation and style of spelling of the original 1923 edition have been maintained.

Lieutenant John Kipling

Reproduced from the *Irish Guards Journal,*
Number 52, 1993

JOHN KIPLING, only son of Rudyard Kipling, was born on 17th August 1897 when his writer father was already famous. The boy, who was the model for Dem in *Puck of Pook's Hill*, was destined by his father for the Navy but his poor eyesight prevented his being accepted.

On the outbreak of war on 4th August 1914, Rudyard Kipling spoke to his friend Lord Roberts of the Irish Guards and, poor eyesight notwithstanding, John Kipling was commissioned second lieutenant in the Irish Guards. After training at Warley he went to France on 12th August 1915 to join the 2nd Battalion. He was then days short of his eighteenth birthday and, because of his youth, Kipling père had to consent to his being sent on active service. He did so, according to his biographer, 'with a heavy heart and was full of foreboding'. John Kipling became commander of Number 5 platoon, 2 Company. On 27th October 1915 he was posted as 'Missing' at Loos. In a letter to Rudyard Kipling, Major John Bird, company commander, described John Kipling as having been wounded in the action and spoke of his gallantry, coolness and ability to handle men and expressed his own affection for the young man. It was at first hoped that Kipling had been taken prisoner and, such was the fame of Rudyard Kipling, the Royal Flying Corps dropped leaflets over the German lines seeking help in ascertaining whether 'this son of a world famous author' was dead or alive. No news came, and in the absence of any information it was assumed that he had been killed and he was eventually listed as such in the appendix of this book.

Kipling and his wife were deeply distressed by the death of their only son. Kipling expressed a stoic resignation. 'I hear he finished well' he wrote. 'It was a short life. I'm sorry that all the years' work ended in that one afternoon'. He went to France and visited Puits Wood where John Kipling had last been seen. 'A bitter business and sad, even for those who know where their boys are laid' he wrote. It was at Kipling's suggestion that the words 'Known unto God' were used on the headstones of the unidentified. He himself died in 1936, not knowing where John was buried.*

* He had arranged for a British gardener, employed by the War Graves Commission, to sound the Last Post every night at the Menin Gate in remembrance of his son. This continued until the Germans overran Ypres in 1940.

In 1919, during the battlefield clearance which followed the end of the war, an examination of the records relating to St Mary's Advanced Dressing Station Cemetery revealed that one of the bodies was that of a lieutenant of the Irish Guards found near Puits 14, east of Loos village. The body had remained in No-man's land from 1915 until 1917 when it lay just within the Allied lines. It was exhumed and re-buried in Plot 7, Row D, Grave 2 and marked by a headstone inscribed 'AN UNKNOWN LIEUTENANT OF THE IRISH GUARDS'.

Then in 1992 an observant and a diligent officer of the Commonwealth War Graves' Commission, researching into officers of the Irish Guards killed or missing in the Battle of Loos on 27th September 1915, noticed an apparent anomaly in the Commissions' Records. The body that lay in St Mary's Advanced Dressing Station Cemetery was recorded as having been recovered from Block G25 C68. The area is mapped into squares and the location given in the records lies five miles west of Loos, an area where the Irish Guards had not been in action. A simple transposition of H for G would give the exact spot where John Kipling had been seen on the day he went missing on 27th September 1915. Because the Battle of September/October 1915 was the only action involving the Irish Guards near Loos, and John Kipling the only Irish Guards Lieutenant whose body was unaccounted for from the action it is beyond doubt that the 'unknown Lieutenant of the Irish Guards' must be John Kipling. The War Graves Commission have replaced the headstone that marked the grave with one bearing the inscription 'LIEUTENANT JOHN KIPLING, IRISH GUARDS, 27TH SEPTEMBER 1915, AGE 18' and have supplied a photograph of the head stone. The misattribution of one letter of the alphabet by a clerk in a Labour Company over seventy years ago led to confusion which has now been settled and the fate of John Kipling with it.

Introduction

THESE VOLUMES try to give soberly and with what truth is possible, the experiences of both Battalions of the Irish Guards from 1914 to 1918. The point of view is the Battalions', and the facts mainly follow the Regimental Diaries, supplemented by the few private letters and documents which such a war made possible, and by some tales that have gathered round men and their actions. As evidence is released, historians may be able to reconstruct what happened in or behind the battle-line; what motives and necessities swayed the actors; and who stood up or failed under his burden. But a battalion's field is bounded by its own vision. Even within these limits, there is large room for error. Witnesses to phases of fights die and are dispersed; the ground over which they fought is battered out of recognition in a few hours; survivors confuse dates, places and personalities, and in the trenches, the monotony of the waiting days and the repetition-work of repairs breed mistakes and false judgements. Men grow doubtful or over-sure, and, in all good faith, give directly opposed versions. The clear sight of a comrade so mangled that he seems to have been long dead is burnt in on one brain to the exclusion of all else that happened that day. The shock of an exploded dump, shaking down a firmament upon the landscape, dislocates memory throughout half a battalion; and so on in all matters, till the end of laborious enquiry is too often the opening of fresh confusion. When to this are added the personal prejudices and misunderstandings of men under heavy strain, carrying clouded memories of orders half given or half heard, amid scenes that pass like nightmares, the only wonder to the compiler of these records has been that any sure fact whatever should be retrieved out of the whirlpools of war.

It seemed to him best, then, to abandon all idea of such broad and balanced narratives as will be put forward by experts, and to limit himself to matters which directly touched the men's lives and fortunes. Nor has he been too careful to correct the inferences of the time by the knowledge of later events. From first to last, the Irish Guards, like the rest of our Armies, knew little of what was going on round them. Probably they knew less at the close of the War than at the beginning when our forces were so small that each man felt himself somebody indeed, and so stood to be hunted through the heat from Mons to Meaux, turned again to suffer beneath the Soupir ridges, and endured the first hideous winter of The

Salient where, wet, almost weaponless, but unbroken, he helped in the long miracle of holding the line.

But the men of '14 and '15, and what meagre records of their day were safe to keep, have long been lost; while the crowded years between remove their battles across dead Belgian towns and villages as far from us as the fights in Homer.

Doubtless, all will be reconstructed to the satisfaction of future years when, if there be memory beyond the grave, the ghosts may laugh at the neatly groomed histories. Meantime, we can take it for granted that the old Regular Army of England passed away in the mud of Flanders in less than a year. In training, morale, endurance, courage and devotion the Earth did not hold its like, but it possessed neither the numbers, guns, nor equipment necessary for the type of war that overtook it. The fact of its unpreparedness has been extolled as proof of the purity of its country's ideals, which must be great consolation to all concerned. But, how slowly that equipment was furnished, how inadequate were our first attempts at bombs, trench-mortars, duck-boards, wiring and the rest, may be divined through the loyal and guarded allusions in the Diaries. Nor do private communications give much hint of it, for one of the marvels of that marvellous time was the silence of those concerned on everything that might too much distress their friends at home. The censorship had imposed this as a matter of precaution, but only the spirit of the officers could have backed the law so completely; and, as better days came, their early makeshifts and contrivances passed out of remembrance with their early dead. But the sufferings of our Armies were constant. They included wet and cold in due season, dirt always, occasional vermin, exposure, extreme fatigue, and the hourly incidence of death in every shape along the front line and, later, in the farthest back-areas where the enemy aeroplanes harried their camps. And when our Regular troops had been expended, these experiences were imposed upon officers and men compelled to cover, within a few months, the long years of training that should go to the making of a soldier – men unbroken even to the disturbing impact of crowds and like experiences, which the conscript accepts from his youth. Their short home-leaves gave them sudden changes to the tense home atmosphere where, under cover of a whirl of "entertainment," they and their kin wearied themselves to forget and escape a little from that life, on the brink of the next world, whose guns they could hear summoning in the silences between their talk. Yet, some were glad to return – else why should youngsters of three years' experience have found themselves upon a frosty night, on an iron-bound French road, shouting aloud for joy as they heard the stammer of a machine-gun over the rise, and turned up the well-known trench that led to their own dug-out and their brethren from whom they had been separated by the vast interval of ninety-six hours? Many have confessed to the same delight in their work, as there were others to whom almost every hour was frankly detestable except for the companionship that revealed them one to another till the chances of war separated the companions. And there were, too, many, almost children, of whom no record remains. They came out from Warley with the constantly renewed drafts, lived the span of a Second Lieutenant's life and were spent. Their intimates might pre-serve, perhaps, memories of a promise cut short, recollections of a phrase that stuck, a chance-seen act of bravery or of kindness. The Diaries give their names and fates with the conventional expressions of regret. In most instances, the compiler has let the mere fact suffice; since, to his mind, it did not seem fit to heap words on the doom.

For the same reason, he has not dealt with each instance of valour, leav-ing it to stand in the official language in which it was acknowledged. The rewards represent but a very small proportion of the skill, daring and heroism actually noted; for no volume could hold the full tale of all that was done, either in the way of duty, under constraint of necessity and desire to keep alive, or through joy and pleasure in achieving great deeds.

Here the Irish rank and file by temperament excelled. They had all their race's delight in the drama of things; and, whatever the pinch – whether ambushed warfare or hand-to-hand shock, or an insolently perfect parade after long divorce from the decencies – could be depended upon to advance the regimental honour. Their discipline, of course, was that of the Guards, which, based upon tradition, proven experience and knowledge of the human heart, adjusts itself to the spirit of each of its battalions. Though the material of that body might be expended twice in a twelvemonth, the leaven that remained worked on the new supplies at once and from the first. In the dingy out-of-date barracks at Warley the Regimental Reserves gathered and grew into a full-fledged Second Battalion with reserves of its own, and to these the wounded officers and men sent home to be repatched, explained the arts and needs of a war which, apparently always at a stand, changed character every month. After the utter inadequacy of its opening there was a period of hand-made bombs and of loaded sticks for close work; of nippers for the abundant wire left uncut by our few guns; of remedies for trench-feet; of medicaments against lockjaw from the grossly manured Belgian dirt, and of fancy timberings to hold up sliding trenches. In due course, when a few set battles, which sometimes gained several hundred yards, had wasted their many thousand lives, infallible forms of attack and defence developed themselves, were tried and generally found wanting, while scientific raids, the evolution of specialists, and the mass of regulated detail that more and more surrounded the life of the trenches, occupied their leisure between actions. Our battalions played themselves into the game at the awful price that must be paid for improvisation, how-ever cheery; enduring with a philosophy that may have saved the war, the deviations and delays made necessary by the demands of the various polit-ical and other organizations at home.

In the same spirit they accepted the inevitable break-downs in the busi-ness of war-by-experiment; for it is safe to say that there was hardly an operation in which platoons, companies, regiments, brigades, or divisions were not left with one or both flanks in the air. Among themselves, officers and men discussing such matters, make it quite clear how and why such and such units broke, were misled, or delayed on their way into the line. But when a civilian presumes to assist, all ranks unite against his unin-formed criticisms. He is warned that, once over the top, no plans hold, for the machine-gun and the lie of the ground dictate the situation to the pla-toon-commander on whom all things depend and who sees, perhaps, fifty yards about him. There are limits, too, of shock and exhaustion beyond which humanity cannot be pressed without paying toll later. For which cause it may happen that a Division that has borne long agony unflinch-ing, and sincerely believes itself capable of yet more, will, for no reason then apparent (at almost the mere rumour of noises in the night), collapse ignominiously on the same ground where, a month later, with two-thirds of its strength casualties, it cuts coolly and cleanly to its goal. And its fel-lows, who have borne the same yoke, allow for this.

The compiler of these records, therefore, has made little attempt to put forward any theory of what might or should have happened if things had gone according to plan; and has been scrupulous to avoid debatable issues of bad staff-work or faulty generalship. They were not lacking in the War, but the broad sense of justice in all who suffered from them, recognizing that all were equally amateurs, saved the depression of repeated failures from turning into demoralization.

Here, again, the Irish were reported by those who knew them best, to have been lenient in their judgements, though their private speech was as unrestrained as that of any other body of bewildered and overmastered men. "Wearing down" the enemy through a period of four years and three months, during most of which time that enemy dealt losses at least equal to those he received, tested human virtue upon a scale that the world had never dreamed of. The Irish Guards stood to the test without flaw.

They were in no sense any man's command. They needed minute com-prehension, quick sympathy and inflexible justice, which they repaid by individual devotion and a collective good-will that showed best when things were at their utter worst. Their moods naturally varied with the weather and the burden of fatigues (actions merely kill, while fatigue breaks men's hearts), but their morale was constant because their unoffi-

cial life, on which morale hinges, made for contentment. The discipline of
the Guards, demanding the utmost that can be exacted of the man,
requires of the officer unresting care of his men under all conditions. This
care can be a source of sorrow and friction in rigid or over-conscientious
hands, till, with the best will in the world, a battalion may be reduced to
the mental state of nurse-harried children. Or, conversely, an adored
Company Commander bold as a lion, may, for lack of it, turn his puzzled
company into a bear-garden. But there is an elasticity in Celtic psychology
that does not often let things reach breaking-point either way; and their
sense of humour and social duty – it is a race more careful to regard each
other's feelings than each other's lives – held them as easily as they were
strictly associated. A jest; the grave hearing out of absurd complaints that
might turn to tragedy were the hearing not accorded; a prompt soothing
down of gloomy, injured pride; a piece of flagrant buffoonery sanctioned,
even shared, but never taken advantage of, went far in dark days to build
up that understanding and understood inner life of the two Battalions to
which, now, men look back lovingly across their civilian years. It called for
a devotion from all, little this side of idolatry; and was shown equally by
officers, N.C.O.'s, and men, stretcher-bearers, cooks, orderlies, and not
least by the hard-bit, fantastic old soldiers, used for odd duties, who faith-
fully hobbled about France alongside the rush of wonderful young blood.

Were instances given, the impression might be false, for the tone and
temper of the time that set the pace has gone over. But while it lasted, the
men made their officers and the officers their men by methods as old as
war itself; and their Roman Catholic priests, fearless even in a community
none too regardful of Nature's first law, formed a subtle and supple link
between both. That the priest, ever in waiting upon Death or pain, should
learn to magnify his office was as natural as that doctors and frontline
commanders should find him somewhat under their feet when occasion
called for the secular, not the spiritual, arm. That Commanding Officers,
to keep peace and save important pillars of their little society, should first
advise and finally order the Padre not to expose himself wantonly in forward posts or attacks, was equally of a piece with human nature; and that
the priests, to the huge content of the men, should disregard the order
("What's a casualty compared to a soul?") was most natural of all. Then the
question would come up for discussion in the trenches and dug-outs, where
everything that any one had on his mind was thrashed out through the
long, quiet hours, or dropped and picked up again with the rise and fall of
shell-fire. They speculated on all things in Heaven and earth as they
worked in piled filth among the carcasses of their fellows, lay out under
the stars on the eves of open battle, or vegetated through a month's feeding and idleness between one sacrifice and the next.

But none has kept minutes of those incredible symposia that made for them a life apart from the mad world which was their portion; nor can any pen re-create that world's brilliance, squalor, unreason and heaped boredom. Recollection fades from men's minds as common life closes over them, till even now they wonder what part they can ever have had in the shrewd, man-hunting savages who answered to their names so few years ago.

It is for the sake of these initiated that the compiler has loaded his records with detail and seeming triviality, since in a life where Death ruled every hour, nothing was trivial, and bald references to villages, billets, camps, fatigues and sports, as well as hints of tales that can never now fully be told, carry each their separate significance to each survivor, intimate and incommunicable as family jests.

As regards other readers, the compiler dares no more than hope that some of those who have no care for old history, or that larger number who at present are putting away from themselves odious memories, may find a little to interest, or even comfort in these very details and flatnesses that make up the unlovely, yet superb, life endured for their sakes.

RUDYARD KIPLING

Then hold your head up all the more,
  This tide,
  And every tide;
Because he was the son you bore,
And gave to that wind blowing and that tide!

1915

LOOS AND THE FIRST AUTUMN

OFFICIALLY, the formation of the 2nd Battalion of the Irish Guards dates from the 15th July 1915, when it was announced that His Majesty the King had been "graciously pleased to approve" of the formation of two additional Battalions of Foot Guards – the 4th Grenadier Guards, and the 2nd Battalion Irish Guards, which was to be made up out of the personnel of the 2nd (Reserve) Battalion. And, officially, on July 18 that formation took place. But those who knew the world in the old days, and specially the busy part of it that had Warley Barracks for its heart, know that the 2nd Battalion was born in spirit as in substance, long ere the authorities bade it to be. The needs of the War commanded it; the abundance of the reserves then justified it; and, though Warley Barracks had been condemned as unfit for use by the Honourable the East India Company a trifle of fifty odd years ago, this was not the hour to stand on ancient tradition. So the old, crazy barracks overflowed; the officers' damp and sweating dog-kennels were double-crammed; and, by sheer good-will and stark discipline, the work went forward to the creation. Officers and men alike welcomed it, for it is less pleasing to be absorbed in drafts and driblets by an ever-hungry 1st Battalion in France, than to be set apart for the sacrifice as a veritable Battalion on its own responsibility, with its own traditions (they sprang up immediately) and its own jealous *esprit de corps*. A man may join for the sake of "King and Country" but he goes over the top for the honour of his own platoon, Company, and Battalion; and, the heart of man being what it is, so soon as the 2nd Battalion opened its eyes, the first thing that it beheld was its 1st Battalion, as an elder brother to measure its stature against in all things. Yet, following the ancient mystery of all Armies, there were not two Battalions, but one Regiment; officers and men interchangeable, and equally devoted to the Battalion that they served for the time, though in their deeper minds, and sometimes confessing it, more devoutly attached to one or the other of the two.

By summer of '15 the tide of Special Reserve Officers was towards its flood, and the 2nd Battalion was largely filled by them. They hailed from every quarter of the Empire, and represented almost every profession and

...though Warley Barracks had been condemned as unfit for use by the Honourable the East India Company a trifle of fifty odd years ago, this was not the hour to stand on ancient tradition. So the old, crazy barracks overflowed;

Recruits at Warley.

state of life in it, from the schoolboy of eighteen to the lawyer of forty odd. They had parted long ago with any delusion as to the War ending that year or the next. The information that came to them by word of mouth was not of the sort dispensed in the Press, and they knew, perhaps a little more than the public, how inadequate were our preparations. One and all they realized that, humanly speaking, unless fortune favoured them with permanent disablement, they were doomed men; since all who recovered from their wounds were returned to the War and sooner or later despatched. He was lucky in those days who survived whole for three months; and six without hurt was almost unheard of. So the atmosphere of their daily lives, underneath the routine and the carefully organized amusements that the world then offered to its victims, had an unreality, comparable in some degree to the elaborately articulated conversation and serious argument over utterly trivial matters that springs up among officers in that last hour of waiting under the thunder of the preliminary bombardment before the word is given that hoists all ranks slowly and methodically into a bone-naked landscape.

Lieut.-Colonel the Earl of Kerry, M.V.O., D.S.O., who commanded the Reserve and whose influence over the men was unbounded, began the work of making the 2nd Battalion, and, later on, Major G. H. C. Madden was recalled from duty in France to be its Senior Major. Captain the Hon. T. E. Vesey was the first Adjutant and, with a tight hand which was appreciated afterwards, showed all that young community how to take care of itself. It was a time for understanding much and overlooking little. "Or else," as the Sergeants explained, "ye'll die before ye've killed a Jerry."

On the 27th of July Major and Brevet Lieut.-Colonel the Hon. L. J. P. Butler took over command, and on August the 6th the Battalion with full transport, and packs, paraded as such for its first route-march, of sixteen miles, in the flat country, filled with training troops, that lies round Warley. The weather was very hot, nor did that Officer who had bethought him to fill his "full pack" with a full-blown air-cushion, take much reward of his ingenuity when his unlucky fraud betrayed him by bursting almost under the Adjutant's eye. Men said that that was their real introduction to the horrors of war.

They were inspected on the 10th August by Major-General Sir Francis Lloyd, commanding the London District, who, after the usual compliments on their physique and steadiness, told them they were due for France in a few days. Lord Kitchener came down and addressed them on the 13th of the month, was photographed with a group of all the Officers of the 2nd Battalion and Reserve Battalions, and expressed his belief that they would be a credit to the Guards Division then, as we know, being formed in France.

On the 16th they left Brentwood Station, that has seen so many thousands depart; and that evening were packed tightly at Southampton in the *Anglo-Canadian* and the *Viper*. Duly escorted by destroyers, for the seas were troubled by submarines, both ships tied up at Havre in stillness and strange "foreign" smells at midnight. The city and its outskirts for miles round had long since been turned wholly to the monotonous business of expediting troops and supplies; and the camps that ringed it spread and linked on almost daily. The French were used, now, to our armed Empire at large flooding their streets. Wonder and welcome had passed. No pretty maids met them with wine or garlands, and their route inland to their work was as worn and smooth as the traffic-burnished metals from Brentwood to the sea. But the country and its habits were new to all those new hands, trained in a strict school; and it filled them with joy to behold the casual manner in which a worn and dusty French sentry was relieved while they were marching to their first wonderful camp outside the city.

They entrained for Lumbres on the 18th August and were bidden, next day, to march to billets at Acquin, a little village on a hill-side a few miles from St. Omer, in a fold of the great Sussex-like downs. It is a place both steep and scattered, cramped and hot, and when the air-war was in full swing had its small share of bombs intended for Army Headquarters at St. Omer, and the adjacent aerodromes. The men were billeted in barns forty and fifty at a time which, specially for a new Battalion, was rather unhandy, as offering many ups and downs and corners, which afford chances for delays and misunderstandings. But it was to be their first and only experience of comfort for any consecutive time, and of French life a little untouched by war. They most deeply enjoyed the simple kindliness of the village-folk, and the graceless comments of the little sharp-faced French children at the halting attempts of the Irish to talk French; the glimpses of intimate domestic days, when sons and brothers of their hosts, returned on a few days' leave from far-away battle-fields in the Argonne or beyond, were shown with pride to the visitors who were helping the villagers to cart their corn – "precisely as our own sons would have done." They talked, too, with veterans of '70 met in the fields and at the cafés, who told them in set and rounded phrases that war was serious. And the French men and women upon whom they were billeted liked them well and remembered them long. Said one, years after, with tears in the eyes: "Monsieur, if you drew a line in the air and asked those children not to cross it, it was as a wall to them. They played, monsieur, like infants, without any thought of harm or unkindness; and then they would all become men again, very serious – all those children of yours."

So things were gracious and kindly about them in that little village where every one had suffered loss, and was making their resolute, curt,

French best of it; and the 2nd Battalion settled down to an eleventh-hour course of instruction in everything that the war of that day might call for – except, it may be, how to avoid their own Cavalry on the march.

The historic first meeting between the 1st and 2nd Battalions took place on the 30th August on a march out to St. Pierre, when the units of the different Guards Brigades were drawing in together for combined work preparatory to the Battle of Loos. The veterans of the 1st were personal in their remarks, deriding the bright cap-stars of the 2nd Battalion, and telling them that they would soon know better than to advertise their rank under fire. The 2nd Battalion Diary notes a point that the 1st, doubtless through delicacy, omits – that when the merry gathering under the trees in the field was at an end, after dinner, the 2nd Battalion fell in and marched off the ground "before the critical eyes of their older comrades, and the 1st followed." No fault was found, but it was a breathless business, compared, by one who took part, to the performances of rival peacocks. ("There was not any one else, that we considered; but we knew that, if we put a foot wrong *that* parade in front of *them* we'd be in the road to hear tell of it the rest of our lives.") And it was on this great day, too, that the Rev. Father Knapp joined as R.C. Chaplain to the Battalion, and thereafter proved himself as far forward on all fields as any of the rest of his brethren.

LOOS

They began to learn something about service conditions when, on the 1st September, they joined up with their Brigade, the 2nd Guards Brigade, and shared a wet day of advancing, on parallel roads, with three Guards Brigades, for practice at coming up into the line. Otherwise, they dug trenches by day and night, developed, more or less, their own system of laying them out in the dark, and their Brigade's idea of storming trenches with the help of bombers who had had very little practice with the live bomb; and kept their ears open for any news about conditions on the front. The "smoke-helmets" issued on the eve of the Battalion's departure from England were new also. Many of the talc eye-pieces had cracked in transit, and had to be replaced, and the men instructed how to slip them on against time. This was even more important than the "attack of villages," which was another part of their curriculum at Avroult, Wismes, Wavrans, Tatinghem, Wisques, Dohem, and the like in that dry autumn weather that was saving itself to break filthily at Loos.

On the 5th September, knowing extremely well what they were intended for, after Battalion drill, Lieut.-General Haking, commanding the Eleventh Corps, addressed all the Officers of the 2nd Guards Brigade at the 1st Coldstream Mess at Lumbres. The summary is set down in the Diary with no more comment than three exclamation points at the end.

He told them that an attack on the German lines was close at hand; that the Germans had but forty thousand men at the selected point to oppose our two hundred thousand; and that behind their firing-line and supports were only six Divisions as a reserve to their whole Western front. This may or may not have been true at the time. What follows has a more direct bearing, perhaps, on the course of events, so far as the Battalion was concerned. General Haking said that almost everything depended on the platoon leaders, and "he instructed them always to push on boldly whenever an opportunity offered, even at the expense of exposing and leaving unguarded their flanks." Hence, perhaps, the exclamation points. From the civilian point of view the advice seems hardly safe to offer to a battalion of at least average courage a few days before they are to meet singularly well-posted machine-guns, and carefully trained bombers.

Ceremonial drill of the whole of the 2nd Guards Brigade followed the next day, when they were inspected by Major-General the Earl of Cavan, marched past in column of double platoons, returned to line in mass, complimented on their appearance and so forth, after which, in the evening the C.O. of the Battalion with General Feilding (1st Guards Brigade), Captain Viscount Gort (B.M. 1st Guards Brigade), and Colonel Corry commanding the 3rd Grenadier Guards, went off in a car to "see the country south-east of Béthune." This was not a sector that improved on acquaintance; and in the days that followed all senior officers looked at and pondered over the unwholesome open scarred ground over which "the greatest battle in the history of the world," as General Haking said, was to take place. Meantime, among the drills held at Acquin appear orders, presumably for the first time, that every one was to fire ten rounds "from his rifle while wearing his smoke-helmet." The result on the targets of this solitary experiment is not recorded; but it takes some time for a man to get used to sighting through dingy talc eye-pieces. Nor is it likely to be known in this world whether the "six young officers" who attended riding-school just before the march towards Loos, derived much benefit from their instruction.

They moved on the evening of the 22nd September and marched to Dohem where they picked up their Brigade Headquarters and some other units, and thence, next day, in heavy rain to billets in Linghem. General Haking delivered another speech at the Corps Conference on the 24th, explaining the broad outlines of the "greatest battle, etc." which at that moment was opening. He dwelt specially on the part to be played by the Eleventh Corps, as well as the necessity for speed and for the use of reserves. It may have occurred to some of his hearers that they were the reserves, but that speed was out of the question, for the roads were clotted with Cavalry, and there did not seem to be any great choice of those "parallel roads" on which they had been exercised, or any vast crush of motor-buses. When they got away from Linghem on the early morning of the 25th and marched with their Brigade to Burbure and Haquin, they enjoyed continuous halts, owing to the Cavalry going forward, which meant, for the most part, through them, and the wounded of the battle being brought back – all on the same road. They billeted (this was merely a form) at Haquin "very wet and tired" about one on the morning of the 26th, having been on their feet standing, marching, or variously shifted about, for twenty odd hours. The men's breakfasts were issued at half-past four that same dawn "as there was a possibility of an early move."

No orders, however, came, the world around them being busied with the shifting phases of the opening of Loos, which had begun with an advance at some spots along the line, and at others was hung up among wire that our two or three hours' bombardment did not seem to have wholly removed. The 2nd Guards Brigade, then, waited on at Haquin till shortly after noon, and moved via Nœux-les-Mines, Sailly-Labourse, Noyelles, and Vermelles, large portions of which were then standing and identifiable, to trenches in front of Le Rutoire. Here the German lines had been driven back a little, and Captains Alexander and Hubbard, commanding the two leading Companies of the Battalion, were sent on to look at them in daylight. The results of the Captains' adventure, when it is recalled that one set of trenches, at the best of times, looks remarkably like another, and that this was far from being a good time, were surprisingly satisfactory. "There was no one to tell them exactly which trenches were to be taken over, but, from instructions given on the map, and in consultation with the 1st Scots Guards who had to occupy ground on their right, they arranged which set of them to inhabit. Owing to congestion of roads, and having to go across much broken country, etc., it was nearly midnight before the Battalion got into the selected spot – an old line of captured German trenches in front of Lone Tree." This, as is well known to all regimental historians, was a mark of the German guns almost to the inch, and, unfortunately, formed one of our dressing-stations. At a moderate estimate the Battalion had now been on foot and livelily awake for forty-eight hours; the larger part of that time without any food. It remained for them merely to go into the fight, which they did at half-past two on the morning of the 27th September when they received "verbal instructions to push forward to another line of captured German trenches, some five hundred yards, relieving any troops that might happen to be there." It was nearly broad daylight by the time that this disposition was completed, and they were much impressed with the permanence and solidity of the German works in which they found themselves, and remarked jestingly one to another, that "Jerry must have built them with the idea of staying there for ever." As a matter of fact, "Jerry" did stay within a mile of that very line for the next three years and six weeks, less one day. They had their first hint of his intentions when patrols pushed out from Nos. 2 and 3 Companies in the forenoon, reported that they were unable to get even a hundred yards ahead, on account of rifle-fire. Men said, long afterwards, that this was probably machine-gun fire out of the Bois Hugo, which thoroughly swept all open communications, for the enemy here as elsewhere had given ground a little without losing his head, and was hitting back as methodically as ever.

The attack of their Brigade developed during the course of the day. The four C.O.'s of the Battalions met their Brigadier at the 1st Grenadier Guards Headquarters. He took them to a point just north of Loos, whence they could see Chalk-Pit Wood, and the battered bulk of the colliery head and workings known as Puits 14 bis, together with what few small buildings still stood thereabouts, and told them that he proposed to attack as follows: At half-past two a heavy bombardment lasting for one hour and a half would be delivered on that sector. At four the 2nd Irish Guards would advance upon Chalk-Pit Wood and would establish themselves on the north-east and south-east faces of it, supported by the 1st Coldstream. The 1st Scots Guards were to advance echeloned to the right rear of the Irish, and to attack Puits 14 bis moving round the south side of Chalk-Pit Wood, covered by heavy fire from the Irish out of the Wood itself. For this purpose, four machine-guns of the Brigade Machine-Gun Company were to accompany the latter Battalion. The 3rd Grenadiers were to support the 1st Scots in their attack on the Puits. Chalk-Pit Wood at that time existed as a somewhat dishevelled line of smallish trees and brush running from north to south along the edge of some irregular chalk workings which terminated at their north end in a deepish circular quarry. It was not easy to arrive at its precise shape and size, for the thing, like so much of the war-landscape of France, was seen but once by the men vitally concerned in its features, and thereafter changed outline almost weekly, as gun-fire smote and levelled it from different angles.

The orders for the Battalion, after the conference and the short view of the ground, were that No. 3 Company (Captain Wynter) was to advance from their trenches when the bombardment stopped, to the southern end of Chalk-Pit Wood, get through and dig itself in in the tough chalk on the farther side. No. 2 Company (Captain Bird), on the left of No. 3, would make for the centre of the Wood, dig in too, on the far side, and thus prolong No. 3's line up to and including the Chalk-Pit – that is to say, that the two Companies would hold the whole face of the Wood.

Nos. 1 and 4 Companies were to follow and back up Nos. 3 and 2 respectively. At four o'clock the two leading Companies deployed and advanced, "keeping their direction and formation perfectly." That much could be seen from what remained of Vermelles water-tower, where some of the officers of the 1st Battalion were watching, regardless of occasional enemy shell. They advanced quickly, and pushed through to the far edge of the Wood with very few casualties, and those, as far as could be made out, from rifle or machine-gun fire. (Shell-fire had caught them while getting out of their trenches, but, notwithstanding, their losses had not been heavy till then.) The rear Companies pushed up to thicken the line, as the fire increased from the front, and while digging in beyond the Wood, 2nd Lieutenant Pakenham-Law was fatally wounded in the head. Digging was not easy work, and seeing that the left of the two first Companies did not seem to have extended as far as the Chalk-Pit, at the north of the Wood, the C.O. ordered the last two platoons of No. 4 Company which were just coming up, to bear off to the left and get hold of the place. In the meantime, the 1st Scots Guards, following orders, had come partly round and partly through the right flank of the Irish, and attacked Puits 14 bis, which was reasonably stocked with machine-guns, but which they captured for the moment. Their rush took with them "some few Irish Guardsmen," with 2nd Lieutenants W. F. J. Clifford and J. Kipling of No. 2 Company who went forward not less willingly because Captain Cuthbert commanding the Scots Guards party had been Adjutant to the Reserve Battalion at Warley ere the 2nd Battalion was formed, and they all knew him. Together, this rush reached a line beyond the Puits, well under machine-gun fire (out of the Bois Hugo across the Lens–La Bassée road). Here 2nd Lieutenant Clifford was shot and wounded or killed – the body was found later – and 2nd Lieutenant Kipling was wounded and missing. The Scots Guards also lost Captain Cuthbert, wounded or killed, and the combined Irish and Scots Guards party fell back from the Puits and retired "into and through Chalk-Pit Wood in some confusion." The C.O. and Adjutant, Colonel Butler and Captain Vesey, went forward through the Wood to clear up matters, but, soon after they had entered it the Adjutant was badly wounded and had to be carried off. Almost at the same moment, "the men from the Puits came streaming back through the Wood, followed by a great part of the line which had been digging in on the farther side of it."

Evidently, one and a half hour's bombardment, against a country-side packed with machine-guns, was not enough to placate it. The Battalion had been swept from all quarters, and shelled at the same time, at the end of two hard days and sleepless nights, as a first experience of war, and had lost seven of their officers in forty minutes. They were re-formed somewhat to the rear along the Loos–Hulluch road. ("Jerry did himself well at Loos upon us innocents. We went into it, knowing no more than our own dead what was coming, and Jerry fair lifted us out of it with machine-guns. That was all there was to it *that* day.") The watchers on the Vermelles water-tower saw no more than a slow forward wave obscured by Chalk-Pit Wood, the spreading of a few scattered figures, always, it seemed, moving leisurely; and then a return, with no apparent haste in it, behind the Wood once more They had a fair idea, though, of what had happened; and guessed what was to follow. The re-formed line would go up again exactly to where it had come from. While this was being arranged, and when a couple of Companies of the 1st Coldstream had turned up in a hollow on the edge of the Loos–Hulluch road, to support the Battalion, a runner came back with a message from Captain Alexander saying that he and some men were still in their scratch-trenches on the far side of Chalk-Pit Wood, and he would be greatly obliged if they would kindly send some more men up, and with speed. The actual language was somewhat crisper, and was supplemented, so the tale runs, by remarks from the runner addressed to the community at large. The demand was met at once, and the rest of the line was despatched to the near side of the Wood in support. The two Companies of the Coldstream came up on the left of the Irish Guards, and seized and settled down in the Chalk-Pit itself. They all had a night's energetic digging ahead of them, with but their own entrenching tools to help, and support-trenches had to be made behind the Wood in case the enemy should be moved to counter-attack. To meet that chance, as there was a gap between the supporting Coldstream Companies and the 1st Guards Brigade on the left, the C.O. of the 2nd Battalion collected some hundred and fifty men of various regiments, during the dusk, and stuffed them into an old German communication-trench as a defence. No counter-attack developed, but it was a joyless night that they spent among the uptorn trees and lumps of unworkable chalk. Their show had failed with all the others along the line, and "the greatest battle in the history of the world" was frankly stuck. The most they could do was to hang on and wait developments. They were shelled throughout the next day, heavily but inaccurately, when 2nd Lieutenant Sassoon was wounded by a rifle bullet. In the evening they watched the 1st Coldstream make an unsuccessful attack on Puits 14 bis, for the place was a well-planned machine-gun nest – the first of many that they were fated to lose their strength against through the years to come. That night closed in rain, and they were left to the mercy of Providence. No one could get to them, and they could get at nobody; but they could and did dig deeper into the chalk, to keep warm, and to ensure against the morrow (September 29) when the enemy guns found their range and pitched the stuff fairly into the trenches "burying many men and blowing a few to pieces." Yet, according to the

. . . it was a joyless night that they spent among the uptorn trees and lumps of unworkable chalk. Their show had failed. . . and "the greatest battle in the history of the world" was frankly stuck.

The support line, Chalk Pit Wood, 1915.

count, which surely seems inaccurate, they only lost twenty dead in the course of the long day. The 3rd Guards Brigade on their right, sent in word that the Germans were massing for attack in the Bois Hugo in front of their line. "All ranks were warned," which, in such a situation, meant no more than that the experienced among them, of whom there were a few, waited for the cessation of shell-fire, and the inexperienced, of whom there were many, waited for what would come next. ("And the first time that he is under *that* sort of fire, a man stops his thinking. He's all full of wonder, sweat, and great curses.") No attack, however, came, and the Gunners claimed that their fire on Bois Hugo had broken it up. Then the Brigade on their left cheered them with instructions that Chalk-Pit Wood must be "held at all costs," and that they would not be relieved for another two days; also, that "certain modifications of the Brigade line would take place." It turned out later that these arrangements did not affect the Battalions. They were taken out of the line "wet, dirty, and exhausted" on the night of the 30th September when, after a heavy day's shelling, the Norfolks relieved them, and they got into billets behind Sailly-Labourse. They had been under continuous strain since the 25th of the month, and from the 27th to the 30th in a punishing action which had cost them, as far as could be made out, 324 casualties, including 101 missing. Of these last, the Diary records that "the majority of them were found to have been admitted to some Field Ambulance wounded. The number of known dead is set down officially as not more than 25, which must be below the mark. Of their officers, 2nd Lieutenant Pakenham-Law had died of wounds; 2nd Lieutenants Clifford and Kipling were missing, Captain and Adjutant the Hon. T. E. Vesey, Captain Wynter, Lieutenant Stevens, and 2nd Lieutenants Sassoon and Grayson were wounded, the last being blown up by a shell. It was a fair average for the day of a debut, and taught them somewhat for their future guidance. Their Commanding Officer told them so at Adjutant's Parade, after they had been rested and cleaned on the 2nd October at Verquigneul; but it does not seem to have occurred to any one to suggest that direct Infantry attacks, after ninety-minute bombardments, on works begotten out of a generation of thought and prevision, scientifically built up by immense labour and applied science, and developed against all contingencies through nine months, are not likely to find a fortunate issue. So, while the Press was explaining to a puzzled public what a far-reaching success had been achieved, the "greatest battle in the history of the world" simmered down to picking up the pieces on both sides of the line, and a return to autumnal trench-work, until more and heavier guns could be designed and manufactured in England. Meantime, men died.

THE HOHENZOLLERN AND TRENCH WORK

The Battalion, a little rested, and strengthened by four officers from the 1st Irish Guards (Lieutenant and Temporary Captain FitzGerald, Lieutenants Rankin and Montgomery, and 2nd Lieutenant Langrishe) as well as a draft of a hundred men under 2nd Lieutenant Hamilton, was introduced to the trenches on the 3rd October, when they moved to Vermelles and hid themselves in the ruins and cellars of as much as the enemy had allowed to remain of it. It was an unpleasing experience. The following comment covers it, and the many others of the same sort that followed: "We was big men for the most part, and this creepin' and crawlin' in and out of what's left of houses, was not our ways of livin'. Maybe some of the little fellows in the Line would have found it easier. And there's a smell to that kind o' billet worse than graves – a smell off the house-plaster where it lies, and the wallpaper peeling off the walls, and what's in the sand-bags that we build acrost the passages an' the sculleries, ye'll understand, and the water on the floors stinkin' and rottin'. Ye hear it drip like dhrums through ceilings in the night. And ye go in an' out of them dark, stinkin' places always stoopin' an' steppin' on bits o' things. Dead houses put the wind up a man worse than trenches."

Next day they were turned down into the multitude of trenches, established or in the making, which lay between Vermelles and the great Hohenzollern Redoubt that swept every line of approach with its sudden fires. They were led out (October 5) at dusk across a muddy field beside a dead town, and entered that endless communication-trench called Central Boyau, whose length was reckoned by hours. It led them to the line held by the East Yorks Regiment and two companies of the K.O.Y.L.I. they were relieving. Men forget much, but no man of any battalion ever forgets his first introduction to the stable, deadly fire-line, as distinguished from the casual field-trench. An hour or so before they moved off, a 5·9 burst in a ruined cottage where all the Battalion Staff was sitting, and might well have destroyed the Sergeant-Major, Drill-Sergeants and Signallers, etc. The only casualty, however, was one pioneer killed, while the officers of the Battalion Staff in the next mound of ruins escaped unhurt.

Then began the slow and repeatedly checked sidle in the dusk, of single men up Central Boyau, which was also a thoroughfare for other units falling, tripping and cursing among festoons of stray telephone wires. From Vermelles to their trenches was a mile and a quarter. They began at seven at night and completed the relief at six in the morning. Not much shelling greeted them, but the darkness was "tickled up," as one man put it, with bullets from all angles, and while No. 3 Company was settling into Reserve trenches just at the point of grey dawn, 2nd Lieutenant Hine showed himself by getting up on to the parapet, and was shot through the head at once, probably by a sniper. Over and above the boy's natural fear-lessness, by which he had already distinguished himself at Loos (for he had helped Captain Alexander to hold the men in Chalk-Pit Wood after the failure of the Coldstream attack on Puits 14 bis), he was utterly convinced he would not be killed in the War. Others of his companions had presentiments of their own death more than once, and yet survived to the end with nothing worse than a wound or gassing. It may be worth noting, as far as this sort of information goes, that a man who felt that he was "for it" on the eve of an engagement was seldom found to be wrong. Occasionally, too, it would come over a man in the trenches that that day or night would be his last. Indeed the very hour would sometimes forespeak itself as with an audible voice, and he, chosen, would go forward to the destined spot – so men have said who saw it – already divorced from this world.

But at the beginning, before nerves wore down, there was hope and interest for every one. The enemy had probably learned of the fresh material before them, for they filled the day of the 6th October with alternate whizz-bangs and large-size H.E. howitzers; the crack and gravel-like smash of the small stuff alternating with the grunt, vomit and stamp of the Jack Johnsons. Every one was hit by the flying dirt, and well-nigh choked by the stench, and some officers visiting the front line had their first experience of crawling in cold blood across bits of broken trench, where the debris of corpses was so mingled with the untidy dirt that one could not be sure till later what hand or foot had met. It struck some of the young officers as curious that they were not more impressed. Others were frankly sick; while others found that the sights lifted from them the dread fear of being afraid which waits at every generous man's shoulder. But they all owned, according to their separate temperaments, that they were quite sufficiently frightened for working purposes, and so – went on with their work.

Between the 5th and the 7th October the Battalion lost one officer (2nd Lieutenant Hine) and six other ranks killed and twenty-one wounded. Their trenches were moderately good, and had been regularly used, and they discovered dug-outs here and there, which enabled some of them to doze lying down instead of propped against the side of a trench full of moving men. This was great luxury to them, though their revolvers punched holes in their hips and their boots drew like blisters. The more imaginative wrote home that the life was something like camping out. The truthful merely said that they were having an interesting time, and gave their families peace. There was no need to explain how their servants brought them up their meals, dodging, balancing, and ducking along a trench as the fire caught it, or how, even while the hungry youngsters waited and watched, both food and servant would be wiped out together, with a stretch of the parapet under which they had decided to eat.

Just where the Battalion lay, our front line was two hundred yards from the enemy – too far for hand-bombing, but deadly for Artillery and machine-gun work. Our Artillery was declared to be more numerous and powerful than the German, which generally showered our supports and reserves with shrapnel, while machine-gulls kept down the heads of the front line with small-arm fire. Orders had been issued at that moment that recesses should be built, at twenty-five-yard intervals in our fire-trench parapets, for mounting gas-cylinders, and the Battalion worked at this new fatigue under the direction of an Engineer Officer, Lieutenant Ritchie. The recesses meant nothing in particular, but gave people a pleasant feeling that there was abundance of gas somewhere in the background. They were regularly shelled, but, mankind being infinitely adaptable, had come in the few days of this new life to look on it as almost normal, and to alleviate it with small shifts and contrivances. "I think," says one of the beginners, "that in those days we were as self-centred as a suburban villa residence. The fact of not being able to put your head up without having a shot through it kept us from worrying about our neighbours." Their first experience of external trouble in their underground world began on the afternoon of the 8th October, when loud bombing and shelling broke out two battalions down the line to the right, and some one from the 3rd Grenadiers came charging round the traverses asking for all available bombers, because the Germans had got into their line and were making rather a hash of things. Bombers were accordingly sent, though their experience with the live bomb was limited, and the two companies on the right got to work on sand-bags to bulkhead their right flank in case of a breakthrough. No one really thought that they would be attacked, possibly for the reason that such a thing had not happened to them personally before. "You see, we had lost count of time even of the days of the week. Every day seemed as long as a year, and I suppose we considered ourselves like aged men – prisoners of Chillon, you know. We didn't think anything could happen." On that occasion they were correct. The riot died down and they fell back into normal night routine, every second man in the fire-trench on sentry, every fifth man in support seventy or eighty yards behind, and relief every hour; one officer sitting, between rounds, on one particular spot of the fire-step (so that every one knew where to find him), discussing life, death, Véry lights, and politics with his C.S.M. and at intervals peering over the parapet; another officer pervading the support-trench where bayonet charges are supposed to be supplied from, and where the men grumble that they are always set to make fancy improvements. Meantime, the dim dark on every hand is marked with distant pin-pricks and dots, or nearer blurs or blasts of fire, that reveal the torn edges of the shell-holes like wave-crests of a petrified ocean. Yet, after a few nights, the men in the front line said their chief difficulty was to avoid dozing off "because there was nothing to do."

They lost three killed and nineteen wounded from all causes between the 7th and 8th October, but completed the recesses for the gas-cylinders, and cleaned out an indescribably old trench, needed for future operations, of its stale corpses mixed with bomb-boxes. While this delicate job was in progress, the enemy started shelling that section with high explosives and shrapnel. They had to shift twenty boxes of bombs under, first, a particular and next a general bombardment, which was connected with a German attack a little farther down the line. Their relief came that same day, on the 12th October, after their first full week in the trenches. It was not a cheerful affair. Three battalions were involved in the chaos, as far as the 2nd Irish Guards were concerned. What befell the rest of their Brigade may be left to the imagination. A reconnoitring party of the 1st Monmouths – four officers and eight other ranks – turned up at a quarter-past five to look over the Irish Guards' trenches before their own men came. They were sitting just outside Battalion Headquarters when a 5·9 killed one of the officers and three of the other ranks, wounded the three other officers, and buried the whole party. The Diary, rightly regardful of the interests of the Battalion, observes: "Another lucky escape for our Battalion H.Q. Staff. For this was the spot in the trench normally occupied by the senior Drill-Sergeant and all the Orderlies." Even so, the Monmouths were the only relieving unit that had any idea where they were or what they were to take over. The others, the 4th and 5th Leicesters, lost themselves on the way and wandered blasphemous among trenches. "The consequent confusion was deplorable." The Battalion were chaperoning themselves and others from half-past ten to a quarter-past four in the morning. Then began the mile and a half of nightmare-like crawl up the seven-foot-deep communication-trench, whose sides took strange Egyptian-desert-like colours in the dawn-light, and whose bends and windings bewildered all sense of direction. They shuffled in file behind each other like migrating caterpillars, silently except for the grunt and jerk of a tired man slipping in mud, and whispers along the echoing cut bidding them always "close up." They were all out, in every way, at five o'clock. The relief had begun at eight. After this, they marched three or four hours to billets at Vaudricourt and Drouvin, within sound but out of reach of the guns, where they dropped and slept and shaved and washed, and their officers were grateful to pig down, six together, on the floor of a loft, and none troubled them till four in the afternoon when they were ordered to parade "clean."

Only two nights were allowed for rest and refit, during which time a draft of fifty men under Lieutenant Kinahan joined, and the Battalion bombers were "organized" (they had not thrown very well lately) and made up to eight per platoon. That was on the 14th October. Next morning the Brigadier called up the C.O.'s of all four Battalions and instructed them that every bomber was, as far as possible, to be given the chance of throwing a live bomb before going into the trenches again. He added that "again" meant next morning. On the morning of the 15th October, then, each one of those one hundred and twenty-eight organized bombers did, at practice, throw one live bomb. Says the Diary, without even a note of exclamation: "With the knowledge, experience and confidence thus gained, they had to face trained German bombers a few days later." They might have had to face them that same evening when they took over some Brigade Reserve trenches, directly behind those of their first tour, from the 7th and 8th Sherwood Foresters; but they were merely shelled as they settled in, and the bombing fell farther down the line. Their new trenches were dirty and badly knocked about, but, by some obscure forethought or other, well provided with small and fairly safe dug-outs which gave cover to almost all. Though they were heavily shelled their first two days, and many direct hits fell on the parapet itself, and many men were buried, only two were killed outright and thirty-two wounded. The sensation of being pinned, even when one has one's head above ground, by a weight of pressing earth, added to natural speculation as to whether the next shell may complete the burial, is a horror that returns to a man in his dreams, and takes the heart out of some even more than dysentery. ("There's something in being held tight that makes you lose hold of yourself. I've seen men screamin' and kickin' like wired hares, and them no more than caught by one leg or two. "Tis against Nature for a man to be buried with his breath in him.")

A RAID

On the 18th October they relieved the 1st Coldstream in the front line on the west face of Hohenzollern Redoubt, which, were there choice, might be reckoned the very warmest sector of all the neighbourhood. Both Battalions knowing their business, the relief was effected in two and a half hours under heavy shelling without casualty, though the Irish lost two killed and three wounded in the earlier part of the day. Their new position ran without definite distinction, except sand-bagged barricades, into the German system, and one might at any time crawl into nests of enemy sentries and bombers. This, again, was a fresh experience to them. Loos had been clean-cut in its boundaries. Their week in Left and Right Boyau from the 8th to the 15th October had not led to undue intimacies with anything worse than Jack Johnsons, but now they were promised a change of methods. Since the great breakthrough had failed that was to carry our triumphant arms to Lille, the authorities seemed to attach immense importance to the possession of a few score yards of enemy trench, commanded, when won, by a few thousand yards of other trenches, and were willing to expend much blood upon the captures. Doubtless there was deep design at the back of the detailed work, but, from the point of view of those who had to carry it through, it was a little wearisome. They were warned that bombing attacks would be the order of the day, and on the 10th October their Brigadier visited them and, as a preliminary, ordered that a trench should be run to connect Guildford Street, on the left of the Redoubt as they faced it, with West Face Trench, a matter of some "sixty yards over ground fully exposed to hostile fire at a range of sixty yards." In this manner, then, was the trench dug. Beginning in the dark at eight o'clock 2nd Lieutenant A. Pym, with a party of No. 1 Company, crept out of West Face, Lance-Sergeant Comesky leading, and the whole chain crawling behind him "extended" (on their stomachs) along the line to be dug. They had noted the bearing very carefully in the daytime, and a party in Guildford Street under 2nd Lieutenant T. Nugent were trying to help them to keep it, in a subdued tone. One must not shout when there are rifles and machine-guns, hands on triggers, fifty yards away. As the party lay they dug and scratched, first with their entrenching implements and then with picks and shovels passed along the line; and Lance-Sergeant Comesky, the curve of whose labouring back in the darkness was their guide, had to keep his direction through broken wire, what had been broken men, shell-holes, and the infinite tangle and waste of war. The Irish have some small reputation for digging when there is need. They dug that night as not even the 1st Battalion had dug, and when light came the new trench was four and a half feet deep, and the sole casualty was Lance-Sergeant Comesky, slightly wounded. They had been suspected and "slated " by machine-gun fire in their direction from time to time, but were not actually located till they were well down. As a point of vantage the new line had its defects. By daylight no periscope could live there half a minute ere it was knocked to shivers by rifle-fire.

Meantime a couple of little reconnaissances had been sent out. Private Horton (he had already shown his gifts in this direction), "supported by a Corporal and another man, made his way along an old blown-in trench that ran up the centre of the mass of the Hohenzollern works, till he heard Germans talking at the far end of it, and so reported. The second reconnaissance by Lance-Sergeant G. McCarthy and Private Kingston of No. 2 Company explored along another blown-in trench to the left of Private Horton's line, which, before our guns had wrecked it, had been a continuation of West Face Trench and had run into Little Willie of unsavoury reputation, which latter in its turn trended almost due north into the German works. They found this trench barricaded just at its junction with Little Willie, were fired on by a German sentry, and came away. So far good. The Brigadier's instructions next morning were for a night-attack to be made along both these trenches which lay parallel to each other; for barricades to be run up at the far end of the lengths gained; and, later, the two points to be joined up by a fresh cut. This, it was hoped, would pinch out about fifty yards of occupied German trench opposite the one which had been dug that night by 2nd Lieutenants A. Pym's and Nugent's party from Guildford Street to West Face. What might arrive after that was a question of luck, comparable to ferreting in a populous warren. The Battalion spent the day under shell-fire that killed one man and wounded nine, in making arrangements for bombs and sand-bags for the barricades, and decided that the chain of men working up the trenches, which barely allowed one and a half men abreast, should consist of two bombers, two riflemen; two bombers and two riflemen again; and four men to carry spare bombs. These were to drive the enemy back and hold them while new barricades were being built in the annexed territory. Then would come an officer and four more bombers to "hold the new barricade in event of the leading bombers being rushed while it was being built, then two men to build the barricade; then a chain of riflemen at two-yard intervals reaching back to the point of departure who would pass up more bombs or sand-bags as need arose," and would clean up the old trench along which our advance was made, "so as to give us free access to our new barricade in daylight." It is to be borne in mind that, at that time, the bombers of the 2nd Irish Guards had thrown just one live bomb apiece at training. ("We went in great dread of our rear-ranks that night. A bomb's no thing – more than fixed bayonets – to go capering up trenches with at *anny* time. And the first time least of all.")

The attack was confided to No. 4 Company (Captain Hubbard), who chose 2nd Lieutenants T. F. Tallents and Hamilton for the left and right attacks respectively. They led out at one in the morning, very carefully, for the men were cautioned to stalk the enemy as much as possible, but the moment they were discovered, to rush him back up the trench. So he had to be listened for in the dark, with a sky full of noises overhead. As soon as "contact had been obtained" – that is to say, as soon as the first crack of a bomb and the yell that accompanies it were heard down the cutting – the Véry lights were sent up for a signal for our guns and the troops on either side to annoy and divert. Bombing affairs of the year '15 were on the most simple lines and unaccompanied by barrage. The left attack, when it had toiled some sixty yards from its starting-point, met a party of German bombers. What followed was inevitable. "Our bombers, who had never had an opportunity of throwing more than one live bomb each at training, were easily outclassed by the German bombers, and they were all either killed, wounded, or driven back immediately on to 2nd Lieutenant Tallents." He was coming up twenty or thirty yards behind them, and had just reached some old smashed girders that had been part of a bridge or a dug-out, and back to this tangle the attack was driven. There a stand was made for a while by Tallents and two privates, Higgins and Brophy, till Brophy was killed and the officer and other private wounded. The Germans bombed their way on down to the barricades whence the attack had been launched, and for twenty minutes it was touch and go whether the Irish could hold it even there. All this while Tallents, though wounded, headed the resistance, urged the men to strengthen the barrier, and then got atop of it, "so as to make a longer or more accurate shot with a bomb." Bombs ran short, as they usually do on such occasions; the bombers were down and between men's feet among the wreckage. Second Lieutenant Coxon, who was sending up fresh men and bombs as best he might over broken ground in darkness down blind trappy trenches, indented on Battalion Headquarters for more, and the 1st Coldstream whirled their bombers in till, by means that no one can quite recall, the German rush was stayed long enough for a steady supply of munitions to arrive. This was about four in the morning, after a couple of hours of mixed rough-and-tumble that had died out for the moment to snaps of rifle-fire round corners, and the occasional glare of a bomb lobbed over some cover in the obstructed trench. Tallents had kept his place at the barrier all the time, and, at what turned out to be the psychological moment, launched a fresh attack down the trench, headed by Lance-Corporals J. Brennan and C. Anstey and backed by Lance-Corporal Cahill. It gave time for the men behind to further strengthen the defence, while more bombs were coming up. Then Tallents collapsed and "was removed to the dressing-station," and 2nd Lieutenant F. Synge was sent up to relieve him. He was hit in the head almost at once, but remained at his post, and "never relaxed his efforts to get the position consolidated and tenable," until he too was withdrawn to the dressing-station after dawn. By this time the barricade was completed, and the communication-trench back to the main body was sufficiently cleared to enable work to be continued in daylight.

The smooth official language, impersonal as the account of an operation in a medical journal, covers up all the horror and sweat of the night, the desperate labour with anything that came to hand to make good the barrier, the automatic measurements of time and space as the struggle up the trench swayed nearer or farther, as well as the unspeakable absurdities that went sometimes with the very act and agony of a man's death between the feet of his comrades. The things that cannot be recorded are those that are never forgotten. ("And a man can go missing in such kind of doings more easy than anything except direct hits from heavy stuff. There's everything handy scraped up against a barricade that will stop a bullet, and in the dark how can one see or – what does one care? Bits of all sorts, as the saying is. And a man will take the wrong turn in a trench and then three or four bombs on him, and that shakes the side of it, the like of deep drains. Then the side all shuts down on what's left, ye'll understand, and maybe no living thing'll come that way again till the war's end. No! There will *not* be much left over to a bomber that's missing.")

The right attack, commanded by Captain Hubbard, which was down the old blown-in trench that ran straight towards the centre of the Hohenzollern, was a much tamer affair than the left. The enemy were not struck till our advance was some eighty yards up the cut. They fell back after a few bombs had been exchanged, and our men were able to build a new barricade across the trench fifty yards from their starting-point, with no serious opposition. Their chief difficulty was to clear the newly gained stretch of the hideous mess that choked it, and forced them into the open where the bullets were coming from three sides at once. The men are described as "slow" in settling to this navvy-work, which, considering their distractions, was quite possible. Dawn caught them "with just enough cover to enable them to continue work in a crouching position, and before very many hours of daylight had passed they made it all good." But their officer, 2nd Lieutenant Hamilton, was shot through the jaw while he was superintending the work (it is impossible to direct and give orders without standing up) and he died an hour later. He was buried on the afternoon of the same day at the lonely, flat little cemetery of Vermelles, which is now so full of "unknown British soldiers killed in action." As the expert has already pointed out, "there's not much left over to a bomber that's missing."

The total loss in the night's fray was Hamilton killed, Tallents and Synge wounded, and about sixty other ranks killed, wounded and missing. The net gain was a few score yards of trench, of which the enemy held both ends, with a "No Man's Land" on either flank of about as far as one could throw a bomb over a barricade. In front, not a hundred yards off, a most efficient German trench with lavish machine-guns sniped them continuously between the breathing-spaces of our shell-fire. Our own big stuff, bursting on and near that trench, shook and loosened the sides of our own. The entire area had been fought over for months, and was hampered with an incredible profusion, or so it struck the new hands at the time, of arms, clothing and equipment – from shreds, wisps and clods of sodden uniforms that twist and catch round the legs, to loaded rifles that go off when they are trodden on in the mud or prised up by the entrenching tools. The bottom and sides of the cuts were studded with corpses whose limbs and, what was worse, faces, stuck out of the mixed offal, and were hideously brought to light in cleaning up. However, as one youngster wrote home triumphantly, "I was never *actually* sick."

The affair could hardly be called a success, and the Battalion did not pretend that it was more than a first attempt in which no one knew what was expected of them, and the men were not familiar with their weapons.

A REST AND LAVENTIE

On the evening of the 21st October they were relieved by the 1st Coldstream, and were grateful to go into Brigade Reserve in the trenches beside the Vermelles railway line, where they were out of direct contact with the enemy and the nerve-stretching racket of their own Artillery shelling a short hundred yards ahead of them. ("The heavies are like having a good friend in a fight behind your back, but there's times when he'll punch ye in the kidneys trying to reach the other fella.") They were put to cleaning up old communication-trenches, and general scavenging, which, though often in the highest degree disgusting, has a soothing effect on the mind, precisely as tidying out a room soothes a tired woman. For the first time in a month the strain on the young Battalion had relaxed, and since it was their first month at the front, they had felt the strain more than their elders. They had a general impression that the German line had been very nearly broken at Loos; that our pressure upon the enemy was increasingly severe; that their own Artillery were much better and stronger than his, and that, taking one thing with another, the end might come at any moment. Since there were but a limited number of Huns in the world, it was demonstrable that by continually killing them the enemy would presently cease to exist. This, be it remembered, was the note in the Press and the public mind towards the close of 1915 – the War then redly blossoming into its second year.

As to their personal future, it seemed to be a toss-up whether they would be kept to worry and tease Huns in trenches, or moved off somewhere else to "do something " on a large scale; for at the back of the general optimism there lurked a feeling that, somehow or other, nothing very great had been actually effected. (Years later the veterans of twenty-five, six, and seven admitted: "We were a bit young in those days, and, besides, one had to buck up one's people at home. But we weren't quite such fools as we made ourselves out to be.")

They were taken away from that sector altogether on the 23rd October, marched to Noyelles, thence to Béthune on the 25th, where they entrained for Lillers and billeted at Bourecq. This showed that they had done with the chalk that does not hide corpses, and that the amazing mud round Armentières and Laventie would be their portion. At that date the

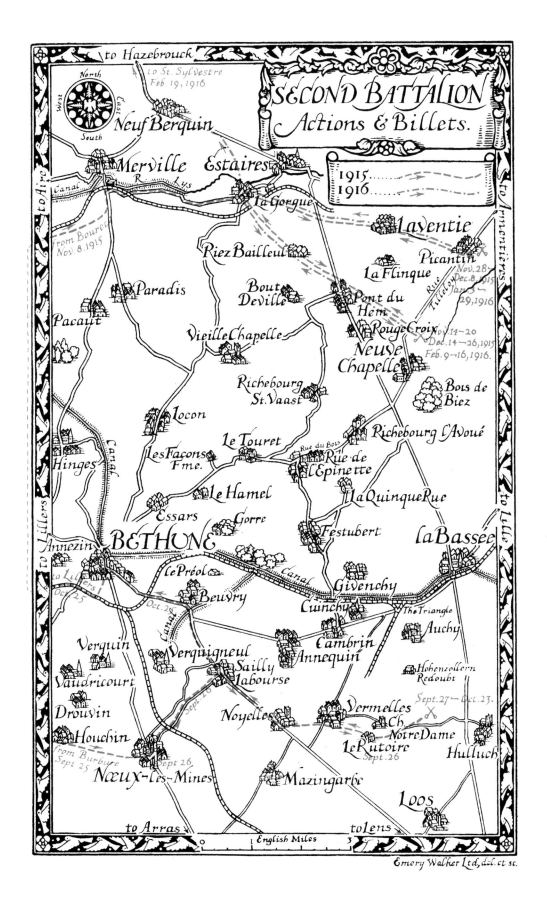

Battalion stood as follows, and the list is instructive as showing how very little the Army of that epoch had begun to specialize. It was commanded by Lieut.-Colonel Hon. L. Butler; Adjutant, Captain (temporary) J. S. N. FitzGerald; Transport Officer, Lieutenant C. Moore; Bomb Officer, 2nd Lieutenant R. E. Coxon; Quartermaster, 2nd Lieutenant J. Brennan. Companies: No. 1, Captain Witts, Lieutenant Nugent, 2nd Lieutenant Pym; No. 2, Captain (temporary) Parsons, 2nd Lieutenants Hannay and James; No. 3, Captain (temporary) R. Rankin, Lieutenant Montgomery, 2nd Lieutenant Watson; No. 4, Captain (temporary) Hubbard, Lieutenant Kinahan, 2nd Lieutenant Brew.

Drafts of eighty-five men in all had come in since they went into Brigade Reserve, and Captain Alexander, who had been sick with influenza and fever for the past fortnight, during which time the 1st Battalion had demanded him urgently, went over to it as Temporary C.O. and Temporary Major.

So they settled down at Bourecq, which in peace-time has few merits, and devoted themselves to eating and to talking about food between meals. In the trenches they had not eaten with discrimination. Out of them, they all demanded variety and abundance, sweets, solids and savouries devoured at any hour, and sleep unlimited to settle it all.

Lord Cavan came on the last day of the month and addressed them as their Divisional Commander; which meant a parade in wet weather. He congratulated them on their fine work of the preceding fortnight (the trench-affairs round Hohenzollern) and on "the fine fighting spirit which had enabled them to persevere and accomplish their task in spite of an initial rebuff." ("He knew as well as we did that if we hadn't hoofed the Hun out of the trench the Hun would have hoofed us," was one comment.) He assured the Battalion that the lives unfortunately lost in the undertaking had not been lost in vain, and that it was only by continually harassing him that we would eventually defeat the German. He said that the Battalion had begun well, and he only wished for it that it might do as well as the 1st, "than which no finer example of a Guards Battalion existed." "And that," said one of those who were young when the speech was made, and lived to be very old and wise, "was at a time when we had literally no troop railways, and relatively no Artillery. And they told us we were going to break through every time we had cleared fifty Jerries out of a front-line trench!"

Two Lewis-guns, which were then new things, had been supplied to the Battalion and teams were made up and instructed in the working by 2nd Lieutenant Hannay, while the Bomb Officer, 2nd Lieutenant Coxon, had his bombing-teams out daily, and it is recorded that on one afternoon the bombers of Nos. 1 and 2 Companies, thirty-two in all, threw fifty live bombs at practice. Then it rained drearily and incessantly for days and nights on end, and there was nothing to do but to eat and attend lectures. A fresh draft of fifty men turned up. Second Lieutenant Keenan, who had been sick, and 2nd Lieutenant Synge, who had been wounded in the bombing attack, rejoined a few days before they marched with the 2nd Guards Brigade to new billets at La Gorgue in mud. Here they had huge choice of mixed discomforts, for the whole sad landscape was sodden with autumn rain. They were to take over from the 60th Brigade at Laventie a peaceful semi-flooded sector, with every promise, for which they were not in the least grateful, of staying in that part of the world the winter long.

The seasonal pause had begun when men merely died without achieving visible result, even in the Press. The C.O.'s and Adjutants of the Brigade, accompanied by the Brigadier-General, made wet and melancholy reconnaissances to their destined stamping-ground – an occasion when every one is forgiven for being in the worst of tempers. The one unpardonable offence was false and bustling optimism. The Battalion's line ran from Winchester Road on the left to South Moated Grange on the right, all "in very bad order owing to the recent rain."

Next day, the 12th November, the Medical Officer and the four Company Commanders were added to the reconnaissance parties. ("It was like going into a cold bath, one toe at a time. And I don't see how looking at it for a week in advance could have made it any better.") Wet days followed the wet nights with Hunnish precision. A wretched Lieutenant (Montgomery) was sent out like Noah's dove to "arrange the route for leading his Company in," the communication-trenches being flooded; and on the 14th November, after Divine Service, the men were paraded in billets and "rubbed their feet with anti-frostbite grease preparatory to going into the trenches." It seems a small matter, but the Battalion had been in the way of hearing a good deal about the horrors of the previous winter in the Ypres Salient, when men were forbidden to stand for more than twelve hours at a time belly-deep in water without relief – "if possible." ("That foot-greasing fatigue, with what the old hands told us was in store, put the wind up us worse than Loos. We was persuaded we would be drowned and frost-bit by whole platoons.")

They paraded that afternoon and marched down to their dreary baptism. Boots – "gum, thigh, long" – had been supplied limitedly to the Companies, and they changed into them in a ruined cottage behind the lines, leaving their marching boots to be picked up on return. "Thus some men were able to wade without getting wet," says the Diary. It was not so with others. For example, the whole of No. 3 Company was taken along one thoroughly flooded communication-trench half-way up their thighs. A platoon of No. 2 was similarly treated, only their guide lost his way, and as all the support-trenches were flooded, 2 and 3 had to be packed in the fire-trenches. Nos. 4 and 1 got off without a complete soaking, and it is pathetic to see how the Battalion, to whom immoderate and omnipresent dampness was still a new thing, record their adventures in detail. But it was not so much water as the immensely sticky mud that oppressed them, with the consequent impossibility of being able to lie down even for a moment. Then it froze of nights. All which are miseries real as wounds or sickness.

They were kept warm for the whole of their tour by repairing the fallen parapets. Shelling was light and not important, but some shrapnel wounded Captain G. Hubbard, and enemy snipers killed three and wounded six men in the forty-eight hours. When the Coldstream relieved them on the evening of the 16th November, which they did in less than four hours, they felt that they could not face the flooded communication-trenches a second time, and made their way home across the open in the dark with no accident. Avoidable discomfort is ever worse than risk of death; for, like the lady in the *Ingoldsby Legends*, they "didn't mind death but they couldn't stand pinching."

On relief, they went into Brigade Reserve in close billets near Rouge Croix, No. 1 Company furnishing an officer and platoon as garrison for the two posts Rouge Croix East and West. Life was reduced to watching the rain drive in swathes across the flat desolation of the land, improving billets under the supervision of the Engineers, which is ever a trial, and sending parties to flounder and dig in the dark at new works behind the firing-line.

Snipers on both sides began to find each other's range and temperament, and "put in good work" according to their lights and opportunities. The enemy developed a taste for mining, and it was necessary to investigate by patrol some craters that appeared spottily on the Battalion's front, and might hide anything. The Germans met these attempts with grenades (minenwerfers not being yet in existence), which fell short; but their burst and direction gave our rifles their line. The days passed with long, quiet intervals when one caught the drawing scrape of a spade or the thicker note of a hammer on revetting stakes – all difficult to locate exactly, for sound runs along trenches like water. A pump would gurgle, a bucket clink, or a shift of the rare sunlight sparkle on some cautiously raised periscope. That crumb of light drawing a shot from an over-keen watcher, half a dozen single shots would answer it. One or other of the four Battalion Lewis-guns would be moved to spray the sector of tumbled dirt which it commanded. In the midst of the stuttered protest, without whoop or wail of warning, a flight of whizz-bangs would call the parapet to order as emphatically as the raps of the schoolmaster's cane silence the rising clamour of a classroom. The hint would be taken, for none was really anxious to make trouble; and silence would return so swiftly that, before the spades had ceased repairing the last-blown gap in the head-cover, one heard the yawn of an utterly bored private in the next bay fretting under his kit because there was no possibility of sneaking a "lay-down."

It was pettifogging work for both sides, varied with detestable cleaning out "the height of the muck," wrestling with sodden sand-bags and throwing up breastworks on exposed ground, so that men might smuggle themselves along clear of the flooded communication-trenches.

The first idea of raiding on a system was born out of that dull time: the size of the forces is noteworthy.

On the 20th November, a misty day when things were quiet, the C.O.'s of the two front-line Battalions (3rd Grenadiers and 2nd Irish Guards) together with the Commandants of Artillery Brigades and Batteries in the vicinity were assembled "to select passages to be cut by Artillery fire at certain places, and for these to be kept constantly open, while raids one or two Companies strong paid surprise visits to the German lines, killing or capturing and returning." Three such places were thus chosen on the Brigade front, one of which was in the line of the centre Company of the 2nd Irish Guards. Having neatly laid out that much trouble for their successors, they were relieved by the 3rd Coldstream, marched to billets at La Gorgue and came into Divisional Reserve at 10.30 p.m. They expected, as they were entitled to, a long night in the Girls' School which they occupied. But, for reasons which have long since passed with dead policies, it was important that the late Mr. John Redmond, M.P., should inspect them next morning. So their sleep was cut and they and their 1st Battalion marched a mile out of La Gorgue, and hung about for an hour on a muddy road in morning chill, till Mr. Redmond, blandly ignorant of his deep unpopularity at the moment, walked down the lines and shook hands after the manner of Royalty with each officer. One of these chanced to be an ex-R.I.C who, on the last occasion they had met, was engaged in protecting Mr. Redmond from the attentions of Mr. O'Brien's followers in a faction-fight at Mallow. Mr. Redmond did not remember this, but the tale unholily delighted the Battalion, on their way to Divine Service afterwards.

Lieutenant T. Nugent left them on the 21st November to join the 1st Battalion with a view to appointment as Adjutant. This was a season, too, when a little leave might be counted on as within the possibilities. Nothing was breathed about it officially, but hopeful rumours arose that they were likely to be in billets well back of the firing-line for the next few weeks. The mere chance of five or six days' return to real life acts as unexpectedly as drink or drugs on different temperaments. Some men it fills with strenuous zeal. Others it placates so that the hardiest "bad character" can take advantage of them; and there are yet those who, fretting and yearning beneath the mask of discipline, are hardly fit to approach on light matters till their date for home has been settled. Moreover, one's first service-leave is of a quality by itself, and in those days was specially precious to parents and relatives, who made themselves cling to the piteous belief that the war might, somehow, end at any moment, even while their beloved was safe with them.

Bomb-practice was taken up seriously while at La Gorgue, and the daily allowance of live bombs increased to sixty. Drums and fifes had been sent out from the Regimental Orderly Room, together with a few selected drummers from Warley. The Battalion promptly increased the number from its own ranks and formed a full Corps of Drums and Fifes, which paraded for the first time on the 23rd November, when they exchanged billets with the 1st Coldstream at Merville. The first tune played was the Regimental March and the second "Brian Boru," which goes notably to the Drums. (In those days the Battalion was overwhelmingly Irish in composition.) Captain the Hon. H. R. Alexander, who had been in hospital with influenza for a week, rejoined on the 23rd as Second in Command.

Merville was a mixed, but not too uncomfortable, experience. The Battalion with the rest of the Guards Division was placed temporarily at the disposal of the Forty-fifth Division as a reserve, a position which meant being neither actually in the trenches nor out of them. They were beyond reach of rifle-fire and in a corner not usually attended to by Artillery. There was a roof to the Officers' Mess, and some of the windows did not lack glass. They ate off tables, with newspapers for cloth, and enjoyed the luxury of chairs. The men lived more or less in trenches, but were allowed out, like well-watched poultry, at night or on misty mornings. All this was interspersed with squad drill, instruction, baths and a Battalion concert; while, in view of possibilities that might develop, Captain Alexander and the four Company Commanders "reconnoitred certain routes from Merville to Neuve Chapelle." But every one knew at heart that there was nothing doing or to be done except to make oneself as comfortable as might be with all the blankets that one could steal, at night, and all the food one could compass by day. Leave was going on regularly. Captain and Adjutant J. S. N. FitzGerald left on the 26th for ten days and Lieutenant A. Pym took over his duties. When Adjutants can afford to go on leave, life ought to be easy.

Then they shifted to Laventie in a full blizzard, relieving the 2nd Scots Guards in Brigade Reserve. Their own Brigade, the 2nd, was taking over from the 3rd Guards Brigade, and Captain Alexander, who not unnaturally caught a fresh attack of influenza later, spent the afternoon reconnoitring the trenches which he would have to occupy on the 28th. The No Man's Land to be held in front of them was marsh and ditch, impassable

Then they shifted to Laventie in a full blizzard...
The No Man's Land to be held in front of them was
marsh and ditch, impassable save when frozen. It
carried no marks in the shape of hedges or stumps to
guide men out or back on patrol...
The old front-line breastworks, Laventie, 1915.

save when frozen. It carried no marks in the shape of hedges or stumps to guide men out or back on patrol, and its great depth – three hundred yards in places from wire to wire – made thorough ferreting most difficult. In this war, men with small-arms that carried twenty-eight hundred yards, hardly felt safe unless they were within half bow-shot of their enemy.

The Battalion's entry into their forlorn heritage was preceded by a small house-warming in the shape of an Artillery bombardment on our side. This, they knew, by doleful experience, would provoke retaliation, and the relief was accordingly delayed till dark, which avoided all casualties. Their general orders were to look out for likely spots whence to launch "small enterprises" against the enemy. It meant patrols wandering out in rain and a thaw that had followed the stiff frost, and doing their best to keep direction by unassisted intellect and a compass. ("Ye'll understand that, in those days, once you was out on your belly in that muck, ye knew no more than a babe in a blanket. Dark, wet and windy it was with big, steep, deep ditches waiting on ye every yard. All *we* took of it was a stiff neck, and all we heard was Jerry gruntin' in his pigstye!") A patrol of No. 4 Company under Lieutenant Brew managed to get up within ear-shot of the German wire on the night of the 29th, crossing a drain by a providential plank. While they lay close, listening to the Huns hammering stakes in their trenches, they saw a German patrol slip home by the very bridge which they themselves had used. Hope ran high of catching the same party next night in the same place, but it rained torrentially, and they found it impossible to move a man out across the bog. They spent their time baling their own trenches as these filled, and were happy to wade only ankle-deep. But their professional lives were peaceful. Though the enemy shelled mechanically at intervals not a soul was even wounded when on the 30th November they came back for the short rest in billets in Laventie.

On their return to the "Red House" where they relieved the 1st Coldstream on the 2nd December, their night patrols discovered, apparently for the first time, that the enemy held their front line very thinly and their support in strength. As a matter of later observation, it was established that, on that sector, the front line mostly withdrew after dark and slept at the back till our unsympathetic guns stirred them up. Our custom seemed always to crowd the front line both with men and responsibility.

The main of the Battalion's work was simple aquatics; draining off of waters that persisted in running uphill, and trying to find the bottom of fluid and unstable ditches where things once lost disappeared for ever. They had not yet seen a man choking in mud, and found it rather hard to believe that such things could happen. But the Somme was to convince them.

The organization of the Front evolved itself behind them as time passed,

and Batteries and Battalions came to understand each other. Too much
enemy shelling on a trench led to a telephone-call, and after a decent interval of from two to six minutes (the record was one minute fifty-five sec-
onds) our Batteries would signify their displeasure by a flight of perhaps
thirty shells at one drench, or several separate salvos. As a rule that was
enough, and this, perhaps, led to the legend that the enemy artillery was
weakening. And, with organization, came the inevitable floods of paper-
work that Authority insists on. There was a conference of the four C.O.'s of
the Brigade on the subject on the 6th December, where suggestions were
invited for "reducing correspondence" and for "saving Company Officers as
much as possible," which seemed, like many other conferences, to have
ended in more paper-work and resolutions on "the importance of keeping a
log-book in the trenches by each Company Officer." The log-book handed
over by every Company Commander to his relief is essential to the conti-
nuity of trench-war life, though nine-tenths of the returns demanded
seemed pure waste.

Yet, there is another point of view. ("Looking back on it, one sees that
that everlasting having to pull yourself together to fill in tosh about rasp-
berry jam, or how men ought to salute, steadies one a good deal. We cursed
it at the time, though!")

On the 7th December patrols reported the enemy with full trenches
working on their front-line wire, upon which our Artillery cut it up, and
the enemy turned out in the evening to repair damages. The local Battery B,
76th Brigade R.F.A., was asked "to fire again." They fired two salvos at
10.15 p.m., and two more one hour later. One Lewis-gun of No. 1 Company
"also fired at this point." So simple and homeopathic was war in that age!

On the 8th their sister Battalion took over from them at Red House, in a
relief completed in ninety minutes, and the Drums of the 1st Battalion
played the Companies through Laventie, while the Drums of the 2nd
played them into billets at La Gorgue. For the first time since they had
been in France all the officers of both Battalions messed together, in one
room, for all the time that they were there; and, as supplies from friends at
home were ample and varied, the tales of some of the meals at La Gorgue
endure to this day.

The system of the Guards' company training always allowed large lati-
tude to Company Officers as long as required results were obtained; and
they fell back on it when bombers and Lewis-gun teams were permanently
added to the organization. With the reservation that bombing-practice
with live bombs was only to take place under the Battalion Bombing
Officer, Company Commanders were made entirely responsible for the
training both of their bombers and Lewis-gunners. It made an almost
immediate difference in the handiness and suppleness of the teams, and

woke up inter-company competition. The teams, it may have been pointed out, were surprisingly keen and intelligent. One officer, finding a nucleus of ex-taxi-drivers among his drafts, treated the Lewis-gun as a simple internal-combustion engine, which simile they caught on to at once and conveyed it in their own words and gestures to their slower comrades.

On the 12th December, the Battalion was paraded while the C.O. presented the ribbon of the D.C.M. to Lance-Corporal Quinn for gallantry in Chalk-Pit Wood at the Battle of Loos, that now seemed to all of them a century distant.

On the 14th they moved to a more southerly sector to take over from the Welsh Guards, and to pick up a Company of the 13th R.W. Fusiliers; one platoon being attached to each Company for instruction, and the Fusiliers' B.H.Q. messing with their own. There is no record what the Welshmen thought of their instructors or they of them, except the fragment of a tale of trench-fatigues during which, to the deep disgust of the Irish, who are not loudly vocal by temperament, "the little fellas sang like canary-birds."

Their new lines, reached across mud, from Pont du Hem, were the old, well-known and not so badly-looked-after stretch from North Moated Grange Street to Erith Street at the lower end of the endless Tilleloy Road which faced south-easterly towards the Aubers Ridge, then held by the enemy. The relief was finished without demonstrations beyond a few shrapnel launched at one of the posts, Fort Erith.

On the 15th, 2nd Lieutenant Brew went out with a patrol to investigate some mine-craters in front of the German firing-line and found them empty, but woke up an enemy machine-gun in the background. Other patrols reported like slackness, but when they tried to take advantage of it, they met the same gun awake, and came home upon their bellies. The ground being so flat, however, the German machines could not get well down to their work of shaving the landscape, and fifteen inches will clear a prostrate man if he lies close. A snipers' team had been organized, and the deep peace of that age may be seen from the fact that at the end of a quiet day, the only claim put in was for "one victim who was passing a gap between two mine-craters."

They were relieved by the 1st Coldstream on the 16th December and went into billets, not more than two miles back, at Pont du Hem and La Flinque Farm, with scattered platoons and single officers holding posts in the neighbourhood of the Rue du Bacquerot. A draft of forty-seven men, which should have been fifty, turned up that same day. The odd three had contrived to mislay themselves as only men on draft can, but were gathered in later with marvellous explanations at the tips of their ready tongues. Officers sent out from Warley also got lost en route, to the wrath of Company Commanders clamouring for them. One writer home complains: "it seems that they are waylaid by some unknown person at the base and sent off for quite long periods to take charge of mysterious parties which dig trenches somewhere unknown." This was the origin, though they knew it not at the Front, of the Divisional Entrenching Battalion – a hated and unpopular necessity.

On the 18th December Captain Eric Greer joined on transfer from the 3rd Reserve Battalion as Second in Command, and a couple of Companies (Nos. 1 and 2) had to start the relief at Winchester Farm by daylight. The authorities had ordered the trenches should be kept clear that evening for a number of gas-cylinders to be placed in the parapets. It meant running the heavy cylinders up a light, man-power, railway to the front line, when they were slung on poles, carried to the recesses that had been dug out for them and there buried beneath sand-bags. ("There was all sorts and manners of gadgets made and done in those days. We was told they was all highly scientific. All us Micks ever took by any of them was fatigues. No! We did *not* like them gas-tanks.")

The next day a shell lit within five yards of a recess apparently stocked with extra gas-tanks. The Officer of No. 2 Company at once telephoned for retaliation. "After a slight lapse during which the Gunners shelled our trench, and were told by the O.C. No. 2 that that was not *exactly* what he wanted, the retaliation was quite satisfactory." They could easily count the number of shells that fell in those days and piously entered them in the Company log-books.

Here follows an appreciation, compiled at first hand, of their surroundings, and the methods by which they kept themselves more or less dry. "Drains are a very difficult problem as there is probably only a fall of three feet in as many miles behind the line. The system is that the men drain the water in the actual trenches or redoubts into a drain slightly in rear. Then there are a number of drains, two or three per Company-area, running straight back. Three men are told off to these and do nothing but patrol them, deepening and clearing where necessary.... From about two hundred yards in rear, the R.E. take and run off the water by larger drains and ditches already in existence into a river some miles in rear. At least that is the theory. The line is now wonderfully dry to live in as the profuse supply of trench-boards has made an enormous difference. Thus men can walk dry-shod up Winchester Street, our main communication-trench, on a path of floorboards built up on piles over, perhaps, three feet of water. Of course, it hits both ways, as you are taken out of the water, but also out of the ground above your waist, and parapets must be built accordingly.... The front line, which is also the only one, as the labour of keeping it habitable absorbs every available man, is composed of a sandbag redoubt about seven or eight feet high, and very thick. It is recessed and traversed. About ten or fifteen yards in rear runs the 'traffic trench,' a boarded path which sometimes runs along the top of black slime, and sometimes turns into a bridge on piles over smelly ponds. Between the redoubt and traffic-trench, rising out of slime, are a weird collection of hovels about three feet high, of sandbags and tin. They are the local equivalents of 'dug-outs' – cover from rain but not from shells. Everywhere there are rats."

Having added gas to their local responsibilities they suffered from the enthusiasms of the specialists attached to, and Generals who believed in, the filthy weapon. As soon as possible after the cylinders which they feared and treated with the greatest respect, were in position, all the talk was of a real and poisonous gas-attack. They were told on the 19th December that such a one would be launched by them on the first night the wind should favour it, and that their patrols would specially reconnoitre the ground that, by the blessing of fortune, the gas would waft across. Then the moon shone viciously and all special patrols were ordered off.

On the 20th the Gunner Officer, Major Young, paid a breakfast call, with the pleasant news that he was going to open an old repaired gap in the enemy wire, and cut two new ones, which, on the established principle of "throwing stones at little brother," meant the infantry would be "retaliated on." He did it. The C.O.'s of the Battalion and the 1st Coldstream, and the Brigade Major, made a most careful periscope reconnaissance of the ground, with particular attention to the smoking gaps that Major Young had blasted, and arranged for a joint reconnaissance by the 1st Coldstream and 2nd Irish Guards for that very evening. The two subalterns told off to that job attended the conference. Second Lieutenant Brew, who had gifts that way, represented our side, for the affair naturally became an inter-regimental one from the first, and 2nd Lieutenant Green the Coldstream. That afternoon everybody conferred – the Brigade Commanders of the 2nd and 3rd Guards Brigades, with their Staffs, all four C.O.'s of the 2nd Brigade, and the C.O. of the 1st Welsh Guards; and between them they arranged the attack in detail, with a simplicity that in later years almost made some of the survivors of that conference weep when they were reminded of it. The gas was to be turned on at first, while machine-guns and Lewis-guns would make a joyous noise together for five minutes to drown the roar of its escape. The Artillery would start heavy fire "at points in rear" simultaneously with the noisy gas. At five minutes past Zero machine-guns would stop, and the Artillery would slow down. But thirty-five minutes later they would "quicken up." Three-quarters of an hour after Zero "gas would be turned off," and, five minutes after that, the attacking parties would start "with gas helmets on their heads but rolled up" and, penetrating the enemy's second line, would "do all possible damage before returning." Then they arranged to reassemble next day, after inspecting the ground. The Battalion was relieved that same evening by the 1st Coldstream, whom they expected to have for their confederates in the attack, and lay up at Pont du Hem.

On the 21st December Brew, who had been out the night before reconnoitring with Green of the Coldstream, started on yet another investigation of the enemy wire at 3 a.m. They got right up to the wire, were overlooked by a German patrol, and spotted by a machine-gun on their way home. "But they lay down and the bullets went over them." There was another conference at Winchester House in the afternoon, where all details were revised, and the day ended with a message to the troops who would be called upon, that the "attack had been greatly modified."

On the 22nd December the notion of following up the gas by a two-Company attack was washed out, and the assailants cut down to a select party, under the patient but by now slightly bewildered Brew, of bombers and bludgeoneers, who were to enter the German trench after three-quarters of an hour of mixed gas and Artillery, "collect information and do all possible damage." If the gas and guns had produced the desired effect, five more bombers and bludgeonists, and a machine-gunner with one crow-bar would follow as a demolishing-party, paying special attention to telephones, the bowels of machine-guns and, which was really unkind, drains. The R.E. supplied the bludgeons "of a very handy variety," and everything was present and correct except the favouring breeze. ("And, all the while, ye'll understand, our parapet stuffed with these dam' gas-tanks the way they could be touched off by any whizz-bang that was visiting there, and the whole Brigade and every one else praying the wind 'ud hold off long enough for some one else to have the job of uncorking the bottle. Gas is no thrick for beginners!")

They called the attack off once more, and the Battalion, with only one night left of their tour, in which to "uncork the bottle," wired to the 1st Coldstream at Pont du Hem, "Latest betting, Coldstream 2 to 1 on (T. and O.) Irish Guards, 6 to 4 against." Back came the prompt answer, "Although the first fence is a serious obstacle, it should not take more than twenty-four hours with such fearless leapers. Best luck and a safe return. No betting here. All broke. We think we have caught a spy." He turned out to be a perfectly innocent Frenchman "whose only offence was, apparently, that he existed in the foreground at the moment when a bombing-school, some miles in rear, elected to send up some suspicious blue lights."

On the 23rd December, after a very quiet night, an entirely new plan of attack came in from an unnamed specialist who suggested that the gas (words cannot render their weariness of the accursed thing at this stage!) should be let off quite quietly without any Artillery fire or unusual small-arm demonstration, at about four in the morning, when the odds were most of the enemy would be asleep, and that of those on duty few would ever have heard the sound of escaping gas. As the expert noted, "It requires a quick decision and a firm determination to give an alarm at 4 a.m., unless one is certain that it is not a false alarm, especially to a Prussian officer." The hope was that the slow-waking and highly-to-his-superiors-respectful Hun would be thus caught in his dug-outs. The Artillery would, gas or no gas, only give a general warning, and the suggested barrage (the first time, oddly enough, that the word is employed in the Diary) in rear of the enemy trenches would prevent his reserves from coming up into the gas-zone, "where there is always a chance that they may be gassed in spite of their gas-helmets." So all the Commanders held yet another conference, and agreed that the gas should be loosed at 4.30, that the barrage in the rear should be abandoned and a bombardment of the enemy's parapet substituted for it, and that no patrols should be sent out. The Companies were duly warned. The wind was not. The enemy spent the day shelling points in the rear till our guns retaliated on their front line, which they returned by shelling our parapet with small stuff. One piece they managed to blow in, and turned a machine-gun on the gap. They also made one flooded dug-out a shade less habitable than before. The wind stayed true south all night, and the rain it brought did more damage to the hovels and huts than any enemy shells; for the Chaplain and the Second in Command were half buried by "the ceiling of their bedroom becoming detached. The calamity was borne with beautiful fortitude." (Even a Second in Command cannot express all his sentiments before a Chaplain.)

Christmas Eve was officially celebrated by good works; for the Battalion, its gas still intact, was warned to finish relief by eight o'clock, because, for the rest of the night, our guns would bombard German communication-trenches and back-areas so as to interfere as much as possible with their Christmas Dinner issues. The 1st Coldstream filed in, and they filed out back to their various billets and posts at Pont du Hem, La Flinque Farm, and the rest. Christmas Day, their first at the front, and in the line, was officially washed out and treated as the 25th of December, dinners and festivities being held over till they should be comfortably settled in Reserve. Some attempts at "fraternization" seem to have been begun between the front-line trenches in the early morning, but our impersonal and impartial guns shelled every moving figure visible, besides plastering cross-roads and traffic lines at the back. Lieut.-Colonel McCalmont, Lord Desmond FitzGerald and Captain Antrobus rode over from the 1st Battalion for lunch, and in the afternoon Lord Cavan spoke to the officers of his approaching departure from the Guards Division to command the Fourteenth Corps; of his regrets at the change, and of his undisguised hopes that the Guards Division might be attached to his new command. "He finished by telling us that we were following in the steps of our great 1st Battalion, which, as he has told the King and Sir Francis Lloyd, was as fine a Battalion as ever trod." Then there was a decorated and be-candled Christmas tree brought out from England by Captain Alexander, which appeared at dinner, and, later, was planted out in the garden at the back of the Mess that all might admire. Likewise, No. 1 Company received a gift of a gramophone, a concertina and mouth-organs from Miss Laurette Taylor. The Irish take naturally to mouth-organs. The gramophone was put under strict control, at once.

On Boxing Day the whole of the 2nd Guards Brigade were relieved by the 1st Brigade, and went back out of reach of the shells to Merville *via* La Gorgue, passing on the road several Companies of the 1st Battalion on their way to relieve the 1st Scots Guards. ("When the like of that happens, and leave is given for to take notice of each other, ye may say that the two Battalions cheer. But 'tis more in the nature of a running roar, ye'll understand, when we Micks meet up.")

Merville billets were thoroughly good, and the Officers' Mess ran to a hard-worked but quite audible piano. Best of all, the fields around were too wet for anything like drill.

The postponed Christmas Dinners for the men were given, two Companies at a time, on the 28th and 29th, whereby Lieutenant Moore, then Acting Quartermaster, distinguished himself by promptitude, resource and organization, remembered to his honour far beyond mere military decorations. At the eleventh hour, owing to the breweries in the back-area being flooded, there was a shortage of beer that should wash down the beef, and the pounds of solidest plum-pudding. "As it would have been obviously preferable to have had beer and no dinners to dinners and no beer, Lieutenant Moore galloped off to Estaires pursued by a waggon, while the Second in Command, having discovered that some of the Eleventh Corps (it is always sound to stand well with the Corps you hope to join) also wanted beer, promised to get it for them if supplied with a lorry, obtained same and bumped off to Hazebrouck. Lieutenant Moore succeeded in getting 500 litres in Estaires and got back in time." So all was well.

Festivities began a little before two, and lasted till eight. They sat at tables and ate off plates which they had not done since leaving England. Food and drink are after all the only vital matters in war.

The year closed with an interesting lecture on the principles of war, delivered at La Gorgue, which dealt with the "futility of ever surrendering the initiative," and instanced some French operations round Hartmannsweillerkopf on the Alsace front, when a German General, heavily attacked, launched a counter-attack elsewhere along the line, forcing his

53

enemy to return to their original position after heavy loss. Another example from the German gas-attack on St. Julien, when the English confined themselves to desperately attacking the captured section, whereby they only lost more men, instead of counter-attacking farther down the ridge. This led to the conclusion that "to sit passively on the defensive with no idea of attacking was so fatuous as not to be worth considering as an operation of war." At present, said the lecturer, we were on the defensive, but purely to gain time until we had the men and materials ready for a great offensive. Meantime the correct action was to "wear down the enemy in every way." Whence the conclusion that the attitude of the Guards Division for the past seven weeks had been eminently proper; since our guns had bombarded "all the time," and had cut the German wire in many places, so that the enemy never knew when he would be attacked. Further, our troops had thrice entered his trenches, besides twice making every preparation to do so (when, finding he was ready, we "very rightly abandoned the enterprise"). Not once, it was shown, had the enemy even attempted to enter our trenches. In fact, he was reduced "to a state of pulp and blotting-paper." The lecture ended with the news that our motor-buses and lateral railways could concentrate one Army Corps on any part of the British front in twenty-four hours and two Corps in forty-eight. Also that the Supreme Command had decided it was useless to break through anywhere on a narrower front than twenty kilometres.

And on this good hearing the year '15 ended for the 2nd Battalion of the Irish Guards; the War, owing to the lack of men and material which should have been trained and prepared beforehand, having just two years, ten months, and eleven days more to run.

1916

THE SALIENT AND
THE SOMME

THE MILD AND RAINY WEATHER loosed floods on all the low-lying fields round Laventie. The 2nd Guards Brigade relieved the 3rd in the Laventie sector, and the 2nd Battalion Irish Guards marched seven miles in wind and wet from La Gorgue, of the battered little church, to its old ground and old routine – first at the north end of Laventie where it took over Dead End, Picantin and Laventie East posts, from the 4th Grenadiers; and, on the evening of the 3rd January, into the well-kept trenches beyond Red House. They relieved the 1st Coldstream here, and their leading Company, in column of route behind Red House, lost six men on the road from a savage, well-timed burst of H.E. One man had an extraordinary double escape. A fragment of shell first hit his ammunition, which exploded, leaving him, for some absurd reason, unhurt. Even as he was trying to find out what had happened, a big shell dove directly under his feet, and, as he said, if it had burst "they wouldn't have found the nails to my boots." But it plumped harmlessly in the muddy ground. The same kind Providence looked after the Orderly-room kitten. Her faithful orderly was carrying the little lady up to war on rats, when two blind shells pitched, one on each side of him.

An unexpected diversion turned up in the front line in the shape of a cinema operator who unlimbered his camera on the parapet behind the sand-bags and took pictures of our guns shelling enemy wire a hundred yards ahead. Then he demanded "scenes in the trenches," which were supplied him, with all the Irish sense of drama, but, as local opinion thought, a little too much "arranged." Notably one picture of a soldier tending a grave. An officer correspondent writes grimly, "We have quite enough work digging graves to mind about tending them." The film duly appeared in the Halls and Revues, sometimes before the eyes of those who would never again behold in life one particular face there.

It turned out a quiet tour of duty; the two lines were so close together that much shelling was inexpedient, and snipers gave no trouble. So all hands were free to attend their own comforts, notably the care and discharge of drains. The R.E. who, contrary to popular belief, sometimes have bowels, had added wooden floors to many of the little huts behind the redoubts. Company Headquarters were luxurious, with real windows, and even window-curtains; the slimy trenches were neatly boarded over and posted and men went about their business almost dry-shod. It was, as we know, the custom of those parts that, before entering the line, troops should dump their ankle-boots at a farm-house just behind Red House and go on in the long trench boots. For no earthly reason that the Irish could arrive at, the Hun took it into his methodical head one night, to shell their huge boot-dump where, as a matter of course, some regimental shoemakers were catching up with repairs. The shoemakers bolted like ferreted rabbits, and all the world, except those whose boots were buried laughed at them. So long as a man comes through it alive, his agonies and contortions in the act of dodging death are fair game.

On the nights of the 4th and 5th January they began to engineer the detail of a local raid which marked progress in the art. Patrols went out from each Company in the front line to hunt for weak places. The patrol from the right Company worked to within fifteen yards of the enemy, got into boggy ground, noisy with loose wire, listened an hour to the Germans working and talking, and came back. The right-centre Company patrol slopped up a ditch for a full furlong, then ran into a cross-ditch fifteen feet wide, with a trip-wire (the enemy disliked being taken unawares), and also returned like the dove of old. Similarly, the left-centre patrol, which found more ditch and trip-wires leading them to a singularly stout section of trench where two Germans looked over the edge of the parapet, and the general landscape was hostile. The left Company had the luck. It was an officer's patrol commanded again by 2nd Lieutenant Brew. Their crawl led them along a guiding line of willows, and to within six feet of a salient guarded by a three-foot wire belt. But a few yards farther down, they came across a gap our guns had made – not clean-cut, but easy enough, in their opinion, to "negotiate." As far as men on their bellies could make out, the line seemed held by sentries at wide intervals who, after the manner of single sentries, fired often at nothing and sent up lights for the pleasure of seeing their support-line answer them. ("As we was everlastingly telling the new hands, the fewer there are of ye *anny*where, the less noise should ye be after making *anny*how. But 'tis always the small, lonely, miserable little man by himself that gives forth noises like large platoons.") Then they were relieved by the 1st Coldstream, and their Acting C.O. (Captain Eric Greer) was instructed to produce a scheme for a really good raid from the left of their line on the weak place discovered. The Coldstream would attend to it during their tour, if the Irish furnished the information. Greer worked it out lovingly to the last detail. Three riflemen and three bombers were to lead off on the right, and as many on the left followed by a "killing and demolition party," armed with bludgeons, of an officer and eight other ranks. A support party of one N.C.O. and five other ranks, with rifles and bayonets, and a connecting party of two signallers with telephones and four stretcher-bearers brought up the rear of what the ribald afterwards called "our mournful procession." It was further laid down that a wire-cutting party (and the men hated wire-cutting) would "improve the gap in the enemy's wire" for the space of one hour. The raiders were to work quietly along the line of the providential willows till they found the gap; then would split into two gangs left and right, and attend to the personnel in the trench "as quickly and silently as possible, never using bombs when they can bayonet a man." The rest were to enter afterwards, and destroy and remove all they could find. "If possible and convenient, they will take a prisoner who will be immediately passed back to our trench by the supporting party. Faces to be blacked for the sake of 'frightfulness,' mutual recognition and invisibility," and electric torches carried. The officer in charge was to be a German linguist, for the reason that a prisoner, hot and shaken at the moment of capture, and before being "passed back," was likely to exude more information than when cold and safe in our own lines.

There was nothing special on at the Front just then; and the 2nd Battalion and the Coldstream discussed and improved that raid at every point they could think of. One authority wanted a double raid, from left and right fronts simultaneously, but they explained that this particular affair would need "so much quietness" in combined stalking that it would be "inconvenient to run it on a time schedule." Then our guns were given word to cut wire in quite other directions from the chosen spot which was no more to be disturbed till the proper time than a pet cover. That was on

OVERLEAF

The 2nd Battalion of the Irish Guards was young throughout, the maker of its own history, and the inheritor of the Guards' tradition; but its common background was ever Warley where they had all first met and been moulded – officers and men together.

Officers of the 2nd Battalion in France, 1916:
Back row, from left to right: LIEUT. H. MONTGOMERY, LIEUT. F.M. HARVEY (*Medical Officer*), CAPT F.H. WITTS, CAPT. J.B. KEENAN, LIEUT. A.R. PYM, LIEUT. C.H. BREW, CAPT. C.J.O'H. MOORE, LIEUT. J. BRENNAN, CAPT. A.G. PARSONS, CAPT. R. RANKIN. *Middle row*: CAPT. REV. FATHER S.S. KNAPP, CAPT. E.B. GREER, COL. HON. L.J. BUTLER, CAPT. J.S.N. FITZGERALD, CAPT. HON. H.R. ALEXANDER. *Front row*: LIEUT. R. HANNAY, LIEUT. F.P. SYNGE, LIEUT. B.B. WATSON, LIEUT. D. HUDSON-KINAHAN.

the 7th January. On the night of the 8th the Twentieth Division on their left announced that they were "going to let off gas" at 2 a.m., and follow up with a raid. The Battalion had to stand to arms, stifling in its respirators, during its progress; and by the glare of the enemy's lights could see our gas drifting low in great grey clouds towards the opposite lines. They observed, too, a number of small explosions in the German side when the gas reached there, which seemed to dissipate it locally. The enemy guns were badly served, opening half an hour late and pitching shell in their own wire and trenches, but they hardly annoyed the Battalion at all. The affair was over in a couple of hours. ("There is nothing, mark you, a man hates like a Division on his flank stirring up trouble. Ye know the poor devils have no choice of it, but it looks always as if they was doing it to spite their neighbours, and not Jerry at all.")

But the pleasure of the Twentieth Division was not allowed to interfere with the business of their own private raid. Before the gas was "let off" 2nd Lieutenant Brew again chaperoned two scouts of the Coldstream to show them the gap in the wire in case they cared to try it on their tour. It was found easily and reported to be passable in single file.

But, as they said wrathfully afterwards, who could have guessed that, on the night of the 10th, after the Coldstream's wire-cutting party had worked for two hours, and their raiders had filed through the gap, and met more wire on the parapet which took more time to cut – when they at last dropped into the trench and searched it for three long hours – they found no sign of a German? The Coldstream's sole trophies were some bombs, a box of loaded M.G. belts and one rocket!

When they relieved the Coldstream on the 11th January, they naturally tried their own hand on the problem. By this time they had discovered themselves to be a "happy" Battalion which they remained throughout. None can say precisely how any body of men arrives at this state. Discipline, effort, doctrine and unlimited care and expense on the part of the officers do not necessarily secure it; for there have been Battalions in our Armies whose internal arrangements were scandalously primitive, whose justice was Neolithic, and yet whose felicity was beyond question. It may be that the personal attributes of two or three leading spirits in the beginning set a note to which the other young men, of generous minds, respond: half-a-dozen superior N.C.O.'s can, sometimes, raise and human-ize the soul of a whole Battalion; but, at bottom, the thing is a mystery to be accepted with thankfulness. The 2nd Battalion of the Irish Guards was young throughout, the maker of its own history, and the inheritor of the Guards' tradition; but its common background was ever Warley where they had all first met and been moulded – officers and men together. So happiness came to them and stayed, and with it, unity, and, to use the modern slang, "efficiency" in little things as well as big – confidence and joyous mutual trust that carries unspoken through the worst of breakdowns.

The blank raid still worried them, and there may have been, too, some bets on the matter between themselves and the Coldstream. At any rate 2nd Lieutenant Brew reappears – his C.O. and the deeply interested Battalion in confederacy behind him.

On the night of the 11th of January Brew took out a small patrol and entered the German trench that they were beginning to know so well. He re-cut the wire, made a new gap for future uses, explored, built two barri-cades in the trench itself; got bogged up among loose wire, behind which he guessed (but the time was not ripe to wake up that hornet's nest), the German second line lay, – and came back before dawn with a periscope as proof that the trench was occupied by daylight. "The enterprise suffered from the men's lack of experience in patrolling by night," a defect that the C.O. took care to remedy.

As a serious interlude, for milk was a consideration, "the cow at Red House calved successfully. Signallers, orderlies and others were present at the accouchement." Doubtless, too, the Orderly-room kitten kept an inter-ested eye on the event.

In the afternoon the Brigadier came round, and the C.O. and the 2nd Lieutenant discussed a plan of the latter to cross the German line and lie up for the day in some disused trench or shell-hole. It was dismissed as "practical but too risky." Moreover, at that moment there was a big "draw" on hand, with the idea of getting the enemy out of their second line and shelling as they came up. The Battalion's private explorations must stand over till it was finished. Three Infantry Brigades took part in this game, beginning at dusk – the Guards on the left, the 114th Brigade in the centre, and the left Battalion of the Nineteenth Division on the right. The 114th Brigade, which was part of the Thirty-eighth Division, had just relieved the 1st Guards Brigade. Every one stood to arms with unlimited small-arm ammunition handy, and, as daylight faded over the enemy's parapets, the 114th sent up a red rocket followed by one green to mark Zero. There was another half-minute to go in which a motor machine-gun got over-tilted and started to gibber. Then the riot began. Both Battalions of the 2nd Guards Brigade, the left-half Battalion of the 114th Brigade, and the left of the Nineteenth Division opened rapid fire with rifles, machine and Lewis guns. At the same time, our Artillery on the right began a heavy front and enfilade bombardment of the German line while our howitzers barraged the back of it. The Infantry, along the Winchester Road, held their fire, but sim-ulated, with dummies which were worked by ropes, a line of men in act to leave the trenches. Last, the Artillery on our left joined in, while the dum-mies were handled so as to resemble a second line attacking.

To lend verisimilitude to an otherwise bald and unconvincing narrative, the guns on the right lifted and began shelling back-lines and communication trenches, as though to catch reinforcements, while the dummies jigged and shouldered afresh on their energetic ropes. The enemy took the thing in quite the right spirit. He replied with rifle-fire; he sent up multitudes of red lights, which always soothed him when upset; and his artillery plastered the ground behind our centre with big shells that could be heard crumping somewhere in the interior of France till our own guns, after a ten minutes' pause, came down once more. Over and above the annoyance to him of having to rush up supports into the front line, it was reasonable to suppose that our deluges of small-arm stuff must have done him some damage. "The men were all prepared and determined to enjoy themselves, the Machine-gunners were out to show what a lot of noise they could really make, and the fire must have been infinitely uncomfortable for German Quarter-master-Sergeants, cookers and others, wandering about behind the line with rations – if they walk about as much as we do. One of the companies alone loosed off 7000 rounds, including Lewis-guns, during the flurry."

They were back at La Gorgue again on the 13th January, in Divisional rest; the 3rd Guards Brigade relieving them. While there the C.O. launched a scheme for each subaltern to pick and train six men on his own, so as to form the very hard core of any patrols or bombing-parties he might have to lead hereafter. They were specially trained for spotting things and judging distance at night; and the tales that were told about them and their adventures and their confidences would fill several unprintable books. (There was an officer who did not so much boast as mount, with a certain air, a glass eye. One night, during patrol, he was wounded in the shoulder, and brought in by his pet patrol-leader, a private of unquestioned courage, with, by the way, a pretty taste for feigning abject fear when he wished to test new men with whom he was working in No Man's Land. He rendered first aid to his officer whose wound was not severe, and then invited him to "take a shquint" at the result. The officer had to explain that he was blind on that side. Whereupon, the private, till the doctor turned up, drew loud and lively pictures of the horror of his wife at home, should it ever come to her knowledge that her man habitually crawled about France in the dark with an officer "blinded on the half of him.")

They rested for nearly a fortnight at La Gorgue, attended a lecture – "if not instructive, at least highly entertaining" – by Max Abbat, the well-known French boxer, on "Sport and what England had done for France," and had a Regimental dinner, when ten of the officers of the 1st Battalion came over from Merville with their Brigadier and the Staff Captain, and Lieutenant Charles Moore, who had saved the Battalion Christmas dinners, looked after them all to the very end which, men say, became nebulous. Some one had been teaching the Battalion to bomb in style, for their team of thirty returned from Brigade Bombing School easy winners, by one hundred points in the final competition. ("Except that the front line is mostly quieter and *always* more safe, there is no differ betwixt the front line and Bombing School.")

They went back into line and support-billets on the 26th relieving the 3rd Guards Brigade; and the Battalion itself taking over from the 1st Grenadiers on the Red House sector, Laventie. Apparently, the front line had been fairly peaceful in their absence, but they noted that the Grenadier Headquarters seemed "highly pleased to go," for the enemy had got in seven direct hits that very day on Red House itself. One shell had dropped in "the best upstairs bedroom, and two through the roof." They took this as a prelude to a Kaiser's birthday battle, as there had been reports of loyal and patriotic activities all down that part of the line, and rumours of increased railway movement behind it. A generous amount of tapped German wireless lent colour to the belief. Naturally, Battalion Headquarters at Red House felt all the weight of the War on their unscreened heads, and all hands there from the Adjutant and Medical Officer to the orderlies and police, strengthened the defences with sand-bags. A Battalion cannot be comfortable if its Headquarters' best bedrooms are turned out into the landscape. No attacks, however, took place, and night patrols reported nothing unusual for the 26th and 27th January.

A new devilry (January 28) now to be tried were metal tubes filled with ammonal, which were placed under enemy wire and fired by electricity. They called them "Bangalore torpedoes" and they were guaranteed to cut all wire above them. At the same time, dummies, which had become a fashionable amusement along the line, would be hoisted by ropes out of our trenches to the intent that the enemy might be led to man his parapets that our guns might sweep them. It kept the men busy and amused, and they were more excited when our snipers reported that they could make out a good deal of movement in the line in front of Red House, where Huns in small yellow caps seemed to be "rolling something along the trench." Snipers were forbidden to pot-shot until they could see a man's head and shoulders clearly, as experience had proved that at so long a range – the lines here were full two hundred yards apart – "shooting on the chance of hitting half a head, merely made the enemy shy and retiring." One gets the impression that, in spite of the "deadening influence of routine" (some of the officers actually complained of it in their letters home!), the enemy's "shyness," at that moment, might have been due to an impression that he was facing a collection of inventive young fiends to whom all irregular things were possible.

They went into Brigade Reserve at Laventie on the 30th of the month, with genuine regrets for the trenches that they had known so long. "We shall never be as comfortable anywhere else," one boy wrote; and the C.O. who had spent so much labour and thought there, lifts up a swan-song which shows what ideal trenches should be. "Handed over in November in a bad state, they are now as nearly perfect as a line in winter can be. The parapets are perfect, the fire-steps all wooden and in good repair. The dug-outs, or rather the little huts which answer to that name in this swampy country, their frameworks put up by the Engineers, and sand-bagged up by the Infantry, are dry and comfortable. The traffic-trench, two boards wide in most places, is dry everywhere. Wherever trench-boards ran on sand-bags or mud they have been painted and put on piles. The wire in front of the line is good."

They were due for rest at Merville, farther out of the way of fire than La Gorgue, for the next week or so, but their last day in Laventie was cheered by an intimate lecture on the origin, nature and effects of poison-gas, delivered by a doctor who had seen the early trials of it at Ypres. He told them in cold detail how the Canadians slowly drowned from the base of the lung upwards, and of the scenes of horror in the ambulances. "Told them, too, how the first crude antidotes were rushed out from England in a couple of destroyers, and hurried up to the line by a fleet of motor ambulances, so that thirty-six hours after the first experience, some sort of primitive respirators were issued to the troops. The lecture ended with assurances that the '15 pattern helmets were gas-proof for three-quarters of an hour against any gas then in use, if they were properly inspected, put on and breathed through in the prescribed manner.

Their only diversion at Merville was a fire in the local chicory factory close to the Messes. Naturally, there was no adequate fire-engine, and by the time that the A.S.C. turned up, amid the cheers of the crowd whom they squirted with an extincteur, the place was burned out. "When nothing was left but the walls and some glowing timbers we heard, creeping up the street, a buzz of admiration and applause. The crowd round the spot parted, and in strode a figure, gaunt and magnificent, attired in spotless white breeches, black boots and gaiters, a blue jacket and a superb silver

...for the enemy had got in seven direct hits that very day on Red House itself. One shell had dropped in "the best upstairs bedroom, and two through the roof."... Naturally, Battalion Headquarters at Red House felt all the weight of the War on their unscreened heads...

Battalion Headquarters, the Red House, near Laventie.

64

helmet. He was the Lieutenant of Pompiers, and had, of course, arrived a bit late owing to the necessity of dressing for the part. He stalked round the ring of urban dignitaries who were in the front row, shook each by the hand with great solemnity, stared gloomily at the remains of the house and departed."

There was no expectation of any imminent attack anywhere, both sides were preparing for "the Spring Meeting," as our people called it; and leave was being given with a certain amount of freedom. This left juniors sometimes in charge of full companies, an experience that helped to bring forward the merits of various N.C.O.'s and men; for no two Company Commanders take the same view of the same Private; and on his return from leave the O.C. may often be influenced by the verdict of his *locum tenens* to give more or less responsibility to a particular individual. *Thus*: *Locum Tenens*. "I say, Buffles, while you were away, I took out Hasken – No, not 'Bullock' Hasken – ' Spud' – on that double-ditch patrol, out by the dead Rifleman. He didn't strike *me* as a fool."

Buffles. "Didn't he? *I* can't keep my patience with him. He talks too much."

L. T. "Not when he's outside the wire. And he doesn't see things in the dark as much as some of 'em." (Meditatively, mouth filled with fondants brought from home by Buffles.) "Filthy stuff this war-chocolate is." (Pause.) " Er, what do *you* think ? He's Lance already."

Buffles. "I know it. I don't think he's much of a Lance either. Well ... "

L. T. "Anyhow, he's dead keen on night jobs. But if you took him once or twice and tried him ... He *is* dead keen ... Eh?"

Buffles. "All right. We'll see. Where's that dam' log-book?" Thus the matter is settled without one direct word being spoken, and "Spud" Hasken comes to his own for better or for worse.

On the 7th February they were shifted, as they had anticipated, to the left of the right sector of the Divisional front, which meant much less comfortable trenches round Pont du Hem, and badly battered Headquarters at Winchester House. They relieved the 1st Coldstream in the line on the 9th, and found at once plenty of work in strengthening parapets, raising trench-boards, and generally attending to their creature comforts. ("Never have I known *any* Battalion in the Brigade that had a good word to say for the way the other Battalions live. We might all have been brides, the way we went to our new house-keepings in every new place – turnin' up our noses at our neighbours.")

And while they worked, Headquarters were "briefly but accurately" shelled with whizz-bangs. On the 11th February the pace quickened a little. There was mining along that front on both sides, and our miners from two mines had reported they had heard work going on over their heads only a hundred and twenty yards out from our own parapets. It might signify that the enemy were working on "Russian saps" – shallow mines, almost like mole-runs, designed to bring a storming party right up to our parapets under cover. The miners were not loved for their theories, for at midnight along the whole Battalion front, pairs of unhappy men had to lie out on ground-sheets listening for any sound of subterranean picks. The proceedings, it is recorded, somewhat resembled a girls' school going to bed, and the men said that all any one got out of the manoeuvres was "blashts of ear-ache." But, as the Diary observes, if there were any mining on hand, the Germans would naturally knock off through the quietest hours of the twenty-four.

In some ways it was a more enterprising enemy than round the Red House, and they felt, rather than saw, that there were patrols wandering about No Man's Land at unseemly hours. So the Battalion sent forth a couple of Lewis-gunners with their weapon, two bombers with their bombs and one telephonist complete with field telephones. These, cheered by hot drinks, lay up a hundred yards from our parapets, installed their gun in an old trench, and telephoned back on pre-arranged signals for Véry lights in various directions to illumine the landscape, and invite inspection. "The whole scheme worked smoothly. In fact it only wanted a few Germans to make it a complete success." And the insult of the affair was that the enemy could be heard whistling and singing all night as they toiled at their own mysterious jobs. In the evening, just as the Battalion was being relieved by the Coldstream, a defensive mine, which was to have been exploded after the reliefs were comfortably settled in, had to go up an hour before, as the officer in charge, fearing that the Germans, who were busy in the same field, might break into his galleries at any moment, did not see fit to wait. The resulting German flutter just caught the end of the relief, and two platoons of No. 1 Company were soundly shelled as they went down the Rue du Bacquerot to Rugby Road. However, no one was hurt. The men of the 2nd Battalion were as unmoved by mines as were their comrades in the 1st. They resented the fatigue caused by extra precautions against them, but the possibilities of being hoisted sky-high at any moment did not shake the Celtic imagination.

While in Brigade Reserve for a couple of days No. 1 Company amused itself preparing a grim bait to entice German patrols into No Man's Land. Two dummies were fabricated to represent dead English soldiers. "One, designed to lie on its back, had a face modelled by Captain Alexander from putty and paint which for ghastliness rivalled anything in Madame Tussaud's. The frame-work of the bodies was wire, so they could be twisted into positions entirely natural." While they were being made, on the road outside Brigade Headquarters at Pont du Hem, a French girl came by and, believing them to be genuine, fled shrieking down the street. They were taken up to the front line on stretchers, and it chanced that in one trench they had to give place to let a third stretcher pass. On it was a dead man, whom no art could touch.

Next night, February 15, between moonset and dawn, the grisliest hour of the twenty-four, Lieutenant Pym took the twins out into No Man's Land, arranging them one on its face and the other on its back in such attitudes as are naturally assumed by the old warped dead. "Strapped between the shoulders of the former, for the greater production of German curiosity, was a cylinder sprouting india-rubber tubes. This was intended to resemble a flammenwerfer." Hand and rifle grenades were then hurled near the spot to encourage the theory (the Hun works best on a theory), that two British patrols had fought one another in error, and left the two corpses. At evening, the Lewis-gun party and a brace of bombers lay out beside the kill, but it was so wet and cold that they had to be called in, and no one was caught. And all this fancy-work, be it remembered, was carried out joyously and interestedly, as one might arrange for the conduct of private theatricals or the clearance of rat-infested barns.

On the 16th they handed over to the 9th Welsh of the Nineteenth Division, and went back to La Gorgue for two days' rest. Then the 2nd Guards Brigade moved north to other fields. The "Spring Meeting" that they talked about so much was a certainty somewhere or other, but it would be preceded, they hoped, by a period of "fattening up" for the Division. ("We knew, as well as the beasts do, that when Headquarters was kind to us, it meant getting ready to be killed on the hoof – but it never put us off our feed.") Poperinghe, and its camps, was their immediate destination, which looked, to the initiated, as if Ypres Salient would be the objective; but they had been promised, or had convinced themselves, there would be a comfortable "stand-easy" before they went into that furnace, of which their 1st Battalion had cheered them with so many quaint stories. Their first march was of fifteen miles through Neuf and Vieux Berquin – and how were they to know what the far future held for them there? – to St. Sylvestre, of little houses strung along its typical pavé. Only one man fell out, and he, as is carefully recorded, had been sick the day before. Thence, Wormhoudt on the 22nd February, nine miles through a heavy snowstorm, to bad billets in three inches of snow, which gave the men excuse for an inter-company snowball battle. The 1st Battalion had thankfully quitted Poperinghe for Calais, and the 2nd took over their just-vacated camp, of leaky wooden huts on a filthy parade-ground of frozen snow, at the unchristian hour of half-past seven in the morning. On that day 2nd Lieutenant Hordern with a draft of thirty men joined from the 7th Entrenching Battalion. ("All winter drafts look like sick sparrows. The first thing to tell 'em is they'll lose their names for coughing, and the next is to strip the Warley fat off 'em by virtue of strong fatigues.") They were turned on to digging trenches near their camp and practice-attacks with live bombs; this being the beginning of the Bomb epoch, in which many officers believed, and a good few execrated. At a conference of C.O.'s of the Brigade at Headquarters the Brigadier explained the new system of trench-attack in successive waves about fifteen yards apart. The idea was that if the inevitable flanking machine-gun fire wiped out your leading wave, there was a chance of stopping the remainder of the company before it was caught.

A lecture on the 1st March by the Major-General cheered the new hands. He told them that "there was a great deal of work to be done in the line we were going into. Communication-trenches were practically non-existent and the front parapet was not continuous. *All* this work would have to be done by the infantry, as the Divisional R.E. would be required for a very important line along the Canal and in front of the town of Ypres." One of the peculiarities of all new lines and most R.E. corps is that the former is always out of condition and the latter generally occupied elsewhere

Their bombing-practice led to the usual amount of accidents, and on the 2nd March Lieutenant Keenan was wounded in the hand by a premature burst; four men were also wounded and one of them died.

Next day, when their Quartermaster's party went to Calais to take over the 1st Battalion's camp there, they heard of the fatal accident at bomb-practice to Lord Desmond FitzGerald and the wounding of Lieutenant Nugent and Father Lane-Fox. They sent Captains J. S. N. FitzGerald and Witts, and their Sergeant-Major and Drum-Major to FitzGerald's funeral.

On the 6th March they entrained at Poperinghe for Calais, where the whole Brigade lay under canvas three miles out from the town beside the Calais–Dunkirk road. "The place would have been very nice, as the Belgian Aviation ground, in the intervals of dodging the Belgian aviators, made a fine parade and recreation ground, but life in tents was necessarily marred by continued frost and snow." More intimately: "The bell-tents are all right, but the marquees leak in the most beastly manner. There are only a few places where we can escape the drips."

Here they diverted themselves, and here Sir Douglas Haig reviewed them and some Belgian Artillery, which, as it meant standing about in freezing weather, was no diversion at all. But their "Great Calais First Spring Meeting" held on Calais Sands, in some doubt as to whether the tide would not wipe out the steeple-chase course, was an immense and unqualified success. Every soul in the Brigade who owned a horse, and several who had procured one, turned out and rode, including Father Knapp, aged fifty-eight. There were five races, and a roaring multitude who wanted to bet on anything in or out of sight. The Battalion bookmaker was a 2nd Lieutenant – at home a barrister of some distinction – who, in fur coat, brown bowler of the accepted pattern, and with a nosegay of artificial flowers in his buttonhole, stood up to the flood of bets till they overwhelmed him; and he and his clerk "simply had to trust to people for the amounts we owed them after the races." Even so, the financial results were splendid. The Mess had sent them into the fray with a capital of 1800 francs, and when evening fell on Calais Sands they showed a profit of 800 francs. The star performance of the day was that of the C.O.'s old charger "The Crump," who won the steeple-chase held an hour after winning the mile, where he had given away three stones. His detractors insinuated that he was the only animal who kept within the limits of the very generous and ample course laid out by Captain Charles Moore. There followed a small orgy of Battalion and inter-Battalion sports and amusements – football competitions for men and officers, with a "singing competition" for "sentimental, comic and original turns." Oddly enough, in this last, the Battalion merely managed to win a consolation prize, for a private who beat a drum, whistled, and told comic tales in brogue. It may have been he was the great and only "Cock" Burne or Byrne, of whom unpublishable Battalion-history relates strange things in the early days. He was eminent, even among many originals – an elderly "old soldier," solitary by temperament, unpredictable in action, given to wandering off and boiling tea, which he drank perpetually in remote and unwholesome corners of the trenches. But he had the gift, with many others, of crowing like a cock (hence his *nom de guerre*), and vastly annoyed the unhumorous Hun, whom he would thus salute regardless of time, place or safety. To this trick he added a certain, infinitely monotonous tom-tomming on any tin or box that came handy, so that it was easy to locate him even when exasperated enemy snipers were silent. He came from Kilkenny, and when on leave wore such medal-ribbons as he thought should have been issued to him – from the v.c. down; so that when he died, and his relatives asked why those medals had not been sent them, there was a great deal of trouble. Professionally, he was a "dirty" soldier, but this was understood and allowed for. He regarded authority rather as an impertinence to be blandly set aside than to be argued or brawled with; and he revolved in his remote and unquestioned orbits, brooding, crowing, drumming and morosely supping his tea, something between a poacher, a horse-coper, a gipsy and a bird-catcher, but always the philosopher and man of many queer worlds. His one defect was that, though difficult to coax on to the stage, once there and well set before an appreciative audience, little less than military force could haul "Cock" Byrne off it.

They celebrated St. Patrick's Day on the 14th March instead of the

17th, which was fixed as their date for removal; and they wound up the big St. Patrick dinners, and the Gaelic Football Inter-Company Competition (a fearsome game), with a sing-song round a bonfire in the open. Not one man in six of that merry assembly is now alive.

THE SALIENT FOR THE FIRST TIME

They marched out of Calais early on the 17th March, through Cassel, and Major the Hon. A. C. S. Chichester joined on transfer from the 1st Battalion as Second in Command. Poperinghe was reached on the afternoon of the 18th, a sixteen-mile march in suddenly warm weather, but nobody fell out. The town, crowded with troops, transport and traffic of every conceivable sort, both smelt and looked unpleasant. It was bombed fairly regularly by enemy 'planes, so windows had long since ceased to be glazed; and at uncertain intervals a specially noxious gun, known as "Silent Susy," sent into its populated streets slim shells that arrived unfairly before the noise of their passage. But neither bombs nor shells interfered with the cinemas, the "music hall," the Y.M.C.A. or other diversions, for every one in "Pop" was *ipso facto* either going into The Salient or coming out, and in both cases needed the distraction of the words and pictures of civilized life. They lay there for a few days, and on the 26th March about midnight, in a great quiet, they entered Ypres, having entrained, also with no noise whatever, from Poperinghe. The Diary, rarely moved to eloquence, sets down: "It was an impressive sight not to be forgotten by those who were present, as we threaded our way through the wrecked and shattered houses. Those of the Battalion who knew it before, had not seen it since the dark days of November '14, when with the 1st Battalion they played their part in the glorious first Battle of Ypres, a fight never to be forgotten in the annals of the Irish Guards."

The impression on the new hands, that is, the majority of men and officers, struck in and stayed for years after. Some compared their stealthy entry to tiptoeing into the very Cathedral of Death itself; and declared that heads bowed a little and shoulders hunched, as in expectation of some stroke upon the instant. Also that, mingled with this emotion, was intense curiosity to know what the place might look like by day. ("And God knows Ypres was no treat to behold, then or after – day or night. The way most of us took it, was we felt 'twas The Fear itself – the same as meeting up with the Devil. I do not remember if 'twas moonlight or dark when we came in that first time. Dark it must have been though, or we felt it was, and there was a lot of doings going on in that darkness, such as Military Police, and men whispering where we was to go, and stretchers, and parties carrying things in the dark, in and out where the houses had fallen by lumps. And

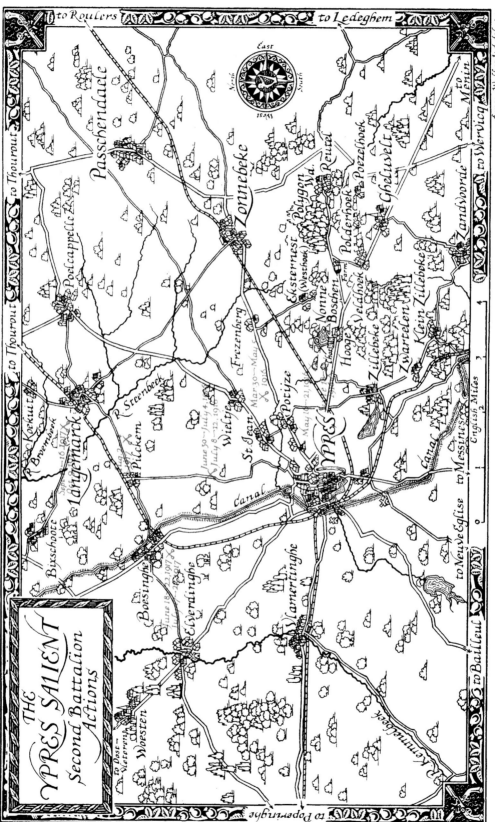

there was little blue lights showing here and there and around, and the whole stink of The Salient, blowing back and forth upon us, the way we'd get it up our noses for ever. Yes – and there was transport on the pavé, wheels going dam' quick and trying, at the same time, not to make a noise, if ye understand.

"And I remember, too, voices out of holes low down betwixt the rubbish-heaps. They would be the troops in cellars over against the Cloth Hall, I expect. And ye could hear our men breathing at the halts, and the kit squeaking on their backs, and we marching the way we was striving not to break eggs. I know. *I* was.")

At the time no one seemed to have noticed the peculiarity of The Salient, which, like Verdun, appears at night surrounded by a ring of searchlights and artillery; so that on going forward one feels as though one were altogether cut off from the rest of the front, a target open to every fire.

They were welcomed on the morning of the 27th March by three shells well and truly placed, one after the other, in the courtyard of the Convent where Battalion H.Q. stood. Six N.C.O.'s and men were wounded, of whom Sergeant McGuinn died a few hours later. This was the prelude to a night-long bombardment from a battery evidently told off for the job, which opening at eleven kept it up till ten of the morning of the 28th, when it ceased, and the remainder of the day was quiet. One must remember that the enemy used Ypres through the years as their Gunnery School officers' training-ground.

The 29th March was also a quiet day for the Battalion. There was, naturally, no walking about, or any distraction from the wonder where the next blast of fire would choose to fall, a sensation of helplessness which is not good for the nerves. They were the right Reserve Battalion of the Right Brigade, which, elsewhere, would have been equivalent to being in the front line, but Ypres had its own scale of sufferings. They worked quietly on repairs from dusk till the first light of dawn in their trenches beyond the Canal. From daylight to dusk again they lay up in dug-outs for the most part, and all fires that showed smoke were forbidden. But a race accustomed to peat can miraculously make hot tea over a few fragments of ammunition-boxes or a fistful of stolen coke, even in the inner bowels of a scaled dug-out. Any signs of life were punished by visits from observation-'planes or a shelling from one flank or the other: for the enemy commanded practically all their trenches, and this implied a constant building and repair of traverses and blindages. It took them three hours to relieve the 1st Coldstream in the front line on the night of the 30th March, and during relief the reserve trench which was being taken over by No. 4 Company under Captain Eric Greer (he had reverted to Company Officer on Major Chichester's arrival as Second in Command) was shelled and badly knocked

73

about. There were only eight men wounded, however, and the Company was "perfectly cool throughout." ("When you know ye may be for it every minute, you can *not* be more frightened than frightened. The same as getting drunk, *I* think. After a while – dead-drunk ye get, and dead-drunk ye stay. Ah, but they was genteel trenches and pleasant-spoken Jerries down at Laventie where we'd come from, in front of Red House and all!")

The last day of March brought them for one breathless half-hour the heaviest shelling they had yet undergone; but it ended, as so many such out-bursts did, in nothing but a few slight wounds, and a searching of the Menin road by night with big stuff that roared and rattled on what remained of the tortured stones. One could always know when Ypres city had been shelled afresh, by the pools of blood on the pavé in the raw morning or some yet undisposed-of horse which told that the night-hawking processions of the Transport had caught it once again. Their daily lives in the front and reserve line were dark, confined and unsavoury. One officer was ill-advised enough to pry into the vitals of his dug-out. ("When I arrived, it did not look so bad, as the floor was covered with sand-bags as usual.") A strong-stomached orderly turned in to remove a few. He found no less than six layers of them, progressively decaying; then floor-boards of a fabulous antiquity, and last the original slime of '14's corruption. It was neglectful, but men who may be blown out of this life any hour of the twenty-four do not devote themselves to the continuities of house-cleaning.

In Ypres city that spring was not one single building habitable, though many of them still retained the shapes of human dwellings. The Battalion Messes were all underground in cellars, a couple of which, with a hole knocked through the dividing walls, make a good anteroom; but their sole light came from a small window which also gave passage to the stove-pipe. A tired man could doze down there, in gross fuggy warmth and a brooding stillness broken only by the footsteps of small parties moving without ostentation till the triple whistle of the aeroplane-watchers sent feet scurrying loudly to cover.

Those who have known of both terrains say Verdun Salient, by reason of its size, contours and elevation, was less of a permanent tax on the morale than the flatness and confinement of Ypres. One could breathe in certain spots round Verdun; look out over large horizons from others; and solid bold features of landscape interposed between oneself and the enemy. The thickness and depth, too, of all France lay behind for support. In The Salient it was so short a distance from Calais or Boulogne that one could almost hear the Channel threatening at one's back, and wherever wearied eyes turned, forwards or flankwise, the view was closed by low, sullen rises or swells of ground, held and used in comfort and at leisure by an established enemy.

They reckoned time in the trenches by the amount of shelling that fell to their share. A mere passage of big stuff overhead seeking its butts in the town did not count, any more than excited local attacks to left or right of the immediate sector; and two or three men wounded by splinters and odds-and-ends, would not spoil the record of "a quiet day." Occasionally, as the tides and local currents of attack shifted, our guns behind them would wake up to retaliation or direct punishment. Sometimes the enemy's answer would be immediate; sometimes he accepted the lashing in silence till nightfall, and then the shapeless town would cower and slide still lower into its mounds and rubbish-heaps. Most usually a blow on one side or the other would be countered, it seemed to the listeners in the trenches between, exactly as in the prize-ring. But the combatants were heavy-, middle-and light-weight guns, and in place of the thump of body-blows, the jar and snap of jabs and half-hooks, or the patter of foot-work on the boards, one heard the ponderous Jack Johnsons arrive, followed by the crump of the howitzers, and then the in-and-out work of field-artillery quickening to a clinch, till one side or the other broke away and the silence returned full of menaces of what would happen next time "if you hit my little brother again." A local and concentrated shelling of the Battalion's second line one day, which might have developed bloodily, was damped down in three minutes, thanks to a telephone and guns that worked almost simultaneously. Nobody but themselves noticed it in the big arena.

Suddenly on the morning of the 9th April (it was due, perhaps, to some change of troops on the front) the enemy snipers and machine-guns woke up; and Lieutenant Kinahan, a keen, well-trusted and hard-working officer, was shot through the head by a sniper, and died at once. By next day, Captain Greer of No. 4 Company had the pleasure to report that his C.S.M.'s little party of snipers had "accounted" for the killer. Sniping on that front just then was of a high order, for the local enemy had both enterprise and skill, with rifle and bomb.

Their trenches were a little below the average of those parts, that is to say, almost impossible. A consoling local legend had it, indeed, that they were so vile that a conference of Generals had decided to abandon them, but that, hearing the Guards Division were under orders for The Salient, forbore, saying: "We'll put the Guards in 'em and if *they* can't make 'em decent we'll give 'em away to Jerry." And in addition to repairs and drainage ("County Council work," as one sufferer called it) there were the regular fatigues which, as has been pointed out many times, more than any battle break down and tire the body and soul of the soldier. Here is one incidental, small job, handed out as all in a night's work. The officer speaks. "It was particularly beastly. We were supposed to make a dummy machine-gun emplacement for the enemy to shell. I took forty men to meet the R.E. officer at a pleasant little rendezvous 'two hundred yards north-west from Hell Fire Corner.' Of course, we were sent to the wrong place to look for that Sapper; and, of course, the Boche was shelling the road on both sides of us. That was about half-past nine. Then we drew our stuff to carry up. There were two sheets of iron, each 12 by 6, and any quantity of sand-bags, shovels and timber. We had to travel a mile and a half by road, then up a communication-trench, and then a few hundred yards across the open. That was all. Well, it took four men to carry each of those cursed pieces of iron on the level open road. You couldn't get 'em up a trench at all. But we hung on to 'em, and about one o'clock we had covered the road-bit of the journey and were half-way from the road to the place where we had to build our blasted dummy. Then we got on to ground absolutely chewed up by shell-holes and old trenches. You couldn't go a foot without falling. When we'd struggled a bit longer with those sheets, we simply had to chuck 'em as unshiftable; and make the best dummy we could of sand-bags only. Imagine two parties of four tottering Micks apiece trying to sweat those tin atrocities across that sort of country! And then, of course, a mist got up and we were lost in the open – lovely! – and our guide, who swore he knew the way, began to lead us round in circles. The R.E. and I spotted what he was doing, because we kept an eye on the stars when we could see 'em. So, after any amount of bother, we all got home. There were bullets flying about occasionally (that's part of the job), and we ran into some shelling on our way back at four in the morning when the Huns could see. But what *I* mean to say is that if it hadn't been for those two dam' sheets which weren't really needed at all, a dozen men could have done the whole business straight off. And that was just one small fatigue!"

Nothing of all this worried the morale of the men. They took it all as part of the inexplicable wonder of war, which orders that the soldier shall do what he is told, and shall stay where he may be put.

A platoon was being inspected that month in Ypres. Suddenly shelling opened some distance off, at first, but methodically drawing nearer to dredge the town, till at last the shrapnel burst almost directly overhead. The men stood rigidly to attention without moving a muscle, till the officer gave them orders to take cover. Then they disappeared into the nearest cellar. Later on, it occurred to the officer that the incident "though commonplace was not without its interesting aspect."

They lay at Poperinghe in Divisional Rest from the 13th till the 19th April, during which time Lieutenant Nutting, and 2nd Lieutenant Reford from the 11th Notts and Derby Regiment, joined for duty. Thence they shifted over to camp near Vlamertinghe in Brigade Reserve as left Battalion of the left Brigade.

On the 21st April Lieutenant R. McNeill joined, and on the 24th they went into the line to relieve the 1st Coldstream in the left sector – as unpleasing a piece of filth as even The Salient could furnish. Five days before their entry it had been raided and blown in, till it was one muddled muck-heap of wreckage and corpses. Front-line repairs, urgently needed, could only be effected in the dark; traffic and communication trenches had to be spasmodically cleaned out between "crumps," and any serious attack on them during their first turn would have meant ruin.

The enemy tried a bombing raid on the night of the 28th–29th, which was beaten off, without casualty, by our bombs, rifles and machine-guns. Nothing worse overtook them, and the bill for their five days' turn was one man killed and ten wounded, of whom three did not quit duty. But the mere strain was poisonous heavy. They handed over thankfully to their opposite number, the Coldstream, on the 29th, and lay up in Ypres Gaol. "The prison is a fine example of the resistance to shell-fire of brick walls if they are thick enough." Verdun forts, at the far end of the line, were learning by now that the best and thickest stone-facings fly and flake beneath the jar of the huge shell that the enemy used against them, while ancient and unconsidered brick-work over deep earth cores, though it collapses into lumps hardly distinguishable from mould, yet gives protection to the men in the galleries beneath.

May-Day at Ypres opened with "a good exhibition" of German shooting. The enemy spent the whole day shelling the water-tower – a metal tank on a brick pedestal – close to the Prison. Every shell fell within fifty yards, till the sole object that escaped – for a while – was the tower itself. The "weather being hot and dry," some of our officers thought good to bathe in the Canal, but, not being water-towers, found it better to come out before a flight of " crumps" found them. Looking back upon this, one of the bathers counted that bath as his own high-water mark of heroism. ("There were Things in the Canal, you know.")

They went up on the 2nd May, relieving the Coldstream in the same evil sector, and the enemy machine-guns filling the dark with bullets as effectively as and more cheaply than artillery, killed one of our Corporals and wounded a couple of the Coldstream. A hint of the various Companies' works shows what they had to contend with nightly. No. 2, which held the right front line "where enough of the trench had been already reclaimed to accommodate the whole company" (it was not superior accommodation), borrowed two platoons from No. 1 and worked till dawn at finishing a traffic-trench behind the blown-in front and at making parapets till "by morning it was possible to get all along this trench, even with a good deal of crawling." No. 4 were out wiring a post against flank and rear attack. It stood out in a wilderness of utterly smashed trenches, which fatigue-parties from the Reserve Battalions dealt with, by the help and advice of the Sappers, and constructed a new trench (Wieltje Trench) running out on the left flank of the weak and unsupported Wieltje Salient. Here was another desert of broken trenches, linked by shallow or wet sketches of new ones. No. 3 Company worked at its own trench, and at the repair of Cardoen Street which "had recently been blown in in several places." An improved trench could be walked along, without too much stooping. Unimproved dittos demanded that men should get out and run in the open, steeple-chasing across wreckage of tinware and timber, the bramble-like embraces of stray wire-ends, and that brittle and insecure foothold afforded by a stale corpse, while low flights of machine-gun bullets has-tened their progress, or shrapnel overhead hunted the party as hawks hunt small birds in and out of hedges. The labour was as monotonous and barren to perform as it seems to record; but it made the background of their lives and experiences. Some say that, whatever future war may bring forth, never again can men be brought to endure what armed mankind faced in the trenches in those years. Certain it is that men, nowadays, thinking upon that past, marvel to themselves that they could by any means have overcome it at the time, or, later, have put it behind them. But the wonder above all wonders is that, while they lived that life, it seemed to them sane and normal, and they met it with even temper and cool heads.

On the 3rd May Major Chichester, who had been suffering for some time from the effects of a wound by a H.E. that burst within a few feet of him, had to go sick, and Captain E. B. Greer was left temporarily in command. Their own Commanding Officer, the Hon. L. J. P. Butler, who had come out with them at the first and taken all that the Gods had sent since, was on the 5th May translated to the command of a Kitchener Brigade. Here is a tribute of that time, from within the Battalion, where they were not at all pleased by the calls of the New Army for seasoned Brigadiers. "Butler, more than any other man, has made this Battalion what it is. Also we all love him. However, I am glad he has got a less dangerous job. He is too brave a man ever to be safe."

On that same day they were relieved and went into one of the scattered wooden camps near Brandhoek for a whole week, which was spoiled by cold weather and classes in wiring under an R.E. corporal attached to them for that purpose. ("We were *not* clever with our hands at first go-off, but when it came to back-chat and remarks on things, and no officers near, begad there was times when I could have pitied a Sapper!")

By the 12th May the Battalion was in Reserve, their Brigade in the line, Major P. L. Reid had assumed command and Lieutenant F. Pym and 2nd Lieutenants A. Pym and Close had joined. Then they began again to con-sider raids of a new pattern under much more difficult conditions than their Laventie affairs. The 2nd Grenadiers and the 1st Coldstream were to do the reconnoitring for them, and "live Germans were badly needed for purposes of intelligence." The authorities recommended, once more, two simultaneous raids symmetrically one from each flank. Their C.O. replied, as at Laventie, that live Germans meant stalking, and wished to know how it was possible to stalk to a time-table, even had the ground been well reconnoitred, and if several nights instead of one, and that a relief-night, had been allowed for preparations. Neither of the raids actually came off, but the projected one on the left flank ended in a most typical and instructive game of blind-man's buff. The idea was to rush a German listening-post known to be held just north of the railway line on the left of Railway Wood, and the point of departure for the Coldstream reconnoitring patrol had been from a listening-post of our own, also on the railway. The patrol's report was perfectly coherent. They had left our listening-post, gone up the railway line, turned half right, crawled fifty yards, found German wire, worked along it, discovered a listening-post "empty but obviously in recent use," had hurried back, recrossed the railway about a hundred yards above our own listening-post, and fifty yards to the north of their crossing had noted the outline of another German listening-post where men were talking. (It is interesting to remember that the entire stage of these tense dramas could almost be reconstructed in a fair-sized garden.) This latter, then, was the post which the Battalion was to attack. Accordingly, they rehearsed the play very carefully with ten men under Lieutenant F. Pym, who had strict orders when they should rush the post, to club the Germans, "trying not to kill them (or one another)." They were to "collar a prisoner and hurry him back if well enough to walk," and, incidentally, as illustrating the fashion of the moment, they were all to wear "brown veils."

With these stage-directions clear in their mind, they went into the line on the 16th May, after a quiet relief, and took over from the Coldstream the sector from Railway Wood, the barricades across the railway, the big dug-out which had been an old mine, under Railway Wood, and disposed their reserves near Hell Fire Corner and the Menin road. It was ground they knew and hated, but since they had last eaten dirt there our own listening-post, which had been the point of departure for the Coldstream patrol, on whose reports the raid would be based, had been withdrawn one hundred and fifty yards down the railway line. Apparently no one had realized this, and the Captain (Platt) of the Coldstream Company, who had this sector when the 2nd Irish Guards relieved, had been killed while out wiring a couple of nights before. Consequently, that patrol had reconnoitred *inside* our own front; had mistaken our own wire for the German, had followed it to one of our own disused posts, and had seen and heard a listening-post of the 2nd Grenadiers which they, quite logically, assumed to be German and reported as such. Everything fitted in like a jigsaw puzzle, but all was based on a line which had been shifted – as the Battalion perceived the moment they took over the sector. So there was no attack with clubs and brown veils by the 2nd Irish Guards on the 2nd Grenadiers' listening-post, then or afterwards, and the moral of the story was "verify your data." ("No living man could tell from one day to the next – let alone nights – which was our line and which was Jerry's. 'Twas broke an' gapped and turned round every way, and each Battalion had its own fancy trenches dug for to make it worse for the next that took over. The miracle was – an' how often have I seen it! – the miracle was that we did not club each other in the dark every night instead of – instead of when we did.")

The Battalion went on, sadly, with its lawful enterprises of running wire and trench from the high ground under Railway Wood toward the shifted barricade on the railway itself; and digging saps to unstable mine-craters that had, some way or other, to be worked into their ever-shifting schemes of defence. All this under machine-gun fire on bright nights, when, as the cruel moon worked behind them, each head showing above ground-level was etched in black for the snipers' benefit. On their right flank, between their own Division and the Canadians, lay a gap of a quarter of a mile or so, which up till then had been imperfectly looked after by alternate hourly patrols. ("And in the intervals, any Germans who knew the way might have walked into Ypres in quest of souvenirs.") It had to be wired and posted, and, at the same time, a huge, but for the moment dry, mine-crater directly in front of the right Company's shattered trench, needed linking up and connecting with another crater on the left. Many dead men lay in the line of that sap, where, at intervals, enemy rifle-grenades would lob in among the sickened workers. The moonlight made the Germans active as rats every night, and, since it was impossible to wire the far sides of the craters in peace, our people hit upon the idea of pushing " knife-rests" – ready-wired trestles – out in the desired direction with poles, after dark. Be it noted, "This is a way, too much neglected, of wiring dangerous places. Every description of 'puzzy-wuzzy' can be made by day by the eight Company wirers, and pushed out. Then on the first dark night, a few metal pegs and a strand or two of wire passed through the whole thing, makes an entanglement that would entangle a train." (The language and emotions of the fatigue-parties who sweated up the unhandy "knife-rests" are not told.) Half the Battalion were used to supply the wants of the other half; for rations and water could only creep to within a couple of hundred yards of Hell Fire Corner, where the parties had to meet them and pack them the rest of the way by hand. The work of staggering and crawling, loaded with sharp-angled petrol-tins of water along imperfect duckboards, is perhaps a memory which will outlast all others for the present generation. "The fatigues kill – the fatigues kill us" – as the living and the dead knew well.

On the 18th May they were drenched with a five hours' bombardment of 4·2's and "woolly bears." It blew in one of their trenches (West Lane) and killed two men and wounded an officer of the Trench-Mortar Battery there. But the height of the storm fell, as usual, round Hell Fire Corner, never a frequented thoroughfare by daylight, and into an abandoned trench. "They could hardly have put down so much shell anywhere else in our line and have got so small a bag. Only one man in the Company was wounded." The race is not always to the swift, nor the battle to the strong; but a Battalion that works strenuously on its parapets and traffic-trenches gets its reward, even in The Salient in '16. Battalion Headquarters, always fair target for a jest, is derided as taking "a severe fright from a shell that pitched twenty yards away, but it was an obvious error in bowling, and was not repeated." Our guns fired throughout the next day, presumably in retaliation, but, like all troops in trenches, the Battalion had no interest in demonstrations that did not directly affect their food and precious water-tins. They were relieved on the 21st of May by the 6th Oxford and Bucks of the Twentieth Division, and went off to camp near Proven for ten days' Corps Reserve, when "almost the entire Battalion was on fatigue, either building military railways or cleaning up reserve-lines of trenches."

AFTER HOOGE

On the 1st June they moved out of that front altogether, to billets at the back of Wormhoudt fourteen miles away, and thence on the next day, June 2, to Bollezeele westward, while the enemy were making their successful attack on the Canadians at Hooge. ("Have ye noticed there is always trouble as soon as you come out of the line; or, maybe, being idle you pay the more attention to it. *Anny*way, the minute *we* was out of it, of course Jerry begins to play up and so Hooge happened, and that meant more fatigue for the Micks.") Meantime, they were in "G.H.Q. Reserve" for a fortnight, busy on a rehearsal-line of English and German trenches which the R.E. had laid down for them to develop. Our G.H.Q. were thinking of the approaching campaign on the Somme. The enemy were intent on disarranging our plans just as our guns were moving southward. Hooge was their spoke in our wheel. It came not far short of success; for it pinned a quantity of shellable troops to weak ground, directly cost the lives of several thousands of them and added a fresh sore to The Salient's many weaknesses in that it opened a fortnight's fierce fighting, with consequent waste, as well as diversion, of supplies. While that battle, barren as the ground it won and lost, surged back and forth, the Battalion at Bollezeele gained a glory it really appreciated by beating the 3rd Grenadiers in the Ring, six fights out of nine, at all weights. Specially they defeated Ian Hague (late heavy-

weight champion of England) whom Corporal Smith of the Battalion settled "on points." There would be time and, perhaps, warning to attend to
Death when He called. Till then, young and active life was uppermost, and
had to be catered for. Indeed, their Brigadier remarked of the social side of
that boxing entertainment that "it reminded him of Ascot."

But at the back of everything, and pouring in hourly by official or unofficial word, was the news of the changing fortunes of Hooge. Would that
postpone or advance the date of the "Spring Meeting," not in the least like
Ascot, that they had discussed so long? Whichever way war might go, the
Guards would not be left idle.

On the evening of the 13th June the order came "telling us that we
would move up next day to Hooge and take over a section of the line from a
Canadian Brigade." They went off in motor lorries, and by the evening of
the 15th the Battalion was once more in the packed Infantry Barracks of
Ypres where the Canadian Officers made Battalion Headquarters their
guests till things could be sorted out. Our counter-attack of the 13th June
had more or less come to rest, leaving the wrecked plinths of the houses of
Hooge, and but very little more, in the enemy's hands, and both sides were
living on the last edge of their nerves. Proof of this came on the night of the
16th, when the Battalion in barracks was waiting its turn. An S.O.S. went
up in the dark from somewhere north of the Menin road, that stony-
hearted stepmother of calamity; some guns responded and, all in one
instant, both sides' artillery fell to it full-tongued, while "to make everything complete a gas-signal was given by one of our Battalions. A terrific
bombardment ensued. Later in the night the performance was repeated,
less the gas-alarm."

The explanation was as simple as human nature. Both sides had taken
bad knocks in the past fortnight. Both artilleries, largely increased, were
standing by ready for trouble, and what else could one expect – save a det-
onation? But local rumour ran that the whole Gehenna had been started
by one stray ration-party which, all communication-trenches being blown
in, was toiling to the front line in the open and showed against the sky-line
– quite enough, at that tension, to convince the enemy that it was the head
of a fresh infantry attack! The rest came of itself: but the gas-alarm was
the invention of the Devil himself! It upset the dignity of all the Staffs concerned, for the Brigadier himself, the H.Q. Staff of the Coldstream, as well
as the C.O. and Company Officers of the 2nd Irish Guards who were visiting preparatory to taking over the sector, found themselves in one tiny
room beneath a brick-kiln, all putting on their helmets at once, and, thereafter, all trying to explain their views of the crisis through them. Some
have since compared that symposium to a mass-meeting of unemployed
divers; others to a troupe of performing seals.

They relieved the 1st Coldstream, very quietly, on the night of the 18th June in an all but obliteratcd section of what had been the Canadians' second line and was now our first, running from the Culvert, on the Menin road, west of Hooge, through Zouave Wood, and into the north end of Sanctuary Wood. Four to eight hundred yards lay between them and the enemy, who were settling down in the old Canadian front line across the little swampy valley. The left of the Irish Guards' sector was, even after the Coldstream had worked on it for three days, without dug-outs, and blown in in places, but it offered a little cover. Their right line, for nearly half a mile, was absolutely unrecognizable save in a few isolated spots. The shredded ground was full of buried iron and timber which made digging very difficult, and, in spite of a lot of cleaning up by their predecessors, dead Canadians lay in every corner. It ran through what had once been a wood, and was now a dreary collection of charred and splintered stakes, "to the tops of which, blown there by shells, hung tatters of khaki uniform and equipment." There was no trace of any communication-trenches, so Companies had to stay where they were as long as the light lasted. Battalion H.Q. lived in the brick-kiln aforementioned, just west of the Zillebeke road, and Company Commanders walked about in the dark from one inhabited stretch to the next, trusting in Providence. So, too, did the enemy, whom Captain Alexander found, to the number of six, ambling promiscuously in the direction of Ypres. They challenged, he fired, and they blundered off – probably a lost wiring-party. In truth, neither front line knew exactly where the other lay in that chaos; and, both being intent upon digging themselves in ere the guns should begin again, were glad enough to keep still. Our observation-parties watched the Germans as they crept over the ridge at dusk and dropped into the old Canadian line, where their policies could be guessed at from the nature of the noises they made at work; but no one worried them.

On the 20th June an unlucky shell pitched into No. 1 Company, killing three, wounding two and shocking five men; otherwise there was quiet, and their Brigadier came round the support-trenches that day and complimented all hands on their honesty as craftsmen. As he said, it would have been easy for them to have slacked off on their last night in a position to which they were not returning, whereas they had worked like beavers, and so the Battalion which relieved them (the Royal Canadian Regiment resting at Steenvoorde, since Hooge where it had lost three hundred men) found good cover and fair wire all along the sector. The Canadians were late, for their motor buses went adrift, somewhere down the road, and the Battalion only "just caught the last train" out of Ypres and reached camp near Vlamertinghe at dawn on the 21st June.

It had been a strange interlude of ash-pits and charnel-houses, sandwiched between open-air preparations, for that always postponed "Spring Meeting." No troops are the better for lying out, unrelieved by active reprisals, among shrivelled dead; and even the men, who love not parades, were pleased at a few days of steady barrack-square drill, when a human being walks and comports himself as though he were a man, and not a worm in the mire, or a slave bound to bitter burdens and obscene tasks. At Vlamertinghe they found, and were glad to see him, Captain FitzGerald, recovered after three weeks' sickness in England, and joyfully back before his time; and Lieutenant R. McNeill, who had acted as Adjutant, returned to the command of No. 2 Company in the absence of Captain Bird, gone sick. They were busied at Battalion H.Q. with the preparation of another raid to be carried out on the night of the 2nd July "as part of the demonstration intended to occupy the attention of the Germans in this locality while more important events were happening elsewhere." Lieutenant F. Pym, a bold, daring and collected officer, was chosen to command the little action, and each Company sent up eight volunteers and one Sergeant, from whom thirty men and one Sergeant were finally picked and set to rehearsing every detail.

On the 28th June they moved up to within four miles of the front and lay at Elverdinghe – two Companies and Battalion H.Q. in the Château itself, where they were singularly comfortable, and two in the Canal Bank, in brick and sand-bag dug-outs. It was true that all furniture and pictures had gone from the Château with the window-glass, and that swallows nested in the cornices of the high, stale-smelling rooms, but the building itself, probably because some trees around blocked direct observation, was little changed, and still counted as one of the best places in the line for Brigade Reserves. Their trenches, however, across the battered Canal presented less charm. The front-line was "dry on the whole," but shallow; the support quite good, but the communication-trenches (it was the Battalion's first experience of Skipton Road) were variously wet, blown in, swamped, or frankly flooded with three feet of water. Broken trenches mean broken Companies and more work for Company Commanders, but some of the platoons had to be scattered about in "grouse-butts" and little trenches of their own, a disposition which tempts men to lie snug, and not to hear orders at the first call.

THE RAID OF THE 2ND JULY

All through the 1st of July our guns bombarded their chosen front with the object of cutting, not too ostentatiously, the wire where our raid was going to take place, and of preparing the way on the right for an attack by the 3rd Guards Brigade on a small German salient that had to be reduced. The enemy answered with a new type of trench-mortar shell, nine inches in diameter, fired from a rifled mortar of high trajectory at a thousand yards range. The shock and smash of it were worse than a 5·9, and did much damage to Nile Trench, but caused no casualties. The 2nd July was the day for the raid itself, and just as Battalion Headquarters were discussing the very last details, an urgent message from Brigade Headquarters came in to them – "Please hasten your report on Pork and Bean rations."

The notion was that our 18-pounders and 4·5 hows. with a couple of trench-mortars, would open heavily at twenty minutes to ten. Ten minutes later the Stokes mortars were to join in. At ten the guns would lift and make a barrage while the Stokes mortars attended to the flanks of the attack. It was a clear evening, so light, indeed, that at the last minute the men were told to keep their jackets on lest their shirts should betray them. (It was *then*, men said later, that the raid should have been postponed.) Everything was quite quiet, and hardly a shot was being fired anywhere, when the party lined up under Lieutenant F. Pym. Our bombardment opened punctually, but drew no answer from the enemy for ten minutes. Then they put down a barrage behind our front line, which was the origin of all the trouble to come. At the last minute, one single unrelated private, appearing from nowhere in particular, was seen to push his way down the trench, climbing over the raiders where they crouched waiting for the life-or-death word. Said an Officer, who assumed that at the least he must bear vital messages. "Who are you?" "R.F.A. Trench-mortar man, sir," was the reply. Then, "Where the devil are you going?" – "Going to get my tea, sir." He passed on, mess-tin in hand, noticing nothing that was outside of his own immediate show; for of such, mercifully, were the Armies of England.

Meantime the enemy barrage increased on Nile Trench, and the front trenches began to gap badly. There was still light enough to give a good view of the German parapets when our raiders went over the top, and several machine-guns opened on them from the enemy second line. This was a bad kick-off, for, with our leading raiders out in the open, it would have been murder to have held the rest back. They all went on into the barrage and the machine-gun fire, and from that point the account of what actually, or supposedly, happened must, as usual, be collected from survivors. The whole attack seems to have reached the German wire which was "well cut in places." Here our men were checked by machine-gun fire (they probably ran up to the muzzles of them), and some bombing. They stopped and began to bomb back. Pym rushed forward through the leading men, jumped into the trench, landed in an empty German bay, shouting to them to follow, turned left with a few men, reached the door of a machine-gun dug-out with its gun in full blast, broke in, found two men at work, knocked one of them off the gun and, with the help of Private Walshe,

85

made him prisoner. Our bombers, meantime, had spread left and right, as laid down, to hold each end of the captured section, but had further to block a communication-trench which entered it about the middle, where the enemy was trying to force his way in. It is difficult to say whether there was not an attack on both flanks as well. At any rate a general bomb-scuffle followed, in which our men held up the enemy and tried to collect prisoners. The captured section of trench only contained one dead and five living. One of these "proved unmanageable and had to be killed." Four were hurried back under escort for samples, but two of these were killed by their own shell-fire on the road. The R.E. officer looked round, as his duty was, to find things to demolish, but the trench was clean and empty. He was hit twice, but managed to get back. Three gas-experts had also been attached to the expedition. Two of them were wounded on the outward run. The third searched the trench but found no trace of gas engines. Some papers and documents were snatched up from the dug-outs, but he who took charge of them did not live to hand over. The barrage grew heavier; the machine-gun fire from the enemy second line never ceased; and the raiders could see the home-parapet going up in lumps. It was an exquis-itely balanced choice of evils when, at about ten past ten, Lieutenant Pym blew his horn for the withdrawal. A minute or two later, men began to trickle over our parapet through the barrage, and here the bulk of the casualties occurred. Our guns ceased fire at twenty past ten, but the enemy battered savagely at our front line with heavies and trench-mortars till eleven. The result was that "the front line, never very good, became chaotic, and the wounded had to be collected in undamaged bays." It was hopeless to attempt to call the roll there, so what raiders could stand, with the two surviving prisoners, were sent up to Brigade Headquarters while the wounded were got across the open to Lancashire Farm, and the trolley-line there. Pym was nowhere to be found, and though some men said, and honestly believed, that they had seen him re-enter our lines, he was not of the breed which would have done this till he had seen the last of his com-mand out of the German trenches. He may have got as far as the German wire on his way back and there, or in that neighbourhood, have been killed; but he was never in our trench again after he left it. Others, too, of that luckless party bore themselves not without credit. For example, a sig-naller, name not recorded, who laid his telephone wire up to the trench across No Man's Land and had it cut by a shell while he was seeking for Lieutenant Pym. On his return he came across a man shot in the legs, and bore him, under heavy shell and machine-gun fire, to our wire which was not constructed for helpless wounded to get through. The signaller dropped into the trench, calling on Sergeant O'Hagan, a busy man that night, for stretcher-bearers, but these had all been hit. The Sergeant suggested that he should telephone to Battalion Headquarters and draw some from there. The telephonist – perhaps because a doctor rarely uses his own drugs – preferred to put the case directly to a couple of men in No. 2 Company, at the same time indicating the position of the wounded man, and those three handed him down into the very moderate safety that our front line then offered. And again, when Sergeant Austen, the Sergeant of the raid, was hit and fell in German wire, one of the raiders stayed with him awhile, and finally dragged him to our line, with the usual demand for bearers. This time they were all busy, but he found Lieutenant F. Greer and that officer's servant, whom he led forth, and "in spite of heavy machine-gun fire," they brought in the Sergeant. Unluckily, just at the end of the German bombardment, Lieutenant Synge was very badly hit while in the front line. The raid had been a fair, flat, but heroic failure, due, as most men said, to its being loosed in broad daylight at a fully prepared enemy. Outside the two prisoners, nothing, not even a scrap of paper, was gained except the knowledge that the Battalion could handle such affairs as these in their day's work, put it all equably behind them, and draw fresh lessons for fresh to-morrows. ("We lost one dam' good Officer, and more good men than was worth a thousand Jerries, but, mark you, we might have lost just that same number any morning in the front line, as we *have* lost them again and again, under the expenditure of half-a-dozen, maybe one, shell the Devil happened to be riding that time. And them that it took, would never have had even the exercise, let alone the glory, of all them great doings of ours. So, ye see, everything in War is good luck or bad.")

Their Brigadier had a little talk with the raiding-party next day on the Canal bank, when he made much of them, and told them that he was very pleased with "their gallant behaviour under adverse circumstances." It was gratifying, because they had done all that they could. But after every raid, as indeed after every action, there follows interminable discussion from every point of view of every rank, as to the "might-have-beens" – what would have happened had you been there, or they been here, and whether the bay where the raid wrecked itself against the barricade none suspected might have been turned by a dash across the top, in the pauses of the shifting and returning overhead machine-gun fire. The messes discuss it, the estaminets where the men talk pick up those verdicts from the mess-waiters and go over them again and again; the front line scratches diagrams on the flank of sand-bags with bits of burned stick, and the more they explain, argue and asseverate, the deeper grows the confusion out of which the historian in due time weaves the accepted version – at which all who were concerned scoff.

The 4th July was a quiet day after a bombardment the night before that had further enlarged the gap of untenable trench which the furious reprisals for the raid had created. They spent their hours repairing damage as much as possible till they were relieved by the 1st Coldstream, and a half of them got into billets at Elverdinghe Château, and the rest in Canal Bank. By this time the enemy had begun to turn their attention to the Château, in spite of its screening trees, and were in the habit of giving it a daily ration of whizz-bangs, which disturb drill-formations. Troops of the Division being fairly thick on the ground, one morning's work (July 7) managed to wound two machine-gunners of the 1st Coldstream and another of the 1st Irish Guards.

On the 5th July Major C. A. Rocke arrived and took over the duties of Second in Command. On the 7th, Captain R. McNeill left the Battalion sick, and Lieutenant R. Nutting took over command of No. 2 Company.

On the 8th they moved up to their old position, relieving the 1st Coldstream across the Canal without casualties, three Companies in the front line that had been a little repaired since their raid, and the fourth (No. 2) in support in Nile Trench. Three quiet days and nights followed, when they could work undisturbed. On the 11th July a happy party was chosen to attend the 14th July celebrations at Paris. The Adjutant, Captain J. S. N. FitzGerald, commanded them, all six, and their names were: Drill-Sergeant Harradine, Sergeants Reid, Glennon and Halpin, and Privates Towland and Dunne. Rumour, which respects naught, said that they were chosen with an eye to the credit of the Battalion at any inter-Allied banquets that might be obligatory, and that they did not fail. On the 12th, after a quiet night, forty large-size shells were sent into Canal Bank, as retaliation, they presumed, for some attentions on the part of our 9·2's the afternoon before. The Battalion was unhurt, but the 1st Scots Guards had several casualties. Their tour ended next day without trouble, and they were back by Elverdinghe Château for two days' light and mostly ineffective shelling preparatory to their move on the 15th July to Camp P, some three miles north of Poperinghe. During this time, 2nd Lieutenant Mylne arrived and was posted to No. 4 Company, and 2nd Lieutenants C. Hyne and Denson to No. 2 Company. Second Lieutenant Hordern also rejoined and was posted to No. 1. Every one understood, without too much being said, that that sector would see them no more till after the great "Spring Meeting," now set for the autumn, which many believed would settle the War. It was a small interlude of "fattening up" before the Somme, which included Battalion sports and company-drill competitions. There was, too, a dinner on the anniversary of the raising of the Battalion, 16th of July, when General Ponsonby dined with the Battalion. (In those ancient days men expected everything in the world except its disbandment as soon as war should be over.)

On the 18th July Captain J. S. N. FitzGerald and his detachment returned from Paris after one joyous week, and took over the Adjutancy again from the Second in Command; and Captain Greer, who had sprained his ankle badly during the raid, was sent down to the base for cure.

It is noted that on the 21st Captain Lord Castlerosse, wounded in the far-off days at Villers-Cotterêts with the 1st Battalion, joined the Battalion from G.S. Ninth Corps. The wild geese were being called in preparatory to their flight for the Somme.

THE SOMME

It began in the usual way, by definite orders to relieve a Battalion in the front line. These were countermanded next day and, the day after, changed to orders to move to Bollezeele, where on the 25th they "received a great welcome from the inhabitants," doubtless for old sakes' sake. Then came the joining up of the last subalterns, and three days' steady route-marching to toughen tender feet. Lieutenant Montgomery rejoined, and was posted to No. 2 Company, and, with him, 2nd Lieutenant Budd; Lieutenant Brew, not without experience in raiding, also arrived and was posted to No. 4 Company. This finished the tale, and on the 29th, the last Sunday of the month, they cleared personal accounts at Mass and Church of England services; and on the 30th marched out to Esquelbecq, where they entrained all together, with their first-line transport, and were shifted, *via* Hazebrouck, Berguette and St. Pol, to Petit Houvain five miles south of the latter town, or, broadly speaking, from the left to the right of the British line. That small trip lasted till evening, after which they marched fourteen miles to Lucheux on the Grouches River above Doullens, into a new world of camps and hutments, at midnight. The Diary says – on such points Diaries are always particular, because it touches the honour of Company Officers – "the Battalion marched splendidly, only six men having to be carried for the last few miles. These were mostly old or previously wounded men." And the month of July ends with the words, "There is nothing to record."

There was, perhaps, not so very much after all.

The Battle of the Somme had been in full blaze now from Maricourt to Hébuterne and Gomiecourt, for one month; and after the expenditure of no one had time to count how many men, our front from Ovillers-la-Boisselle to Fricourt and below Montauban had been advanced in places to the depth of three miles on a front of ten. It was magnificent, for the whole of the Press said so; and it was also extensively advertised as war.

From Ovillers-la-Boisselle to the north the German line, thanks to its clouds of machine-guns, had not been shifted by our attack, and the Battalion came, for the time being, under the orders of the Twenty-fifth

Division (7th Brigade) which lay against the southern shoulder of the Gomiecourt salient just where the sweeping bare uplands break back to the valley of the Authies. They were turned in to dig trenches on the sector, four or five miles from their bivouac in the little wood to the south of Mailly-Maillet. They left the crowded Lucheux camp in lorries at three on the afternoon of the 1st August ("In those days we knew we were for it, but we did not know what the Somme was going to be"), reached bivouac at eight, marched to their trenches and came back at daybreak with one N.C.O. and four men wounded. It was a most gentle introduction to the scenes of their labours. The enemy were using shrapnel mostly part of the 3rd August; 2nd Lieutenant Hordern was dangerously and eight men were slightly wounded by one shell while at work. Second Lieutenant Vaughan joined on this date and was posted to No. 2 Company. Whether, as some said, the authorities did not know what to do with them for a few days, or whether they were part of a definite scheme of attack, no one cared. The machine had taken possession of their lives and fates, and as they went from trench to bivouac and back again they could both see and hear how extremely little a battalion, or for that matter a brigade, mattered in the present inferno. The fortnight's battle that had opened on the 14th of July had finished itself among erased villages and woods that were already all but stumpage, while the big guns were pounding the camps and bivouacs that held our reserves, and one stumbled on old and fresh dead in the most unlikely and absurd places.

On the 6th August their turn ended, and they came back, for a couple of days, to the 2nd Guards Brigade in the Bois de Warnimont hutments – none too good – outside Authie. Here His Majesty the King visited them on the 9th August, and, after a three "quiet" days spent in reconnoitring the trenches in front of Mailly-Maillet and Auchonvillers, the Battalion on the 13th relieved the 1st Coldstream in the front line.

It was a featureless turn of duty, barring some minenwerfer work by the enemy once or twice in the dawns, which effected nothing.

They were relieved by a Battalion of the K.O.Y.L.I. on the 15th, and hutted in the wood near Mailly-Maillet. Here began their more specialized training for the work that lay ahead of them. It included everything that modern warfare of that date could imagine, from following up drum-barrages at twenty-five yards distance, to the unlovely business of unloading ammunition at railheads.

Domestically, there were not many incidents. Captain E. B. Greer rejoined from the base on the 15th August. The Second in Command and the Adjutant went sick on the 18th and 19th consecutively. (These ranks are not in the habit of noticing their personal complaints when regimental life is crowded. They were back in ten days.) Second Lieutenants Lysaght and Tomkins arrived from the base on the 30th, and 2nd Lieutenant Zigomala on the 31st August.

One little horror of a life where men had not far to look for such things stands out in the record of preparations that went on through the clangour and fury of the Somme around them. On a windy Sunday evening at Couin, in the valley north of Bus-les-Artois, they saw an observation balloon, tethered near their bivouacs, break loose while being hauled down. It drifted towards the enemy line. First they watched maps and books being heaved overboard, then a man in a parachute jumping for his life, who landed safely. "Soon after, something black, which had been hanging below the basket, detached itself and fell some three thousand feet. We heard later that it was Captain Radford (Basil Hallam). His parachute apparently caught in the rigging and in some way he slipped out of the belt which attached him to it. He fell near Brigade Headquarters." Of those who watched, there was not one that had not seen him at the "Halls" in the immensely remote days of "Gilbert the Filbert, the Colonel of the Nuts."

Before the end of the month they had shifted from their congested camp near Bus-les-Artois to Méricourt under Albert, which they reached circuitously by train, and there lay in Corps Reserve. The weather was against drills. It rained almost every day, and they slipped and swore through their rehearsals, wave-attacks and barrage-huntings across the deepening mud.

On the 9th September, at Happy Valley, they had their first sight of the tanks, some thirty of which were parked, trumpeting and clanking, near their camp. At that date the creatures were known as "creepy-crawlies" or "hush-hush birds" and were not as useful as they learned to become later. Then came the Battalion's last dispositions as to the reserve of officers, who were to be held till needed with the first-line Transport. The C.O., Lieut.-Colonel Reid, was down in hospital with *pukka* trench-fever and a temperature to match, and Lieutenant Nutting, sick with dysentery, had to be sent to England. Lieutenant Dollar, who had rejoined a few days before on recovery from the same disease, Captain Greer and Lieutenant Brew represented the Reserve, and even so (for the Somme was merciless throughout) Captain Witts, who had fallen ill at Carnoy, had to change places with Lieutenant Brew. Captain Alexander had rejoined the Battalion after two days' (jealously noted as "three nights") Paris leave.

The field-wastage began at once. They relieved the 4th Grenadiers on the evening of the 12th September in the new, poor and shallow trenches dug a few days before, as our troops had worked their way into the German system, in the salient east of Ginchy; but ere that relief was completed, 2nd Lieutenant Zigomala and ten men had been wounded. Next day saw forty casualties from shrapnel and snipers, and 2nd Lieutenant

Vaughan and several men in No. 1 Company were killed by a single shell. The enemy, well aware of what was intended, did all that they could to cripple, delay and confuse, and waste the men and material on our side. Their chief reliance was their "pocketed" machine-guns with which the whole ground was peppered; and their gunners' instructions, most gallantly obeyed, were, on the withdrawal of any force, to remain and continue killing till they themselves were killed. Consequently it was necessary at frequent intervals to hunt up these pests by hand rather as one digs out wasps' nests after dark.

On the night of the 13th September it fell to the lot of the Battalion to send out No. 2 Company upon a business of this nature – machine-guns in a strong trench on their right. After a bombardment supposed to have cut the wire, the Company had to file across a stretch of the open Ginchy–Morval road, and there were enfiladed by machine-gun fire which killed 2nd Lieutenant Tomkins, who had joined less than a fortnight before, and wounded a good many of the men. This was while merely getting into position among the cramped trenches. Next, it was discovered that our bombardment had by no means cut enough wire, and when the attack was launched, in waves of two platoons each, undisturbed machine-guns in a few dreadful minutes accounted for more than three-quarters of the little host. Almost at the outset, Lieutenant Montgomery was killed close to our own parapet, and those who were left, under 2nd Lieutenant Hely-Hutchinson, lay down till they might crawl back after dark. That wiped out No. 2 Company, and next day, its thirty survivors were sent back to the first-line Transport – a bleak prelude to the battle ahead. But it passed almost unnoticed in the failure of an attack launched at the same time by the 71st and 16th Infantry Brigades in the direction of Leuze Wood. Names of villages and salient points existed beautifully on such maps as were issued to the officers, and there is no doubt that the distances on these maps were entirely correct. The drawback was that the whole landscape happened to be one pitted, clodded, brown and white wilderness of aching uniformity, on which to pick up any given detail was like identifying one plover's nest in a hundred-acre bog.

GINCHY

But the idea of the battle of the 15th September was, as usual, immensely definite. Rawlinson's Fourth Army was to attack between Combles and Martinpuich and seize Morval, Lesbœufs, Gueudecourt, and Flers; the French attacking at the same time on the right, and the Reserve Army on the left. Immediately after our objective had been won the Cavalry would advance and, apparently, seize the high ground all round the Department, culminating at Bapaume. The work of the Guards Division, whose views of Cavalry at that particular moment are not worth reproducing, was to support the Cavalry "on the above lines." The 2nd Guards Brigade would take the right of the attack on Lesbœufs; the 1st the left, with the 3rd Brigade in reserve, and the 71st Infantry Brigade on the right of the 2nd Guards Brigade. The 3rd Grenadiers and 1st Coldstream were respectively right and left leading battalions, with the 1st Scots Guards and the 2nd Irish Guards as right and left supporting battalions; each advancing in four waves of single rank; two machine-guns accompanying each leading battalion and four each the supporting ones. Three other machine-guns were to bring up the rear flanked, on either side, by two Stokes mortar guns. The Brigade's allotted front was five hundred yards to the north-east of Ginchy, and since the normal enemy barrage between Guillemont and Ginchy was a thing to be avoided if possible, they were assembled east of the latter village and not behind it. Their objectives were duly laid down for them in green, brown, blue and red lines on the maps, or as one young gentleman observed, "just like a game of snooker except that every one played with the nearest ball as soon as the game began." But every one understood perfectly the outlines of the game. Their predecessors had been playing it by hundreds of thousands since the 1st of July. They knew they would all go on till they were dropped, or blown off the face of the earth.

They dug themselves in on the night of the 14th in shallow trenches about ten paces apart, a trench to each wave which was made up of two half-companies. The 2nd Irish Guards having expended one (No. 2) Company on the 13th September, their No. 3 Company was distributed between Nos. 1 and 4 who accordingly went over in two enlarged waves.

The Brigade lost hardly a man from enemy bombardment during the long hours that passed while waiting for the dawn. At six o'clock on the 15th our heavies opened; and, as far as the 2nd Brigade was concerned, brought down the German barrage exactly where it was expected, between Guillemont and Ginchy, which, by German logic, should have been crowded with our waiting troops. Thanks, however, to the advice of Major Rocke and Captain Alexander as to the massing-point, that blast fell behind our men, who thus lived to progress into the well-laid and unbroken machine-gun fire that met them the instant they advanced. Their first objective (Green line) was six hundred yards away through the mists of the morning and the dust and flying clods of the shells. A couple of hundred yards out, the 3rd Grenadiers and 1st Coldstream came upon a string of shell-holes which might or might not have started life as a trench, filled with fighting Germans, insufficiently dealt with by our guns. This checked the waves for a little and brought the Irish storming into the heels of the leading line, and as the trench lay obliquely across the advance, swung the whole of the 2nd Brigade towards the left, and into the 1st Brigade, who had already met a reasonable share of trouble of their own. Indeed, during this first advance, one party of the 2nd Irish Guards, under Major Rocke and Lieutenant G. Bambridge and 2nd Lieutenant Mylne, found themselves mixed up among the men of the 1st Battalion. Moreover, the attack of the Sixth Division which was taking place on the right of the 2nd Guards Brigade had been held up, and it seemed as though the whole of the machine-gun fire from the low fortified Quadrilateral dominating that end of the line was sweeping like hail into the right of the 2nd Guards Brigade. This still further, though they were not aware of it at the time, turned them towards the left.

The Battalion, without landmarks to guide, did what they could. Under Captain Alexander and 2nd Lieutenant Greer, the Germans in the first unexpected trench were all accounted for. Greer also shot down and put out of action an enemy machine-gun, and the thinned line went on. There had been instructions, in Brigade Orders, as to the co-operation of nine tanks that were to assist the Guards Division that day and would, probably, "start from each successive line well in advance of the attacking troops." Infantry were warned, however, that their work "would be carried out whether the Tanks are held up or not." It was. The Tanks were not much more in evidence on that sector than the Cavalry which, cantering gaily across the shell-holes, should have captured Bapaume; and long before the Brigade were anywhere near their first objective, companies and battalions were mixed up in what with other troops would have been hopeless confusion; but the Guards are accustomed to carry on without worrying whether with their own units or not. In due time, and no man can say what actually happened outside his own range of action, for no man saw anything coherently, their general advance reached the German trench which was their first objective. Its wire had not been cut properly by our guns, and little gasping, sweating parties dodged in and out and round the wings of it, bombing enemies where they sighted them. There were many Germans, too, in the shell-holes that they overpassed, who fired into their backs, and all the while from their right flank, now wholly in the air, came the lashing machine-gun fire of the Quadrilateral which was so effectually holding the Sixth Division. So the wrecked trench of the first objective was, as one man said, "none too bad a refuge even if we had to bomb ourselves into it."

They tumbled in, as they arrived, about a hundred and twenty of all units of the Brigade with Captain Alexander of the Battalion, Captain F. J. Hopley, 3rd Grenadiers, Lieutenant Boyd-Rochfort, Scots Guards, Lieutenant M. Tennant, Scots Guards, attached to the machine-guns, and 2nd Lieutenants Greer and Lysaght, of the Battalion. A few minutes later

Colonel Claude de Crespigny of the 2nd Grenadiers of the 1st Brigade arrived with about fifty men. They had fairly lost the rest of their Brigade in the dust and smoke, and had fetched up, fragmentarily, among the 2nd Brigade, at what was fast becoming a general rendezvous. Finding that the first objective still needed a great deal more combing out, the mixed parties of officers and men divided and began to bomb left and right along the trench. Then Colonel Godman of the Scots Guards appeared (it was all one whirling vision of breathless men and quickly passing faces), and took over general command of the Brigade. With him were Lieutenant Mackenzie and Captain the Hon. K. Digby, the Adjutants of the 1st Scots Guards and 1st Coldstream; while Captain FitzGerald, Lieutenant Keenan and 2nd Lieutenant Close of the Battalion were bombing and taking prisoners up an offshoot of the trench in the direction of Lesbœufs. The Germans who had fought so well among the shell-holes did not seem to be represented here, for they surrendered with ease. Their own people machine-gunned them so purposefully as they scuttled towards our lines that sometimes they bolted back to the comparative decency of the trench whence they had been digged.

Meantime the situation did not clear itself. The uncut wire of the first objective and the general drift of the whole attack to the left had made a gap between the two front Battalions of the 2nd Brigade's attack, that is to say, the 3rd Grenadiers and the 1st Coldstream. A party of a hundred of the former Battalion were pushed up into it, and seem to have disappeared into the general maelstrom. At the same time, the 3rd Grenadiers were trying to get touch with the Sixth Division, on their sorely hammered right. Major Rocke, Lieutenant Bambridge and 2nd Lieutenant Mylne and their party of the 2nd Irish Guards, were far out towards the left where the 2nd Brigade's advance had outrun that of the 1st, so much that the 1st Coldstream's left flank was in the air and there was a gap between the two Brigades. Here Major Rocke's party found Colonel Guy Baring (he was killed a little later) commanding the 1st Coldstream, and at his suggestion formed a defensive flank on the left of the Coldstream until the 1st Brigade drew level. This precaution was rewarded by a satisfactory bag estimated at over two hundred Huns who, being incommoded by the 2nd Brigade's action, were trying to slip through the gap between the two Brigades and escape round the rear of the 2nd Brigade, and who were mostly killed by small-arm fire.

More men kept dribbling in to the first-objective trench from time to time ("Like lost hounds, only they'd been fighting every yard of their way home"), and the remnants of the Battalions of the Brigade were sorted out and apportioned lengths of trench to hold. Thus: "Grenadier Guards, 60 on the right; Scots Guards, 60 next; Irish Guards, 40 next; Coldstream

Guards, 10, on the left in touch with the 1st Brigade," or, at least, as far as any touch could be made. The fighting, of course, continued all round them, and various parties devoted themselves to this as need arose. Everything was in the air now, left and right flanks together, but the Guards Division, as an extremely mixed whole, had pushed forward and taken the ground it had been ordered to take, while the enemy, attacking here, bombing there and bolting across the shell-holes elsewhere, seemed to be desirous to pull out of action and break away towards Bapaume. Our guns, of which the fighting infantry were unconscious at the time, had helped them towards this decision. There was some question and discussion in the trench as to whether they should now push on to their second objective, or whether our artillery would, as originally laid down, bombard that before a fresh move. But signs of German withdrawal across the bare down and the sight of some of their field-guns trotting back suggested a sporting chance of pushing on towards Lesbœufs, which Captain Ian Colquhoun of the Scots Guards and Captain Lyttelton of the 3rd Grenadiers thought worth taking. Their view was shared by Major Rocke, Captain Alexander and Lieutenant Mylne of the Battalion, so between them they amassed some hundred men and went out nearly half a mile into an unoccupied trench in a hollow, with standing crops in front. Here they halted and sent back demands for reinforcements. As they were utterly detached from an already detached force, they might as well have indented for elephants. The day went on, and the enemy, realizing that our push had come to an end, began to steal forward in small bodies which first outflanked and then practically surrounded the detachment. At last a whole company, hidden in the tall crops, made a rush which should have killed or captured every one in the position. Somehow or other – and again, no coherent account was ever rendered, but it was probably due to our controlled rapid fire – they failed. Our men fought their way out and back to the main body with surprisingly few casualties; and the enemy excitedly following them, came under a limited but well-directed machine-gun fire from the main trench. The Diary enters it as "a weak attack from Lesbœufs easily driven off, Lieutenant M. Tennant doing good work with his machine-gun which was well placed on the right." But nothing is more difficult than to dissect and sift out the times and the values of linked or overlapping episodes throughout one desperate day, where half-a-dozen separated detachments are each profoundly certain that they, and they alone, bear the weight or turn the tide of the local war. The minuteness of the field of action adds to the confusion; when one remembers that the distance from Ginchy to Lesbœufs was about the extreme range of a service rifle and that the whole of that day's work had won them about eight hundred yards. For that advance they had paid three hundred casualties among the men, and the following officers: Captain Parsons, Lieutenants Purcell and Walters, both the latter attached to the Machine-Gun Company, killed; Major Rocke, Lieutenant Brew (seriously), and 2nd Lieutenants M. R. FitzGerald, Mylne and Cutcliffe Hyne wounded. In addition 2nd Lieutenants Vaughan and Tomkins and Lieutenant Montgomery had been killed in the preliminary work on the 13th September. A total of six officers dead and five wounded.

A partially successful attempt on a German trench ahead of them by a battalion of the Durham Light Infantry a little after dark, brought the very long day to an end. The night was quiet, while some units of the Twentieth Division came up and dug themselves in outside their parapet in readiness for the fresh attack which was to begin the next morning. Men could not help admiring, even at the time, the immense and ordered inhumanity of the system that, taking no count of aught except the end, pushed forward through the dead and the debris of war the fresh organizations which were to be spent next day as their predecessors had been. ("Atop of it all, when a man was done with he felt that he was in the road of the others. The same with the Battalions. When they was used they was heaved out of the road like a broke lorry, and only too glad of it. But, as I was saying, when we was expended, we all felt ashamed of blocking the traffic with our wounds and our carcasses. The only fun for us afterwards was telling them that came up what was awaiting them. But they knew – they knew it already!")

The 16th September was an almost continuous bombardment of whizz-bangs and 5·9's on the trench where they still lay; but in the intervals of the shelling men kept turning up and reporting themselves with tales of adventure and extremity among the shell-holes outside. They were relieved a little before midnight and left their battered lair eighty-eight strong, *via* Ginchy, Guillemont and Trônes Wood for the Citadel, which when they reached, their total had been increased by strays to one hundred and six. Lieutenant Bambridge, eminently capable of looking after himself and his party, turned up later with another sixty. Next day, the weary work of re-making the Battalion began. Lieutenant Dollar had to be sent down to hospital with a return of the dysentery from which he had reported himself recovered. This further reduced the few available officers on their feet. A draft of a hundred and fifty men came in. By absorbing the still effective digging-platoon into the active line, a Battalion of four Companies of a hundred each was put together and turned out for the next week in the Carnoy mud to drill under new Company Commanders.

MUD-FIGHTING ON THE SOMME

The second move of the Guards Division opened on the 25th September, and this time the ball was with the 1st Battalion. The work on the 15th of the month had carried the Fourteenth Division's front on to the naked ridge towards Morval and Lesbœufs where it had been held, but without advance, for the past ten days. Now Brigade Orders came "to renew the attacks" over what remained untaken of the ground. "The Guards Division will capture Lesbœufs. The 1st Guards Brigade will attack on the right, the 3rd on the left," while the Fifth Division was to attack Morval on the right of the Guards Division and the Twenty-first Division (62nd Brigade) would take Gueudecourt on the left. The 2nd Guards Brigade would be in reserve; and the Battalion hoped, as men may who know what war means, that they would not be needed. Nor were they till the evening of the 26th September, when they moved from Trônes Wood and its dead, to relieve the 1st Battalion, used and broken for the second time in ten days, the day before, with the 2nd Grenadiers who "after the attack on Lesbœufs had dug themselves in to the east of that town." Caesar himself does not equal the sublime terseness of the Diary. All their world from the King downwards was to crown them with praise later on, but in the meantime reliefs must be orderly conducted and touch must be kept through the shell-tormented darkness with the battalions on either side, while they themselves settled in the reeking front line under certainty of vicious bombardment, and the possibility of suddenly launched counter-attack. They were shelled all that night from their relief on and throughout the next day (the 27th) "by every type of shell, but mostly by 5·9's." In the afternoon when it became necessary to help an attack on their left by launching a creeping barrage from in front of Lesbœufs towards Transloy, the enemy retaliated with a barrage on the Battalion's front that blew the line in in several places. They received the same attentions on the 28th, and this in an uptorn isolated land where water was scarce; but, on their demand, retaliation arrived in the shape of heavies and some aeroplanes. "This had the effect of stopping the enemy's fire completely except for a few whizz-bangs." For the rest of the day they merely took their share of the general necessary shellings on a vast and disputed front. Men grow quick to differentiate between the punishment they should accept without complaint, and the personal direct "hate" which sets the newly strung telephones buzzing to Brigade Headquarters for the guns. But, even so, it is said, a hypnotic sense of helplessness comes over troops which are being shelled continuously, till sometimes they will sit and suffer, the telephone under their hand, while parapets fly up and fall down on them. Yet, one single small casualty may break that spell as suddenly as it was cast, and the whole line, grumbling and uneasy, wants to know whether their Artillery are dead too.

The 1st Coldstream relieved them late at night and without one single casualty on the 28th September, and they lay up in bivouac in Trônes Wood on the 30th. Their old C.O. Colonel, now General, Butler lunched with them in the Headquarters dug-out, where they compared experiences. The 3rd Londons relieved them, and an enemy aeroplane bombed them, but without effect, on their way back to camp in Carnoy Valley; and four officers, Lieutenant Gunstone and 2nd Lieutenants Heard, Crawford and Black, arrived on that uneventful day. Naturally, in a district alive with troops, German aeroplanes did all the harm they could in our back-areas, and nothing will persuade harried infantry on the ground that our aircraft are properly protecting them. A draft of fifty men came in on the 1st October, a Sunday, and on the 2nd they withdrew altogether with the Division out of the battle for intensive training. Their own camp was Méricourt-en-Vimeux west of Amiens, but – more important than all else – the leave-season opened.

It was an ordinary month of the ordinary work demanded by the war conditions of the age. Steady drill was the background of it, and specialist classes for Lewis-gunners, Bombers, Intelligence, and Gas filled the hours, varied by night and day outpost and wire work as well as map-reading for officers. Company Commanders, whose men were taken from lawfully ordained parade, swore and complained, and not without justification; for the suave, unget-at-able shirker has a much better chance of evading the burdens of mere battalion routine when every one is a "specialist," than when, as a marching unit, he is under the direct eye of his own unimaginative N.C.O.'s. ("There was times, if you will believe me, when we was sorry for Platoon Sergeants. What with this and that and the other special trick, every mother's son of us Micks had the excuses of his life to his hands all the time.") Hence the disgraceful story of the Sergeant who demanded whether "those somethinged spe-*shy*-lists "could" lend him as much as three wet-nurses, just to make a show with the platoon."

Rewards began to come in. Captain Harvey, their M.O., was awarded the Military Cross for a little more than the usual bravery that a doctor has to exhibit in the ordinary course of his duty, and 2nd Lieutenant Greer received the same honour for, incidentally, dealing with enemy machine-guns in the advance of the 15th. General Feilding, on the 6th, also distributed ribbons of medals won, and said what he thought of the work of the Guards Division during the previous month. The formal acknowledgement of the Commander of the Fourth Army (General Rawlinson) arrived on October 17. He said that the "gallantry and perseverance of the Guards Division in the battles of the 15th and 25th were paramount factors in the success of the operations of the Fourth Army on those days." Of the 15th September, specially, he observed, "The vigorous attacks of the Guards in circumstances of great difficulty, with both flanks exposed to the enfilade fire of the enemy, reflect the highest credit on all concerned, and I desire to tender to every officer, N.C.O., and man, my congratulations and best thanks for their exemplary valour on that occasion." They knew that they had not done so badly, though every one above the rank of drummer could say now how it could have been done much better; but the official word was grateful to those who had lived, and cheering for those about to die.

On the 23rd October they route-marched to a fair field south of Aumont with their cookers and their water-carts (all the Division more or less was being trained in that neighbourhood), met their 1st Battalion, dined well together, and embarked on a football match which the 1st won by two goals to nothing. "The men thoroughly enjoyed meeting each other, and spent a very happy day." It might be a Sunday-school that the Diary describes, instead of two war-used Battalions drawing breath between engagements.

H.R.H. the Duke of Connaught was to inspect the Division on the 1st of November, which meant rehearsals for the ceremonial – a ritual of value for retaining a hold on "specialists," and taken advantage of by Company Officers and N.C.O.'s who held that it did men no harm to disport themselves occasionally in slow time with a properly pointed foot. The rain and break-up of autumn made training very difficult, but, the Diary notes, though many denied it at the time, "We endeavoured to make every man a bomber rather than to concentrate on the production of a number of specialists." The Inspection rewarded the trouble taken – there was nothing their sternest critics could lay a finger on – and at the end of it, those officers and men who had won decorations in the war, lined up before the Duke who addressed them. Méricourt days ended with a Battalion dinner in the 1st Battalion billets at Hornoy to General Butler, their old commandant whose Brigade was in rest near by. Somehow the memory of such dinners remains with the survivors long after more serious affairs, as it seemed then, have faded. ("It's a curious thing that, on those occasions, one was drunk before one sat down – out of sheer good-fellowship, I suppose, and the knowledge that we were all for it, and had all come through it so far. The amount of liquor actually consumed has nothing to do with the results. I've put away four times as much since Armistice and only got a bit of a head.")

On the 10th and 11th of November the Division returned to school. They were to take over a stretch of the Fourteenth Corps' front near Gueudecourt and Lesbœufs. For tactical purposes the Division was now divided into two "Groups" of six battalions each. The right Group was made up of the 1st Guards Brigade as a whole, with the 1st Coldstream and the 2nd Irish Guards additional. The left was the 3rd Guards Brigade plus the 3rd Grenadiers and the 1st Scots Guards, so that the 2nd Brigade was absorbed for the while. The Battalion left Méricourt-en-Vimeux "with considerable regret" for it was good billets, and was packed into a large fleet of French motor-buses, many of which were driven by Senegalese – "an example of the Frenchmen's ability in saving up their men. A particularly engaging ape was the conductor of the officers' bus. He was fed by the Adjutant on chicken-legs which he greatly appreciated and entirely devoured. He appeared to speak no word of any human language." Medals should have been awarded for this affair; to be driven forty miles by Senegalese chauffeurs is an experience deadly almost as warfare. Méaulte, their destination, was then an "entirely unattractive town." Gangs of Hun prisoners shovelled mud from roads a foot deep in grey reeking slime. Every road was blocked with limbers and lorries that offered no way to the disgusted infantry wedged up impatiently behind them. Their billets were crowded and bad, and they regretted the fleshpots of Méricourt while they cleaned them or froze in tents beside the Carnoy–Fricourt road where they kept warm by trying to make roads out of frosty mud.

Mud, filth, cold, exposure and the murderous hard work necessary to mere existence, were their daily and nightly fare from now on. It must be duly set down for that reason, and that the generations to come may judge for themselves what the war of a people unprepared, against a race that had made provision for war, cost in the mere stage-setting and scene-shifting of actual warfare.

On the 18th November they were shifted from their chill tents at "Mansell Camp" to Camp A, only four miles off, at Trônes Wood. The roads which were not roads and the traffic that was trying to treat them as such,

OVERLEAF

You followed a duckboard track of sorts through Trônes Wood, between ghastly Delville and the black ruins of Ginchy, and across the Ginchy ridge... where, if you were not very careful, the engulfing mud would add you to its increasing and matured collection of "officers and other ranks." These accidents overcome, you would discover that the front line was mud with holes in it.

Ginchy ridge on a wet afternoon, September 1916.

101

made this a matter of three and a half hours' continuous marching, mainly in single file. They found themselves at last in dark and pouring rain, hunting across a morass for holes in the ground inadequately covered with pieces of tarpaulin and five hundred yards away from any firm foothold. This was the "camp." The cookers frankly dared not leave the road and the men had to flounder across the bog to get their teas. For that reason, the next day being fine and all hands "thoroughly wet and uncomfortable," they "sang loudly as they slopped about in the mud."

Their wholly unspeakable front line was five miles distant from this local paradise. You followed a duckboard track of sorts through Trônes Wood, between ghastly Delville and the black ruins of Ginchy, and across the Ginchy ridge where the chances of trouble thickened, through a communication-trench, and thereafter into a duckboarded landscape where, if you were not very careful, the engulfing mud would add you to its increasing and matured collection of "officers and other ranks." These accidents overcome, you would discover that the front line was mud with holes in it. If the holes were roundish they were called posts; if oblong they were trenches with names, such as Gusty Trench and Spectrum Trench. They connected with nothing except more mud. Wiring peered up in places, but whether it was your own or the enemy's was a matter of chance and luck. The only certainty was that, beyond a point which no one could locate, because all points were wiped out by a carpet-like pattern of closely set holes, you would be shelled continuously from over the bleak horizon. Nor could you escape, because you could never move faster than a man in a nightmare. Nor dared you take cover, because the mud-holes that offered it swallowed you up.

Here, for instance, is what befell when No. 1 Company went up to relieve a Grenadier Company on the night of the 19th November. They started at 3 p.m. in continuous mud under steady shelling. Only three out of their four platoon guides turned up. The other had collapsed. Ten men were hit on the way up; a number of others fell out from sheer exhaustion or got stuck in the mud. The first man who set foot in the front-line trench blocked the rest for a quarter of an hour, while four of his comrades were hauling him out. This was five hours after they had begun. The two Lewis-guns and some stragglers, if men hip-deep in mud and water can straggle, were still unaccounted for. Lance-Sergeant Nolan brought them all in by hand at three in the morning under shellfire. Then they were heavily shelled (there was hardly any rifle-fire), and three men were wounded. Luckily shells do not burst well in soft dirt. It was Private Curran's business to shift two of them who were stretcher-cases to Battalion Headquarters one mile and a half distant. This took two relays of eight men each, always under shell-fire, and Curran's round trip was completed in nine hours. When they were relieved by the soft-spoken Australians, on the evening of the 21st, they spent the whole of the night, from 8 p.m. to 6 a.m., getting back to camp, where it is not surprising that they arrived "utterly exhausted." Owing to an orderly losing his way, one isolated trench or hole held by Sergeant Murphy, Lance-Sergeant Nolan and seven men, was not relieved, and they stayed on for another twenty-four hours. No. 2 Company, a few hundred yards away, were fairly dead to the world by the time that they had worked their way to their line, which possessed, nominally, a trench and some posts. The trench was a gutter; their posts had no protection at all from shells, and when they arrived they found that no sand-bags had been sent up, so they had nothing to work with. They also spent their time pulling men out of the mire. Supervision of any sort was impossible. It took the officer three hours to get from the left to the right of his short line. The posts could not be reached by daylight at all, and during bombardments of the trench "it often seemed as though what little there was must disappear, and (the Battalion, as we know, was mostly new hands) the coolness of the young N.C.O.'s was invaluable in keeping up the spirits of the men." There was one time when a Sergeant (Lucas) was buried by a shell, and a brother Sergeant (Glennon) "though he knew that it meant almost certain death" went to his aid, and was instantly killed, for the enemy, naturally, had the range of their own old trenches to the inch. To be heroic at a walk is trying enough, as they know who have plowtered behind the Dead March of a dragging barrage, but to struggle, clogged from the waist down, into the white-hot circle of accurately placed destruction, sure that if you are even knocked over by a blast you will be slowly choked by mud, is something more than heroism. Equally, to lie out disabled on a horror of shifting mud is beyond the sting of Death. One of our Corporals on patrol heard groaning somewhere outside the line. It proved to be a Grenadier, who had lain there twenty-four hours "suffering from frost-bite and unable to move." They saved him. Their stretcher-bearers were worn out, and what sand-bags at last arrived were inadequate for any serious defence. "We were fighting purely against mud and shells, as the German infantry gave us no trouble." When No. 2 was relieved at the same time as No. 1 Company, they dribbled into camp by small parties from two till ten in the morning, and three of the men never turned up at all. The Somme mud told no tales till years later when the exhumation parties worked over it. The Australians, of whom it is reported that the mud dragged every national expletive out of them by the boots, relieved the Division as a whole on the 22nd November, and, pending the new arrangements for taking over more of the French line, the Guards were transferred first to a camp between Carnoy and Montauban, which for those parts was fairly comfortable. At all events, the huts though stoveless were water-tight, and could be "frowsted up" to something like warmth. For ten days they worked, two days out of three, on the Carnoy–Montauban road in company with a Labour Battalion surnamed "The Broody Hens," owing to their habit of scuttling at the very last moment from under the wheels of the multitudinous lorries. "On off days we made paths through the mud for ourselves." But these were dry, and by comparison clean.

The trench-line taken over by the Guards Division ran, roughly, from Morval to Sailly-Saillisel (locally "Silly-Sally") when their Groups were split into two (right and left) sections. The right, to which the Battalion was attached, was made up of themselves, their sister Battalion and the 2nd Grenadiers. A spell of hard winter weather had frozen the actual trenches into fairly good condition for the minute, but there were no communications, nor, as they observed, much attempt at fire-steps. The French trusted more to automatic rifles – the Battalions the Irish relieved had thirty-two each – and machine-guns than to infantry, and used their linesmen mainly as bombers or bayoneteers. Accommodation was bad. When not on tour, two Companies were billeted in old dug-outs that contained the usual proportion of stale offences, on the west side of Combles: one in cellars and dug-outs in the town itself; and one in dug-outs in Haie Wood three thousand yards behind the front. Their front line ran along the east edge of the obliterated village, their support a hundred yards or so behind it through the mounds of brick and earth of the place itself, while the Reserve Company lay up in mildewy dug-outs in a chalk quarry three-quarters of a mile back. (One peculiarity of the Somme was its most modestly inconspicuous cave-dwellings.) For the rest, "The whole area was utterly desolate. West of the village, rolling ground, the valleys running east and west a waste of mud with shell-holes touching one another. Here and there the charred stumps of trees. Equipment, French and German, dotted the ground, and rifles, their muzzles planted in the mud, showed where, in some attack, wounded men had lain. The village was just mounds of earth or mud and mere shell-holes." Later on even the mounds were not suffered to remain, and the bricks were converted into dull red dust that in summer blew across the dead land.

The Battalion was not in position till the 11th December, when it relieved the 2nd Grenadiers after three or four days' rain which wiped out what communication-trenches had been attempted, and pulped the front line. As to the back-breaking nature of the work – "Though the first Company (on relief) passed Haie Wood about 4 p.m. it was 11.30 before they had floundered the intervening 3000 yards." One of the Grenadiers whom they relieved had been stuck in the mud for forty-three hours. Unless the men in the trenches, already worn out with mud-wrestling to get there, kept moving like hens on hot plates, they sank and stuck. ("It is funny, maybe, to talk about now, that mud-larking of ours; but to sink,

sink, sink in the dark and you not sure whether they saw ye or could hear you, puts the wind up a man worse than anything under Heaven. Fear? Fear is not the word. 'Twas the Somme that broke our hearts. Back, knees, loins, acrost your chest – you was dragged to pieces dragging your own carcass out of the mud. 'Twas like red-hot wires afterwards – and all to begin it again.")

A mystery turned up on the night of the 12th December in the shape of a wild-looking, apparently dumb, Hun prisoner, brought before Captain Young of the Support Company, who could make naught of him, till at last "noticing the likeness between his cap and that affected by Captain Alexander"[1] he hazarded "Russky." The prisoner at once awoke, and by sign and word revealed himself as from Petrograd. Also he bolted one loaf of bread in two counted minutes. He had been captured at Kovel by the Huns, and brought over to be used by them to dig behind their front line. But how he had escaped across that wilderness that wild-eyed man never told.

They got back on the 13th December to a hideous tent-camp near Trônes Wood. Thence, thoroughly wet, they were next day solemnly entrained at Trônes Wood, carted three miles by train to Plateau and thence, again, marched two more to Bronfay. There, done to the last turn, chilled to the marrow and caked with mud, they found the huttage allotted them already bursting with a Brigade of Artillery. Short of turning out themselves, the gunners did their kindest to help the men dry and get their food, while the various authorities concerned fought over their weary heads; some brilliant members of the Staff vowing that the camp intended for them had not even been built; which must have been vast consolation to the heavy-eyed, incurious sick, of whom there were not a few after the last tour, as well as to the wrathful and impeded Cooks and Sergeants. They got their sick away (the Adjutant, Captain J. S. N. FitzGerald and Lieutenant D. Gunston among them), and somehow squashed in all together through another day of mere hanging about and crowded, cold discomfort, which does men more harm and develops more microbes than a week's blood and misery.

On the 16th December they returned afoot through eight miles of snowstorm to "some of the most depressing scenery in Europe." The "men had had but little rest and few of them had got any of their clothes in the least dry." But they were left alone for one blessed night at Combles and Haie Wood in their cellars and their dug-outs, and they slept where they lay, the stark corpse-like sleep of men too worn-out even to mutter or turn.

Except that shelling was continuous over all the back-areas and

---

[1] This was pure prophecy. Captain, as he was then, Alexander was credited with a taste for strange and Muscovitish headgear, which he possibly gratified later as a General commanding weird armies in Poland during the spasms of reconstruction that followed the Armistice.

approaches, the enemy as a fighting force did not enter into their calculations. Or it might be more accurate to say, both sides were fighting ground and distance. The sole problem of the lines was communication; for every stick, wire and water-tin had to be backed up by brute bodily labour across the mud. All hands were set to laying trench-boards from the support and reserve lines and Haie Wood. Without these, it had taken two and a half hours to carry a load eight hundred yards. With them, the same party covered the same distance under an equal burden in twenty minutes. The enemy used their prisoners and captives for these ends. Ours were well tended, out of harm's range, while His Majesty's Foot Guards took their places. The front line – they relieved the 2nd Grenadiers there on the 17th – was "mere canals of mud and water with here and there a habitable island." The defences had been literally watered down to a string of isolated posts reached over the top across stinking swamp, and the mounds and middens called parapets spread out dismally and collapsed as they tinkered at them.

All dirt is demoralizing. The enemy's parapets had melted like ours and left their working-parties exposed to the waist. Since the lines were too close to be shelled by either artillery, the opposing infantry on both sides held their hands till there grew up gradually a certain amount of "live and let live," out of which, but farther down the line, developed attempts at fraternization, and, in front of the Guards, much too much repair work and "taking notice" on the part of the enemy. The Hun never comprehends unwritten codes. Instead of thanking Heaven and the weather for a few days' respite, he began to walk out on the top of his mounds and field-glass our wire. Therefore, on the 19th December, the dawn of a still freezing day, two obviously curious Germans were "selected and shot" by a sniper who had been detailed for that job. "The movement then ceased," and doubtless our action went to swell the wireless accounts of "unparalleled British brutalities."

Their next tour, December 23, which included Christmas Day, saw them with only seven officers, including the C.O. and the Acting-Adjutant, Lieutenant Denson, fit for duty. Captain Bambridge and Lieutenant Hely-Hutchinson had to be left behind sick at the Q.M. stores in Maricourt, and two officers had been detached for special duties. The M.O. also had gone sick, and those officers who stood up, through the alternations of biting frost and soaking thaw, were fairly fine-drawn. Whether this was the vilest of all their War Christmasses for the Battalion is an open question. There was nothing to do except put out chilly wire and carry stuff. A couple of men were killed that day and one wounded by shells, and another laying sand-bags round the shaft of a dug-out tripped on a telephone wire, fell down the shaft and broke his neck. Accidents in the front line always carry more weight than any three legitimate casualties, for the absurd, but quite comprehensible, reason that they might have happened in civilian life – are outrages, as it were, by the Domestic Fates instead of by the God of War.

The growing quiet on the sector for days past had led people to expect attempts at fraternization on Christmas. Two "short but very severe bombardments" by our Artillery on Christmas morning cauterized that idea; but a Hun officer, with the methodical stupidity of his breed, needs must choose the top of his own front-line parapet on Christmas Day whence to sketch our trench, thus combining religious principles with reconnaissance, and – a single stiff figure exposed from head to foot – was shot. So passed Christmas of '16 for the 2nd Battalion of the Irish Guards. It had opened with Captain Young of No. 1 Company finding, when he woke in his dug-out, "a stocking stuffed with sweets and the like, a present from the N.C.O.'s and the men of his Company."

They were relieved by the 1st Battalion on Christmas night, but returned on the 29th to celebrate New Year's Day by baling out flooded trenches and slapping back liquid parapets as they fell in. The enemy had most accurately registered the new duck-board tracks from the support-lines, and shelled the wretched carrying-parties by day and night. ("If you stayed on the track you was like to be killed; if you left it, you had great choice of being smothered.") The Acting-Adjutant (Lieutenant Denson) and the Bombing Sergeant (Cole) attended a consultation with the Brigade Bombing Officer on the morning of the 30th at Support Company's Headquarters in the Quarry. Business took them to the Observation Post in the wreckage of the church; and while there, the enemy opened on the support-line. They tried to get to the Support Company's dug-out; but on the way a shell pitched in among them, wounding the Brigade Bombing Officer (Lieutenant Whittaker), the Sergeant and Lieutenant Denson. The other two were able to walk, but Denson was hit all over the body. Hereupon Lieutenant Black and his orderly, Private Savage, who were in the Support dug-out, ran to where he lay, and, as they lifted him, another shell landed almost on them. They did not dare to risk taking Denson down the nearly vertical dug-out stairs, so Private Savage, with a couple more men from No. 3 Company, in case of accidents, carried him on his back six hundred yards to the dressing-station. Thrice in that passage their track was blown up, but luckily none of the devoted little party was hit. To be hunted by shell down interminable lengths of slimy duckboard is worse than any attempt on one's life in the open, for the reason that one feels between the shoulder-blades that one is personally and individually wanted by each shouting messenger.

Another escaped prisoner, C.S.M. J. B. Wilson of the 13th East Yorks, managed to get into our lines that night. He had been captured at Serre on the 13th November, and had got away from a prisoners' camp at

Honnecourt only the night before. He covered sixteen kilometres in the darkness, steered towards the permanent glare over the front, reached the German line at dawn, lay up in a shell-hole all through the day and, finally, wormed across to us by marking down an N.C.O. of ours who was firing some lights, and crawling straight on to him. Seeing his condition when he arrived, the achievement bears out the Diary's tantalizingly inadequate comment: "In private life he was a Bank accountant, and seemed to be very intelligent as well as a man of the greatest determination. We fed him and warmed him before sending him on to Haie Wood whence an ambulance took him to Brigade H.Q."

So the year ended in storm and rain, the torn, grey clouds of the Somme dissolving and deluging them as they marched back to Maltz Horn Camp, across an insane and upturned world where men of gentle life, unwashen for months at a stretch, were glad to lie up in pigsties, and where ex-Bank-accountants might crawl out of shell-holes at any hour of the hideous twenty-four.

1917

RANCOURT TO
BOURLON WOOD

THE NEW YEAR changed their ground, and, if possible, for the worse. It opened with black disappointment. They were entrained on the evening of the 2nd January for Corbie in a tactical train, whose tactics consisted in starting one hour late. On the two preceding days the Germans had got in several direct hits on its rolling stock; so that wait dragged a little. But they were uplifted by the prospect, which some one had heard or invented, of a whole month's rest. It boiled down to less than one week, on the news that the Division would take on yet another stretch of French line. There was just time to wash the men all over, their first bath in months, and to attend the Divisional Cinema. By this date Lieutenant Hanbury had joined, the Adjutancy was taken over by Captain Charles Moore, Lieutenant-Colonel P. L. Reid had to go down, sick, and the command of the Battalion had devolved on Major E. B. Greer.

By the 10th January they were at Maurepas, ready to move up next day *via* Combles and Frégicourt into their new sector, which lay the distance of one Divisional front south of the old Sailly-Saillisel one. It lay on the long clean-cut ridge, running north from Rancourt, to which the French had held when they were driven and mined out of St. Pierre Vaast Wood, facing the north-west and west sides of that forest of horrors. It was of so narrow a frontage that but one Brigade at a time went into the line, two Battalions of that Brigade up to the front, and but one Company of each Battalion actually to the front-line posts. These ran along the forward slope of the ridge, and were backed by a sketchy support-line a hundred yards or so on the reverse with the reserve five or six hundred yards behind it. "Filthy but vital" is one description of the sector. If it were lost, it would uncover ground as far back as Morval. If held, it screened our ground westward almost as far as Combles. (Again, one must bear in mind the extreme minuteness of the setting of the picture, for Combles here was barely three thousand yards from the front line.)

The reports of the Eighth Division who handed it over were not cheering. The front-line posts had been ten of ten men apiece, set irregularly in the remnants of an old trench. The only way to deal with them was to dig out and rebuild altogether on metal framings, and the Sappers had so treated four. The other six were collapsing. They needed, too, a line of efficient support-posts, in rear, and had completed one, but wire was scarce. All support and reserve trenches were wet, shallow and badly placed. A largish dug-out a hundred yards behind the front had been used as Battalion Headquarters by various occupants, German and French, and, at one stage of its career, as a dressing-station, but it seemed that the doctors "had only had time to pull upstairs the men who died and dump them in heaps a few yards away from the doorway. Later, apparently, some one had scattered a few inches of dirt over them which during our occupation the continual rain and snow washed away. The result was most grisly." The French have many virtues, but tidiness in the line is not one of them.

The whole situation turned on holding the reverse of the ridge, since, if the enemy really meant business, it was always open to him to blow us off the top of it, and come down the gentle descent from the crest at his ease. So they concentrated on the front posts and a strong, well-wired reserve line, half-way down the slope. Luckily there was a trench-tramway in the sector, running from the Sappers' dump on the Frégicourt road to close up to the charnel-house-ex-dressing-station. The regular trains, eight trucks pushed by two men each, were the 5, 7, and 9 p.m., but on misty days a 3 p.m. might also be run, and of course trains could run in the night. This saved them immense backaches. ("But, mark you, the easier the dam' stuff gets up to the front the more there is of it, and so the worse 'tis for the poor devils of wiring-parties that has to lay it out after dark. Then Jerry whizz-bangs ye the rest of the long night. All this fine labour-saving means the devil for the Micks.")

The Germans certainly whizz-banged the working-parties generously, but the flights as a rule buried themselves harmlessly in the soft ground. We on our side made no more trouble than could be avoided, but worked on the wire double tides. In the heat of the job, on the night of the 11th January, the Brigadier came round and the C.O. took him out to see Captain Alexander's party wiring their posts. It was the worst possible moment for a valuable Brigadier to wander round front lines. The moon lit up the snow and they beheld a party of Germans advancing in open order, who presently lay down and were joined by more. At eighty yards or so they halted, and after a short while crawled away. "We did not provoke battle, as we would probably have hurt no one, and we wanted to get on with our wiring." But had the Brigadier been wasted in a mere front-line bicker, the C.O., not to mention Captain Alexander, would have heard of it.

By the time that the 1st Coldstream relieved them on the 14th January, the Battalion had fenced their private No Man's Land and about six hundred yards of the line outside the posts, all under the come-and-go of shell-fire; had duckboarded tracks connecting some of the posts; systematized their ration and water supply, and captured a multitude of Army socks whereby Companies coming down from their turn could change and be dry. Dull as all such detail sounds, it is beyond question that the arrangement and prevision of domestic works appeal to certain temperaments, not only among the officers but men. They positively relish the handling and disposition of stores, the fitting of one job into the next, the race against time, the devising of tricks and gadgets for their own poor comforts, and all the mixture of house making and keeping (in which, whatever may be said, the male animal excels) on the edge of war.

For the moment, things were absurdly peaceful on their little front, and when they came back to work after three still days at Maurepas, infantry "fighting" had become a farce. The opposing big guns hammered away zealously at camps and back-areas, but along that line facing the desolate woods of St. Pierre Vaast there was mutual toleration, due to the fact that no post could be relieved on either side except by the courtesy of their opponents who lay, naked as themselves, from two hundred to thirty yards away. Thus men walked about, and worked in flagrant violation of all the rules of warfare, beneath the arch of the droning shells overhead. The Irish realized this state of affairs gradually – their trenches were not so close to the enemy; but on the right Battalion's front, where both sides lived in each other's pockets, men reported "life in the most advanced posts was a perfect idyll." So it was decided, now that every one might be presumed to know the ground, and be ready for play, that the weary game should begin again. But observe the procedure! "It was obvious it would be unfair, after availing ourselves of an unwritten agreement, to start killing people without warning." Accordingly, notices were issued by the Brigade – in English – which read: "*Warning. Any German who exposes himself after daylight to-morrow January 19 will be shot. By order.*" Battalions were told to get these into the enemy lines, if possible, between 5 and 7 a.m. They anticipated a little difficulty in communicating their kind intentions, but two heralds, with three rifles to cover them, were sent out and told to stick the warnings up on the German wire in the dusk of the dawn. Now, one of these men was No. 10609 Private King, who, in civil life, had once been policeman in the Straits Settlements. He saw a German looking over the parapet while the notice was being affixed, and, policeman-like, waved to him to come out. The German beckoned to King to come in, but did not quit the trench. King then warned the other men to stand by him, and entered into genial talk. Other Germans gathered round the first, who, after hesitating somewhat, walked to his side of the wire. He could talk no English, and King, though he tried his best, in Chinese and the kitchen-Malay of Singapore, could not convey the situation to him either. At last he handed the German the notice and told him to give it to his officer. The man seemed to understand. He was an elderly person, with his regimental number in plain sight on his collar. He saw King looking at this, and desired King to lift the edge of *his* leather jerkin so that he in turn might get our number. King naturally refused and, to emphasize what was in store for careless enemies, repeated with proper pantomime: "Shoot! Shoot! Pom! Pom!" This ended the palaver. They let him get back quite unmolested, and when the mirth had ceased, King reported that they all seemed to be "oldish men, over yonder, and thoroughly fed up." Next dawn saw no more unbuttoned ease or "idyllic" promenades along that line.

As the days lengthened arctic cold set in. The tracks between the posts became smears of black ice, and shells burst brilliantly on ground that was as pave-stones to the iron screw-stakes of the wiring. One shell caught a carrying-party on the night of the 20th January, slightly wounding Lieutenant Hanbury who chanced to be passing at the time, and wounding Sergeant Roddy and two men. The heavies behind them used the morning of the 21st to register on their left and away to the north. By some accident (the Battalion did not conceive their sector involved) a big shell landed in the German trench opposite one of their posts, and some thirty Huns broke cover and fled back over the rise. One of them, lagging behind the covey, deliberately turned and trudged across the snow to give himself up to us. Outside one of our posts he as deliberately knelt down, covered his face with his hands and prayed for several minutes. Whereupon our men instead of shooting shouted that he should come in. He was a Pole from Posen and the East front; very, very sick of warfare. This gave one Russian, one Englishman and a Pole as salvage for six weeks. An attempt at a night-raid on our part over the crackling snow was spoiled because the Divisional Stores did not run to the necessary "six white night-shirts" indented for, but only long canvas coats of a whity-brown which in the glare of Véry lights showed up hideously.

A month of mixed fatigues followed ere they saw that sector again. They cleaned up at Morval on the 22nd, and spent a few days at the Briquetterie near Bernafay Corner, where three of the Companies worked at a narrow-gauge line just outside Morval, under sporadic long-range shell-fire, and the fourth went to Ville in Divisional Reserve. The winter cold ranged from ten to twenty degrees of frost in the Nissen huts. Whereby hangs this tale. The Mess stove was like Falstaff, "old, cold and of intolerable entrails," going out on the least provocation. Only a few experts knew how to conciliate the sensitive creature, and Father Knapp, the R.C. chaplain, was *not* one of them. Indeed, he had been explicitly warned on no account whatever to attempt to stoke it. One bitter morning, however, he found himself alone in the Mess with the stove just warming up, and a sand-bag, stuffed with what felt like lumps of heaven-sent coal, lying on the floor. Naturally, he tipped it all in. But it was the Mess Perrier water, which had been thus swaddled to save it from freezing – as the priest and the exploding stove found out together. There were no casualties, though roof and walls were cut with glass, but the stove never rightly recovered from the shock, nor did Father Knapp hear the last of it for some time.

From the close of the month till the 19th of February they were in Divisional Reserve, all together at Ville in unbroken frost. While there (February 1), Lieutenant F. St. L. Greer, one of the best of officers and the most popular of comrades, was wounded in a bombing accident and died the next day. In a Battalion as closely knit together as the 2nd Irish Guards all losses hit hard.

Just as the thaw was breaking, they were sent up to Priez Farm, a camp of elephant huts, dug-outs and shelters where the men were rejoiced to get up a real "frowst" in the confined quarters. Warriors do not love scientific ventilation. From the 16th to the 25th February, the mud being in full possession of the world again, they were at Billon, which has no good name, and on the 25th back at St. Pierre Vaast, on the same sector they had left a month ago. Nothing much had been done to the works; for the German host – always at its own time and in its own methodical way – was giving way to the British pressure, and the Battalion was warned that their business would be to keep touch with any local withdrawal by means of patrols (*Anglice*, small parties playing blind-man's buff with machine-gun posts), and possibly to do a raid or two. But it is interesting to see that since their departure from that sector all the ten posts which they had dug and perspired over, and learned to know by their numbers, which automatically come back to a man's memory on his return, had been re-numbered by the authorities. It was a small thing, but good men have been killed by just such care.

They watched and waited. The air was full of rumours of the Germans' shifting – the home papers called it "cracking" – but facts and news do not go together even in peace. ("What annoyed us were the newspaper reports of how we were getting on when we weren't getting on at all.")

The Twenty-ninth Division on their left were due to put in a two-Battalion attack from Sailly-Saillisel on the dawn of the 28th February, while the Battalion in the front line was to send up a smoke-screen to distract the enemy and draw some of his barrages on to themselves. So front-line posts were thinned out as much as possible, and front companies sent out patrols to see that the Hun in front of them was working happily, and that he had not repaired a certain gap in his wire which our guns had made and were keeping open for future use. All went well, till the wind shifted and the smoke was ordered "off," and when the Twenty-ninth to Béthune   to Len

Vimy

Chelers   Béthonsart
Mar. 9
Ap. 2   22   Villers-Brulin
Tinques   Bethencourt
Ecoivres   Farbu

Tinquette
to St Pol   Bray   Ecurie
Averdoingt   Feb. 12—   Mar. 9.
17
Penin   Anzin
Maizières
Ambrines   Agnez-les-Duisans   St Nicolas

Givenchy-le-Noble
Avesnes-le-Comte   Wanquetin   Warlus   ARR
from St. Pol   Beaufort   Jan. 1.
Mar. 22   Liencourt   Hauteville   Dec. 6   Berneville
Simencourt   31
Gd Rullecourt
May 11   Barly   Beaumetz   Bretencourt
June 11   les-Loges
Ap 1.   Bavincourt   Rivière   Blaireville
Sombrin   June 11   July 9   Ransart   Boisleux-
Saulty   au-Mont   Boi
Bailleulmont   Berles-   Hendecourt   Boiry-
au-Bois   Adinfer   St. Martin   Han
La Cauchie   Monchy-   Wd   Moyenneville   co
July 9   Pommier   au-Bois   May 26—30
from St Omer   Warlincourt   Mar 30   Douchy   Ayette
to Crécy Plage   Bienvillers-   Nov 19—20
May 20   au-Bois   Courcelles-
Aug.   Mondicourt   Ablainzeville   le-Comte
Thièvres   Couin   Bucquoy   Gomiecourt
Aug. 17 → 21
Sarton   Achiet-le-Grand
July 31   Authie   Bois de Warnimont   Bapaum
Bus-les-Artois   Courcelles-au-Bois
Vauchelles   Serre
Louvencourt   Colincamps   Beau
Bertrancourt   Auchonvillers   Gueudecou
Aug.   Flers
13-15
Mailly-Maillet   Hamel
Aug. 1-6.
Englebermer   Delville
Wood
Dec. 6   Guillemont
Montauban   Bern
Albert   Fricourt   Mametz   Hond
Meaulte   Carnoy   court
Citadel   Billon Fm.   Mar
Dernancourt   Bronfay Fm.   Ma
from Méricourt-en-Vimeu   Treux   Ville   Happy
Heilly   Valley
Nov. 11   Morlan-   Somme
to Arques, May 30   Méricourt   court   Bray
to Araines, Oct   l'Abbé   from Corbie
to Corbie Jan. 2   Jan. 9

to Douliens   to Amiens

North   East
West   South

Eng
0   1   2   3   4

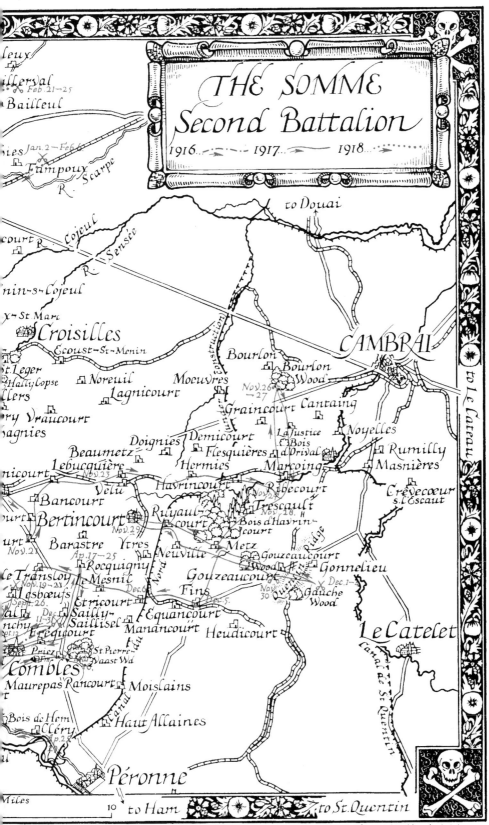

THE SOMME
Second Battalion
1916 — 1917 — 1918

leux
illerval Feb. 21→25
Bailleul
ies Jan. 2→Feb 6
Fampoux R. Scarpe

to Douai

court R. Cojeul
R. Sensée
nin-s-Cojeul
X—St Marc
Croisilles
Ecoust-St-Menin
St Leger
Hally Copse   Noreuil
lers   Lagnicourt
ry Vraucourt
agnies
Beaumetz   Doignies Demicourt
Lebucquière   Hermies Flesquières
nicourt   Velu   Havrincourt
Bancourt   Ruyaul-
urt Bertincourt   court
urt   Nov.29
Nov.21 Barastre Ytres   Metz
Ap.17→25   Neuville
le Transloy Rocquigny
Nov.19→21 le Mesnil   Gouzeaucourt
asbœufs Sept.26.   Dec.6   Fins
al Dec. Sailly-   Dec.5.
nchy Saillisel   Equancourt
ept.11 Frequcourt   Manancourt Heudicourt
Priez   St Pierre
Vaast Wd
Combles
Maurepas Rancourt Moislains
Bois de Hem
Cléry   Haut Allaines
Ap.26

Péronne

Bourlon   Bourlon
Nov.26   Wood
→27
Graincourt Cantaing
La Justice   Noyelles
Bois
d'Orival   Rumilly
Marcoing   Masnières
Ribecourt   Crèvecœur
Nov.21   s.l'Escaut
Trescault
Nov.18. H
Bois d'Havrin-
court
Gouzeaucourt
Wood   Gonnelieu
Nov.   Dec.1→2
30   Gauche
Wood

Moeuvres

CAMBRAI

to Le Cateau
to Le Cateau

Le Catelet

Canal de St Quentin

Miles
10   to Ham   to St. Quentin

Division attacked, the tail of the enemy barrage caught the Battalion unscreened but did no harm. A heavy fog then shut down sarcastically on the whole battle, which was no success to speak of. Through it all, the Battalion kept guard over their own mouse-holes and the gap in the wire. Sudden activities of our guns or the enemy's worried them at times and bred rumours, all fathered on the Staff, of fantastic victories somewhere down the line. They saw a battalion of Germans march by platoons into St. Pierre Vaast Wood, warned the nearest Artillery group, and watched the heavies searching the wood; heard a riot of bombing away on their left, which they put down to the situation at Sailly-Saillisel (this was on the 1st of March), and got ready for possible developments; and when it all died out again, duly sent forth the patrols, who reported the "enemy laughing, talking and working." There was no sign of any withdrawal there.

On the 6th March, in snow and frost, they took over from the 1st Coldstream a new and unappetizing piece of front on the left which the Coldstream had taken over from the Twenty-ninth Division. It consisted of a line of "about twelve so-called posts which were practically little more than shell-holes." The Coldstream had worked like beavers to get them into some sort of shape, but their predecessors had given the local snipers far too much their head; and the long flat-topped ridge where, under an almost full moon, every moving man offended the sky-line, was as unwholesome as could be desired. The Coldstream had lost six men sniped the night before their relief, and it was impossible to reach two of the posts at all. Another post was practically untenable, as the enemy had direct observation on to it, and one sniper who specialized in this neighbourhood had accounted for fourteen men in one tour. The Battalion settled down, therefore, to fire generously at anything that fired. It was noisy and, maybe, wasteful, but it kept the snipers' heads down.

On the 7th March it was clear that the troops in front of them had been replaced by a more cautious and aggressive enemy. So the Battalion turned a couple of their most untenable posts into listening-posts, occupied by night only, and some one suggested that the new Artillery which had just come in behind them might put down a creeping barrage for the greater discouragement of snipers. They cleared out a post or two first, in anticipation of stray shots, and lost one man killed and one wounded; but when the barrage arrived it was weak and inaccurate. Guns need time to learn to work in well with their brethren ahead, and the latter are apt to be impatient when they think they are being experimented on.

THE GERMAN WITHDRAWAL

Not till towards mid-March did the much-written-of German "crack" affect their chilly world. The C.O.'s of the Battalions conferred at Brigade Headquarters on the 13th to discuss the eventuality, and in the middle of it the Major-General came in and announced there was good reason to think that the retirement in front of them would begin that night. In which case, so soon as scouts had reported that the enemy trenches were held very lightly or had been abandoned ("But Jerry never abandoned his dam' machine-guns till we was on top of 'em"), two patrols from each Company in the front line, of an officer and twelve men apiece, would go forward on schedule time and occupy. They would be followed by the two front Companies, who would make good the enemy's old front and support lines. With two Battalions in the front line to draw from, this made a force of four Companies, all of whom were to be under the command of the Senior Lieut.-Colonel in the Battalions engaged. He would be known as "O.C. Situation Centre," and would issue all orders, acting as in command of an advanced guard. *But* the two reserve Companies of the Battalions in line would be with the main body of the Brigade and would not move without the Brigadier's direct orders. In other words, no one was to be drawn into anything like a vulgar brawl. And on the 14th March, from a hill near by, a vast fire could be seen far off, which was Péronne a-burning. That same afternoon the enemy began shelling their own front line along the western edge of St. Pierre Vaast Wood. The situation betrayed itself. An officer's patrol out from the 1st Scots Guards reported the enemy gone from in front. Whereupon the Battalions in the line, the 2nd Irish Guards and the 1st Coldstream, moved out cautiously at dusk and established themselves partly in the first of the enemy's abandoned trenches, with supports, more or less, in our old front line. When their relief came it was a pitch-black night, and the Coldstream had pushed out some patrols into bits of the German trench beyond the chaos of No Man's Land, who, naturally, did not even themselves know where in France they might be, but had to be discovered and relieved just the same, which took the relieving Battalion till two o'clock in the morning. At three o'clock the C.O. of the 2nd Irish Guards – Colonel E. B. Greer – was warned that "Situation Centre" – the two advanced Companies who were to beat out hidden snipers – would be formed at 7 a.m. By the accident of Lieut.-Colonel Godman of the Scots Guards being sick, it fell to Greer to command that advanced force. Captain Alexander took our two forward Companies, and Captain Sir Ian Colquhoun the two Companies of the Scots Guards. The general advance was to begin all along the Divisional front at 10 a.m. By that hour the

German shelling was intense. They used 5·9's and larger, as they were firing from a long way back. The trouble for the 2nd Irish Guards Companies developed almost at once on their left, where their patrol was fired at by machine-guns from a German trench on the edge of the wood. Their own 1st Battalion, trying to push out of Sailly-Saillisel, was hung up too – they heard and saw it – for the same reason. The Division could have driven through at the cost of fairly heavy casualties, but nothing was to be gained by wasting men in rushes on hidden machine-guns that can lay out thirty good lives in two minutes. The Scots Guards got on into the Wood without much trouble at first, till they too ran on snipers between tree-stumps and up and down the defaced trenches, or opened some single machine-gun slinking from cover to cover. It was all slow "feeling," with alternating advances at walking pace, and long checks – "something like drawing a gorse for wolves instead of foxes." The shelling through the day was heavy, but ineffective. With such a broken line as ours advancing, the enemy could not tell where any portion was in strength. The force lay up where they happened to stop, and before dawn on the 16th March were told to feel ahead, while the Scots Guards on their right got into touch with the Eighth Division. Progress was slow as the day before, under heavy shelling – sometimes considered and dealt out with intention – at others evidently from a battery using up ammunition before going back. As they worked their way more into St. Pierre Vaast Wood came the sensation, which there is no mistaking, that they were being played with by the Hun, and losing touch as he intended them to do. Certain vital trenches would be controlled by a few snipers and machine-guns; a sunk road offering shelter would be plastered with heavies, and a full Company would be held in it, digging for more cover, by dead accurate long-range fire; while far and far behind, the orderly German withdrawal of the main body continued in peace.

On the 17th March, for example, "we were never really in touch with the enemy's rear-guard during the day except for one or two snipers." On the 18th, "by daybreak we were out of touch with the enemy, and Cavalry patrols of King Edward's Horse and the 21st Lancers went through us." Here is the comment of the time and the place on our advance: "The German retreat was conducted very skilfully. One cannot say that we caused them to leave one position an hour before they intended. They inflicted upon us a considerable number of casualties (twenty in this Battalion, while on our left the 1st Battalion lost considerably more). On the other hand, we saw no evidence that in the actual retirement we had even damaged one German. They left little or nothing behind."

And the professional judgement is equally fair. "But of course it must be remembered that the task of the (German) Regimental Officers was an easy one, however difficult it may have been for the Staff. Given time, there is no difficulty in withdrawing Battalions from trenches by night, for a few snipers and machine-gunners, knowing the ground, and retreating from trench to trench, can hang up an advance indefinitely unless the troops advancing have strong reserves and are prepared for heavy losses."

This last was not our situation. The Fourteenth Corps had no divisions in immediate reserve; the sector the Guards Division was working on had been greatly thinned out, and their Artillery was relatively small. With tremendous losses in the past and the certainty of more to come, things had to be done as cheaply as possible. "Hence our mode of advance." It led them into a stale hell which had once been soil of France but was now beyond grace, hope or redemption. Most of the larger trees in St. Pierre Vaast were cut down, and the smaller ones split by shell or tooth-brushed by machine-gun fire. The ground was bog, studded with a few island-like formations of fire-trench, unrevetted, unboarded, with little dug-outs ten or twelve feet deep, all wet and filthy. There were no regular latrines. Numberless steel helmets and heaps of stick-bombs lay about underfoot. The garrisons must have been deadly uncomfortable, and there was good evidence that the enemy had economized men beyond anything that we dared. The ground had been cut to bits by our fire, and in one place yawned what had been a battery position wiped out, unseeing and unseen, weeks ago, as the dead teams round it testified. Very few booby-traps were left behind. The Battalion only lost five men in all through this cause.

FATIGUES ON THE SOMME

And on March 19 they came away from the filth and the multitudes of scattered, distorted dead who grimaced at them over their victory, and were laid off at Montauban next day, to be railway navvies for a few weeks. Their camp had last been occupied by a "Labour" battalion. "It would be quite impossible to exaggerate the state of filth in which we found this place. No tins had apparently been burned or buried for months, and rotting matter lay all over the ground." Something like this has been observed before by other Battalions about Labour Corps. However, they mucked it out into moderate decency, and went daily with the 3rd Grenadiers and the 4th Coldstream to make the broad-gauge line from Trônes Wood to Rocquigny and eventually into Ypres. Eventually, when the Sappers had taught them a little, they slapped it down at the rate of more than half a mile a day. It meant at the least four hours' marching to reach railhead, and as many hours of strenuous work when they got there. But "the men were quite happy in spite of the long hours and the absolutely vile weather." They could acquire all the fuel they needed, and had no drills or parades. To toil with your belts or braces disposed as you please; and to wear your cap at outrageous civilian angles; to explain to your desk-bred N.C.O. (with reminiscences, till he cuts you short) that you have had experience on this job in civil life, repairing Dublin trams; to delve in a clean dirt uncumbered by stringy bundles that have once been the likes of yourself; to return, singing, down the road to bountiful meals and a satisfactory "frowst" afterwards, are primitive pleasures far above pay or glory.

Their navvying at one camp or another along the rail lasted till almost the end of April. They were rather pleased with the country round them near Rocquigny, because there was grass on it, and they found passable football-grounds. It was a queer, part rural, part mechanical, part military life, in which people grew fat and jovial, and developed sides of their character that the strain of responsibility had hid. The Battalion made friendships, too, with troops in the railway trade – men whom they met day after day at the same place and job, just as though people on the Somme lived for ever. They were taught how to ballast permanent ways, or lever the eternally derailed troop and construction trains back on to the sprawling metals.

On the 27th April they were all called in from their scattered labours, reminded that they were Guards once more, and promised a long programme of field-training. Inevitably, then, the evening after, came orders to strike their camp at Bois de Hem, pitch it on the Lesbœufs road and get back to road-work between Ginchy, Lesbœufs and Le Transloy. The march was hot and dusty; which impressed them, for they had forgotten heat. Camp lay close to where the right of the 2nd Guards Brigade had reached, in the battle of September 15, 1916. Here is the picture. The site "had been under severe shell-fire all the winter, so little burying could be done. Before we could pitch the camp we had to get rid of several dead men, and all the country between Lesbœufs and Le Transloy, as well as towards Morval, was dotted with corpses. In one morning, No. 4 Company, incidental to its work on the roads, buried no less than seventy Germans, English and French. On Ginchy crest we found the body of Lieutenant Montgomery. He had been killed commanding No. 2 Company on September 13 of last year" (that was when No. 2 was wiped out on the eve of the battle of the 15th), "but we had never been able to find him. He was buried on the crest."

The desolation struck them with continuous horror. Most of the troops had been moved on into the comparatively unspoiled country to the eastward, but the Battalion was forced to sit down among the dead in "mile on mile of tumbled earth, collapsing trenches with their fringe of rotting sand-bags, tangles of rusted wire, and everywhere little crosses. For variety, an occasional wood, in which the trees were mere skeletons, shattered stumps with charred branches." It is a perfect etching of the Somme. They were impressed, too, by the fiendish forethought and thoroughness with which all signs of civil life and work, and, as far as might be, all means of reviving them, had been wiped out, burned up, blasted off, cut down or removed by the Hun. Details of destruction and defilement, such as would only occur to malignant apes, had been attended to as painstakingly and lovingly in the most unlikely corner of some poor village, as in the fields and among the orchards and factories. They had to fill all shell-holes in camp to make even standing ground for themselves, and, of course, a football "field" came next. Every man returning from work brought back his load of timber or iron out of the pitiful old trenches, not to mention flowers from wrecked gardens, and "we built a regular village." Their road-mending consisted in digging out the shell-holes till they reached firm ground, filling up with timber and brick (easy to find), and topping off with road-metal brought up by rail. And thus they worked till the 9th May. But this was the last that was required of them in that form.

They were turned down to training-camp at Curlu, almost on the banks of the Somme, in a clean and cleaned-up country where "dead men, even, were hard to find." By this time specialization had run its course through our armies till the latest platoon-organization acknowledged but one section that was known as a "rifle" section. The others, although behung with the ancient and honourable weapons of their trade, were Bomb, Lewis-gun, and Rifle (Sniper) Sections. But the Battle of Arras had proved what angry Company Commanders had been saying for months past – that infantry lived or died by their knowledge of the rifle. These Somme officers were accordingly told that most of their time should be given to platoon-training, fire direction and musketry. ("We did what we were told, but we always found out when it came to a pinch – suppressing machine-guns in a pill-box and stuff of that kind – if you could rush your men into proper position, good shooting did the rest.") And just as they were buckling down to the new orders, word came, on Sunday, May 13, that they had better prepare for an inspection by the King of the Belgians on Tuesday, May 15. The Brigade put up one long "agony" of rehearsal, and to its own surprise managed to achieve a creditable parade. Unlimited British Generals attended the Royal visitor, and for the first time in the Battalion's history their pipers in their Celtic kilts were present. These had arrived about a fortnight before, when the Battalion solemnly invited Captain Hugh Ross of the Scots Guards to tea in his capacity of a "pipe expert" to pronounce on their merits. And civil war did not follow!

On the 17th May they set out *via* Billon Farm camp to Méricourt l'Abbé, where for the first time in six months, barring a few days at Corbie in January, they were billeted in real houses such as human beings use. Méricourt in summer is quite different from the cramped, windy, damp Méricourt of winter. All the land smiled with the young crops that the old,

...word came that they had better prepare for an inspection by the King of the Belgians... The Brigade put up one long "agony" of rehearsal, and to its own surprise managed to achieve a creditable parade.

The 2nd Guards Brigade march past King Albert, 15th May 1917.

indefatigable French women and men were cramming it with. Here, while the Guards Division was concentrating preparatory to their move into war again, the Battalions were trained hard but *not* as specialists.

General Ivor Maxse, commanding the Sixteenth Corps (none but Corps Generals can say certain things in public), lectured on some of the teachings of the Battle of Arras. He gave instances of what comes of divorcing the soldier from his rifle. On one occasion, said he, men were met sidling down a road with the simple statement that the Germans were advancing to counter-attack them, and that they were retiring "because their own supply of bombs had run out." Patrols sent up to verify, found the counter-attack was being made by four Huns furiously trying to surrender to some one. Again, a Company was heavily fired on from a wood about two hundred yards off. Not a man returned the fire. They simply shouted down the trench, "Pass the word for the snipers." All of which proves what every Company Commander knows, that the human mind under stress of excitement holds but one idea at a time, or, as the drill books of forty years ago laid down, "men will instinctively act in war as they have been trained to act in peace."

In spite of the growing crops and intense agriculture, the Battalion found rifle ranges and did "a great deal of much-needed musketry."

They wound up their stay at Méricourt in great glory at the Brigade sports, sweeping off everything in sight – flat races, steeple-chase, tug-of-war and the rest, and winning their Brigadier's trophy to the Corps with the greatest number of firsts by a clear "possible" against the whole Guards Division. (" 'Tis this way. A good Battalion will do what is wanted; but a happy Battalion, mark you, takes on from that. Did we work at the Sports? Remember, we was all in the pink, trained on that dam' railway an' fatted up for Boesinghe. What chance had the rest of the Division against us at all?")

THIRD YPRES AND BOESINGHE

They entrained on the 30th May as part of the vast concentration that was crystallizing itself for the third Battle of Ypres, and, after twelve hours, breakfasted at Arques, near St. Omer, and marched all day to their crowded billets, which, like the rest of the landscape, were loaded up with crops and difficult to train in. They knew nothing of what was expected of them till the 11th June, when C.O.'s were told at Brigade Headquarters that they were to practise assaults from trench to trench instead of "open warfare." A battle, including earthquakes, had taken place at Messines which had unkeyed the situation to a certain extent, and the Guards Division would be needed to develop it.

The screw would be applied next in The Salient, and they would go up to Elverdinghe, on a sector that had long been notoriously quiet. But they were assured that as soon as "Jerry" had word of their arrival they would not feel neglected. All this on the top of their open-warfare exercise was disappointing. They knew more than they wanted to about the Ypres areas, and had hoped that something was going to crack on the high and windy Somme and let them triumphantly into Cambrai. "Fatted troops" are ever optimistic.

Their march towards their new-ground was a hot and villainously dusty one, with packs and steel helmets, of eleven miles and the wind at their backs, so they moved in a sweating pillar of cloud. Not a man of theirs fell out, and the Brigade knew it, for the C.O. of the 3rd Grenadiers, who were bringing up the rear, sent along written congratulations with word that he had not seen one single Irish Guardsman panting by the wayside. To have won that little record had meant the hardest sort of work for officers and N.C.O.'s.

On the 15th June they lay at Cardoen Farm, in shelters and huts round the place on which the enemy had no direct observation, though it was not four miles behind the line. Brigade Headquarters were more or less underground at Elverdinghe Château, and the enemy attended to it the instant the Guards Division relieved the Thirty-eighth Division. The front lines, as usual hereabouts, were too close together for unrestricted artillery work; but supports, communications, railways and battery positions were open to him, and he dosed them by day and night. The Divisional sector had a frontage of about twelve hundred yards, which ran from the point where our line, bending back from the Ypres Salient, turned across the Yser Canal some five thousand yards north-north-west of Ypres itself, and thence straight along the Canal bank to where the Belgians took on. The Battalion relieved the 1st Coldstream on the 18th June, and found their front, which was on top of the Canal embankment and within fifty yards of the enemy's, fairly good. Owing to water showing at two feet, trenches were protected by breast-works and well revetted, but liable, from their make, to be badly blown by direct hits when, since it crowned the breast-works, their own wire would hamper the occupants. The Canal bed, empty and overgrown with high grass and weeds, was all dead ground. The most that could be said for the position was that it gave fair protection against shell, but might be awkward to hold, as support and back lines were much too much under direct observation. Battalion Headquarters were regularly shelled, and in Boesinghe village itself, the most dangerous area of all, there was no cover, and one had to skirmish about in the open, with both eyes and ears on what might be coming next. The front, as usual, under these conditions was the safest. They were so close to the enemy that they were not shelled at all. What little stuff fell near them was the enemy's own shorts, upon receipt of which the German front line would loose protesting rockets. Support and reserve companies were regularly shelled, with the ration and water parties pushing supplies up the railway in trucks from Elverdinghe to B.H.Q. The Battalion's normal work was repairing blown head-cover and breast-work, and reporting, with oaths, that it was impossible to dig on account of subsoil water. They indulged the enemy every early morning with five minutes' "rapid" of Lewis-guns or rifles, and their Stokes mortars were busy day and night. Machine-guns (nothing can keep a machine-gunner quiet long) sprayed enemy dumps intermittently all night long. It was an intimate, if uneasy dog's life of dodging and ducking; yet with reliefs and all it only cost them twenty-four casualties, mostly slight, in the four days' turn. Their rest at Cardoen Farm afterwards meant fatigues of carrying sand-bags and six casualties to show for it; a brisk shelling of the camp; and a brawl between their Lewis-gun battery and one of the wandering Hun 'planes with which the camps were so infested that they were hardly noticed in reports or letters.

Their next tour, June 27 to 29, was in support behind the Canal, in dug-outs round Bleuet Farm; Battalion Headquarters in the remnants of the farm itself. Our own Artillery seemed, from the Infantry point of view, to be devoting its attention to building up dumps and bringing in more guns; so the enemy had it rather their own way in shelling working-parties and communications. The relief was a bad one, and that tour worked out at nineteen casualties, of whom six were dead.

They ended June in wet bivouacs at a camp near International Corner, which had an unsavoury reputation for being shelled, and under the shadow of a specially heavy fatigue of burying a cable in a forward area. But – Army fashion – nothing happened. No shells arrived; it was too wet even for parades, and some other lucky Battalion had that cable-picnic all to itself.

On the 2nd July they were marched off twelve miles to Herzeele, where as no billets were ready they dined in a field, and shook down afterwards among a crowd of gunners. Many tales have been told of happy Herzeele, for it boasted at that time no less than three Town Majors, every one of them a Colonel! Hence some small muddle as to billets.

The immense preparations for what was to be the third Battle of Ypres included, for the Guards Division, ten days' special training over trenches such as they would have to deal with when their turn came. These were duly dug by fatigue-parties in an open stretch of country near the town, and "the whole model was on the same scale as the actual German front-line system." Although the existing features of the ground were puzzling at first, the model proved to be extremely useful as teaching all ranks the lie of the land.

The only features not included were the hidden concrete "pill-boxes" supporting each other behind his line, on which the enemy was basing his new and unpleasant system of elastic defence. But, allowing for inevitable unrealities, there is no doubt that training "on the model" supples and brings a Battalion to hand better than any other device. The men grow keen as they realize by eye what is to be expected; talk it over afterwards (there are certain analogies between trench-to-trench attack and "soccer"); the N.C.O.'s discuss with the officers, and the Battalion Commander can check some preventible errors before the real thing is loosed.

His Majesty the King came on the 6th July to watch a Brigade attack in the new formation. It was a perfect success, but the next week saw them sweated through it again and again in every detail, till "as far as the Battalion was concerned the drill of the attack was reduced almost to perfection." In their rare leisure came conferences, map and aeroplane study, and, most vital of all, "explaining things to the N.C.O.'s and men." They wound up with a model of a foot to a hundred yards, giving all the features in the Battalion's battle area. The men naturally understood this better than a map, but it was too small. (" 'Twas like a doll's-house garden, and it looked you would be across and over it all, in five minutes. But we was not! We was not!")

On the 14th, in hot weather, the move towards the cockpit began. They bivouacked in certain selected woods that gave cover against searching 'planes, who knew as much about it as the enemy Staff did, and bombed all movements on principle.

On the 17th they went into line "for a tour which proved to be one of the most unpleasant and most expensive" since the Battalion came to France. They held the whole of the 2nd Guards Brigade frontage, with a Battalion of the 3rd Guards Brigade on their left, so the Companies were necessarily broken up, as their platoons were detached to the separate trenches. All No. 4 Company and two platoons of No. 3 were in the front line, and a platoon of No. 3 and Company H.Q. in the support-line near Hunter Street. In Walkrantz Trench was another platoon of No. 3; No. 1 Company was in an unwholesome support-trench; and working with it, one platoon of No. 2. In Bleuet Farm were the remaining three platoons of No. 2 Company; and Battalion Headquarters were in Chasseur Farm, about a hundred and fifty yards behind No. 1 Company. Altogether, it might fairly be called a "hurrah's nest" to relieve, hold or get away from. The enemy, even without being stirred up by our first series of preliminary bombardments, which had opened on the 15th, were thoroughly abreast of things. They began by catching No. 2 Company coming up to Bleuet Farm in a barrage of gas-shells, which meant putting on box-respirators in the dark and going ahead blind. Only one man was knocked out, however. The Transport was gassed late at night on the Elverdinghe road, and held up for two hours under fumes of lachrymatory and phosgene. But Transport is expected to get in, whatever happens, and the fact that Lieutenant R. Nutting, its officer, was badly gassed too, was an incident. From the official point of view he should have put on his respirator at the first, which is notoriously easy when rounding up hooded men and panicky horses. So he suffered. But as he was the only person who knew where Bleuet Farm might be in that poisonous blackness, he lay on the mess-cart, and between upheavals, guided the convoy thither. Next morn, after spending the night in a dug-out, he had to be carried back to the dressing-station. That same night 2nd Lieutenant Lofting, while on patrol along the Canal bank, was slightly wounded in the leg.

The next three days were one nightmare of stores of all kinds for the battle-dumps, pouring into the front line while the platoons there stacked and sorted them out, under continuous fire. Our hourly increasing force of heavies (the field-guns were not yet called upon) took as much of the burden off our men as they could, but the enemy were well set and knew just what they had to bowl at. The front-line companies' work was to repair a very great deal of trench damage; make assembly trenches for the coming attack; pile up the dumps, praying that the next salvo would not send them all sky-high, and keep the crawling communication-lines clear of corpses, wreckage, wounded and traffic-blocks. The Diary puts it all in these cold words: "Some of the carrying-parties under N.C.O.'s did very fine work under fire. In no case did any party fail to perform the work set it." Other pens have described that tour as "house-moving in Hell." They lost men in the dark who were not missed till morning. On the night of the 18th, probably through a misreading of the many lights which were going up everywhere and might have been read as S.O.S.'s, our big guns suddenly put down a bitter barrage just behind the German front line. They replied by one just behind ours, and a searching bombardment round our wretched Battalion Headquarters. One shell went through the roof of an officer's dug-out in No. 1 Company trench and killed Lieutenant James (he had joined the Battalion, for the second time, not a month ago) and 2nd Lieutenant Wilson, only a few weeks joined. Lieutenant Paget was also wounded in the knee. The casualties among the men were heavy also; and next night, as our field-guns came into play, a "short" from one of them killed an irreplaceable C.S.M. – Grimwood of No. 4 Company – which on the eve of engagement is equivalent to losing an officer.

On the morning of the 20th, No. 4 Company sent out four raiding parties across the Canal bank to see how strongly the enemy was holding things, and, quaintly enough, to "accustom them to our temporary occupation of their front line." The inventive Hun had managed to raise the water-level of the Canal, and two of the parties had to abandon the attempt altogether. The others, led by their sergeants, floundered across, sometimes up to their chins, found the enemy line held, and came back with useful news and no casualties, for which their Corps Commander and their Brigadier congratulated them. On the afternoon of the same day, the C.O. (Byng-Hopwood) and Second in Command (Stephen Bruton) of the 1st Coldstream came up to look at the line, and were both killed by the same shell in a communication-trench.

On the 21st, at the discomfortable hour before earliest dawn, our R.E. Company began to send over gas from four-inch Stokes mortars and projectors, and our own two-inch Stokes in the front line strove to cover the noise by separate rapid fire. Thanks to past practice with the box-respirators, in which our perspiring men had at last learned to work, there were no casualties when a gas "short" burst just behind the front line. It was their first acquaintance with gas-shells but, all told, only one officer and five men were gassed, nearly all of whom returned to duty in a few days. The relief was a small action in itself, for the Companies had to be extricated one by one, and "the dispositions of the relieving Battalions were different from ours." Nor was it a clean departure, since the back lines were more and more crowded with fatigue-parties, each claiming right of way, and the Battalion was held up in Hunter Street, which at its widest was perhaps four feet and a half, by a couple of hundred men shifting trifles such as mats and bridges towards the firing-line. When they were getting away between Bleuet and Marguerite Farms, Lieutenant Keenan was hit in the thigh by a splinter of shell.

That tour cost the Battalion six officers killed or wounded and sixty casualties in other ranks. Considering the shelling, the heavy traffic and the back-line "furniture removals," the wonder was that they had not suffered thrice as much; but for the eve of a first-class engagement it was ample.

Their last preparations for the attack were put in in bivouac in the wooded area about half a mile north-west of De Wippe Cabaret, where half the Battalion was requisitioned for long, heavy and unpleasant fatigues across shelled ground into forward areas, which led to a small crop of casualties. Accommodation in the wood was insufficient, and many slept where they could under the trees (no bad thing with wandering 'planes at large); but the weather held fine and hot. And then, with everything ready to loose off, the attack was delayed. The reason given was that the French were to spend a few days more in making sure of success before carrying out their end of it. A Battalion takes the smallest interest in its neighbours at any time, and on the edge of battle less than usual. All that the men knew was that the French were on their left, where the Belgians had been, and they hoped that they were strong in 75's. ("Ye can hear the French long before ye can see them. They dish out their field-gun fire the way you'd say it was machine-guns. A well-spoken, quiet crowd, the French, but their rations are nothing at all.")

There is pathetic interest in the entry of the 26th July that the C.O. (Eric Greer) "wrote out Operation Orders for Father Knapp" – a dead man, as the Fates were to decree it, for a dead man. Those orders were as simple as the problem before the Battalion. They had to advance straight to their front, with the 1st Scots Guards on their right, the latter Battalion's right being neatly bounded by the Langemarck–Staden railway, which again was the dividing line between the Guards and the Thirty-eighth Division. If luck held, and pill-boxes did not turn out to be too numerous, they would all fetch up eventually on the banks of the Steenbeek River, three thousand five hundred yards north-east by east from their starting-point.

A happy mixture of chance and design had shown that the enemy were in the habit of abandoning their front line along the Canal during daylight, and of manning it lightly at night. General Feilding, commanding the Guards Division, promptly took advantage of the knowledge to throw the 3rd Coldstream across and establish them on the far bank. The coup was entirely successful, and it saved the Division the very heavy casualties that would have followed a forcing of the Canal had that been held in strength.

On the 27th, at a conference of C.O.'s, they were told that the enemy had further withdrawn on that sector, about five hundred yards up the stage, so to speak, and were resting their front line on a system known to us as Cariboo and Cannon trenches. One of our scouting-aeroplanes had been searching the ground at two or three hundred feet level, and was of opinion there was nobody there who cared to shoot back. It was a curious situation, for though the Battalion had rehearsed and rehearsed what they were to do till, as men said, they could have done it in their sleep, nobody was at ease. (This, by the way, disproves the legend that Battalions know by instinct whether they are going to win or lose.) Late that night a hostile 'plane came over the forest area and woke them up with bombs. Lieutenant Arthur Paget, attached to the M.G.C., was slightly wounded. On the same day a draft of ninety men arrived as reinforcements. Their position was that of supers, for in a corps trained as the 2nd Irish Guards had been to carry out this one affair in a certain way, no amateurs were allowed. Greer had seen to it that every soul over whom he had authority should study the glass, sand, tin and twig model of the ground till he knew it by heart, and had issued, moreover, slips of paper with a few printed sentences ("like home post-cards") to serve for Unit Commanders' reports in action. On the back of these was a map of the sector itself, and "every one was instructed to mark his position with an X." The results were superb, though Greer did not survive to see them.

The Division had its battle-patrols out and across the Canal on the night of the 28th July, pressing forward gingerly, digging themselves in or improving existing "slits" in the ground against shell-fire. The Battalion did much the same thing at the back, for all the world where they walked with cautious shoulders was very unwholesome, and the barrages clanged to and fro everlastingly. Yet, had they been asked, they would have said, "Our guns were doing nothing out of the way." Men were so broke to the uproar they hardly noticed it.

On the 29th July two Companies (1 and 2) of the Battalion moved out to relieve the leading Companies of the 3rd Coldstream, who had been for some time on the far side of the Canal. All went well in the summer after-noon till a hostile aeroplane saw them filing across, and signalled a bar-rage which killed or wounded forty men, wounded Lieutenant Hannay of No. 2 Company, and killed Captain Synge in command of No. 1. Synge was perhaps one of the best Company Commanders that the Battalion had ever known, and as popular as he was brave.

Colonel Greer went up into the line directly afterwards with Captain D. Gunston as his Second in Command, and Lieutenant Hanbury as Adjutant. They were cruelly short of combatant Officers – past casualties had reduced the number to ten; and the only ones left in reserve were Major Ferguson and Lieutenant Hely-Hutchinson. The day and night were spent by the two Companies in digging in where they were, while Nos. 3 and 4 waited on.

Early on the morning of the 30th July the French on their left and the whole of the Fifth Army put down a half-hour barrage to find out where the enemy would pitch his reply. He retaliated on the outskirts of Boesinghe village and the east bank of the Canal, not realizing to what an extent we were across that obstacle. In the evening dusk the remaining two Companies of the Battalion slipped over and took up battle positions, in Artillery ("pigtail") formation of half-platoons, behind Nos. 1 and 2 Companies, who had shifted from their previous night's cover, and now lay out in two waves east of the Yper Lea. By ten o'clock the whole of the Guards Division was in place. The 2nd and 3rd Guards Brigades were to launch the attack, and the 1st, going through them, was to carry it home. A concrete dug-out in the abandoned German front line just north of the railway was used as a Battalion Headquarters. It was fairly impervious to anything smaller than a 5·9, but naturally its one door faced toward the enemy and had no blind in front of it – a lack which was to cost us dear.

July 31st opened, at 3.30 a.m., with a barrage of full diapason along the Army front, followed on the Guards sector by three minutes of "a carefully prepared hate," during which two special Companies projected oil-drums throwing flame a hundred yards around, with thermit that burned every-thing it touched. The enemy had first shown us how to employ these scien-tific aids, and we had bettered the instruction.

July 31st opened, at 3.30 a.m., with a barrage of full diapason along the Army front... His barrage in reply fell for nearly an hour on the east bank of the Canal.

The Yser Canal after the attack, 31st July 1917.

His barrage in reply fell for nearly an hour on the east bank of the Canal. Our creeping barrage was supposed to lift at 4.10 a.m. and let the two leading Battalions (2nd Irish Guards and 1st Scots Guards) get away, but it was not till nearly a quarter of an hour later that the attack moved forward in waves behind it. Twelve minutes later, Nos. 1 and 2 Companies of the Battalion had reached the first objective (Cariboo and Cannon trenches) "with only one dead German encountered"; for the enemy's withdrawal to his selected line had been thorough. The remaining Companies followed, and behind them came the 1st Coldstream, all according to schedule; till by 5.20 a.m. the whole of the first objective had been taken and was being consolidated, with very small loss. They were pushing on to the second objective, six hundred yards ahead, when some of our own guns put a stationary barrage on the first objective – Cariboo trenches and the rest. Mercifully, a good many of the men of the first and second waves had gone on with the later ones, where they were of the greatest possible service in the annoying fights and checks round the concreted machine-gun posts. Moreover, our barrage was mainly shrapnel – morally but not physically effective. No. 2 Company and No. 4 Company, for example, lay out under it for half and three-quarters of an hour respectively without a single casualty. But no troops are really grateful for their own fire on their own tin hats.

About half-past five, Colonel Greer, while standing outside advanced Battalion Headquarters dug-out in the first objective line, was killed instantly by shrapnel or bullet. It was his devoted work, his arrangement and foresight, that had brought every man to his proper place so far without waste of time or direction. He had literally made the Battalion for this battle as a steeple-chaser is made for a given line of country. Men and officers together adored him for his justice, which was exemplary and swift; for the human natural fun of the man; for his knowledge of war and the material under his hand, and for his gift of making hard life a thing delightful. He fell on the threshold of the day ere he could see how amply his work had been rewarded. Captain Gunston took command of the Battalion, for, of the seniors, Captain Alexander was out ahead with No. 4 Company, and Major Ferguson was in Regimental Reserve. Headquarters were moved up into Cariboo trench, and by six o'clock the second objective had been reached, in the face of bad machine-gun fire from Hey Wood that had opened on us through a break in our barrage.

No. 3 Company on the right of our line, next to the Scots Guards, found themselves at one point of this advance held up by our own barrage, and had the pleasure of seeing a battery of German field-guns limber up and "go off laughing at them." Then they came under oblique machine-gun fire from the right.

Lieutenant Sassoon, commanding No. 3, got his Lewis-gun to cover a flank attack on the machine-gun that was doing the damage, took it with seven German dead and five wounded prisoners, and so freed the advance for the Scots Guards and his own Company. As the latter moved forward they caught it in the rear from another machine-gun which had been over-looked, or hidden itself in the cleaning-up of Hey Wood.

Sassoon[1] sent back a couple of sections to put this thing out of action (which they did) and pushed on No. 4 Company, which was getting much the same allowance from concrete emplacements covering machine-guns outside Artillery Wood. Captain Alexander launched an attack at these through a gap in our barrage, outflanked them and accounted for three machine-guns and fourteen Germans. There was some slight difficulty at this point in distinguishing between our barrage, which seemed to have halted, and the enemy's, which seemed to be lifting back. So Captain Alexander had to conduct his advance by a series of short rushes in and out of this double barrage, but somehow or other contrived to consolidate his position without undue delays. ("Consolidatin' positions at Boesinghe meant being able to lie down and get your breath while the rest of ye ran about the country hammerin' machine-gun posts an' damnin' our bar-rages.") Thus occupied, he sent back word to Captain Gunston that in the circumstances he waived his seniority and placed himself under the lat-ter's command. "The pace was too good to inquire."

This was in the interval before Ferguson, acting Second in Command, who by regulation had been left behind, could get word of Greer's death, reach Battalion Headquarters and take over, which he did a little later. On his way up, their Brigadier (Ponsonby) told him that "he could not find words strong enough to express his appreciation of the way in which the Battalion had behaved, and for its dash and devotion to duty." Indeed, they admitted among themselves – which is where criticism is fiercest – that they had pulled the scheme off rather neatly, in spite of their own bar-rages, and that the map and model study had done the trick. By ten o'clock of the morning their work was substantially complete. They had made and occupied the strong points linking up between their advanced Companies and the final objectives, which it was the business of the other Brigades to secure. As they put it, "everything had clicked"; and, for a small reward, Fate sent to Battalion Headquarters the Commanding Officer and Adjutant

---

[1] In those peaceful days when the Division was "fattening" for the fight Greer had kept a sym-pathetic eye on Sassoon, who had gone down very sick some time before Greer came to com-mand the 2nd Battalion, and was convalescing in the Entrenching Battalion, where his heart was not. Greer, who had a keen eye for good officers, said of him: "He writes me pitiful letters protesting that he is now completely fit, and asking that he should be allowed to come up to this Battalion.... He is a stout-hearted savage, and a life-sentence with the Entrenching Battalion would certainly be an awful prospect." So Sassoon was rescued, and Greer's faith in his "stout-hearted savage" abundantly justified.

of the 73rd Hanoverian Fusiliers who had been captured near the second objective, and who wore in gold braid on their left sleeve the word "Gibraltar" in commemoration of the siege when that regiment, as Hanoverian, fought on the English side. The Adjutant spoke English well, and thought that the U.S.A., coming into the war at last, would be bad for Germany. When they asked him if he wanted peace he replied: "The country wants peace. The men want peace, but *I* am an officer, and an officer never wants peace." Herein he spoke more truly concerning his own caste than was ever realized by the British politician.

He was immensely interested, too, in our Zero hour and its arrangements, but seemed unable to grasp the system. "How," he asked, "do you manage your – love hour, your nought hour – how do you call it?" He appeared to think it was something like lawn-tennis, and they explained to him in the wet-floored dug-out, which had already received two direct high-explosive souvenirs, that there was, as he might have observed, very little of "love" about a British Zero.

Then there fell, most naturally, a great thirst upon all the world, for bottles had been drained long ago, and a carrying-party of the 3rd Grenadiers had gone astray in that wilderness, and word had come in from Brigade Headquarters that the pontoon-bridge over the Canal was not yet finished, so they would have to draw on the water-dump on its west bank. Fatigue parties were sent off at once from the two Companies panting there. The other two in the second objective farther on would . . . but orders had scarcely been issued when Lieutenant Nutting pushed up with a string of pack-beasts and made a forward water-dump just behind the first objective, which saved trouble and that exposure which means men's lives. ("All that time, of course, the battle was ragin' – that is to say, we was being shelled and shot over as usual – but, ye'll understand, we wanted water more than we minded the shells. Thirst is stronger than death with the need on ye.")

They disposed themselves for the afternoon, Nos. 1 and 2 Companies taking over from the 1st Scots Guards in the first objective, and Nos. 3 and 4 in the second, with linked strong posts connecting both lines. They also withdrew a couple of platoons sent forward from Nos. 1 and 2 Companies to the final objective (all objectives had now been reached) to rejoin their Companies. At three o'clock Father Knapp appeared at Battalion Headquarters – that most insanitary place – and proposed to stay there. It was pointed out to him that the shelling was heavy, accommodation, as he could see, limited, and he had better go to the safer Advanced Dressing-station outside Boesinghe and deal with the spiritual needs of his wounded as they were sent in. The request had to be changed to a reasonably direct order ere he managed to catch it; for, where his office was concerned, the good Father lacked something of that obedience he preached. And a few hours after he had gone down to what, with any other man, would have been reasonable security, news arrived that he had been mortally wounded while tending cases "as they came out" of the dressing-station. He must have noticed that the accommodation there was cramped too, and have exposed himself to make shelter for others. Captain David Lees, the Battalion's M.O., seems to have been equally careless, but luckier. He walked through what is described as "an intensely hostile" barrage (there were not very many friendly ones falling that day) to the corner of Artillery Wood, where he found a batch of wounded exposed to barrages and machine-guns. He was shelled all the time he was dressing them, and when he had finished, he carried, in turn, Lieutenant Buller, Sergeant McNally and Private Donoghue to a safe trench just outside the barrage zone. To do this he had to go four times through the barrage before he could continue his round of professional visits which took him through it yet a fifth time.

During the afternoon, though there was a general bombardment by the enemy of the first and second objectives for ten minutes every half-hour, the bulk of the shelling was aimless and wandering, as though the gunners could not hang on to any target. Men were killed, but not with intention, and the living could feel that the sting had gone out of the affair. They finished the interminable day under a barrage of gas-shells and H.E., which suggested at first a counter-attack behind it. At that moment, Nos. 2 and 4 Companies were holding an advanced position near Captain's Farm towards the last objective; and it looked as though they would have to be left there all night, but by eleven o'clock the shelling had died out, the mopping-up Companies of the 1st Coldstream relieved our outlying two, and, a quarter of an hour later, dripping and muddy, the whole Battalion got away to a low, wet and uncomfortable camp in the Roussel area, whose single mitigation was a rum-issue.

They had lost in the past three days three officers (Greer, their C.O.; Synge, by shrapnel, on the 29th; and 2nd Lieutenant Armfield, found shot on the 31st, not far from the dug-out they had converted into Battalion Headquarters). Lieutenants Crawford, Buller and Vaughan-Morgan were the wounded. Casualties in other ranks came to 280, a large part due to machine-gun fire. It was a steadying balance-sheet and, after an unde-cided action, would have been fair excuse for a little pause and reconstruc-tion. But a clean-cut, all-out affair, such as Boesinghe, was different, though it had been saddened by the loss of an unselfish priest who feared nothing created, and a Commanding Officer as unselfish and as fearless as he. The elder and the younger man had both given all they had to the Battalion, and their indomitable souls stayed with it when, next day

(August 1), the Authorities inquired whether it felt equal to going into the line again for what would certainly be an unusually abominable "sit and be hit" tour. The Battalion replied that it was ready, and spent the day cleaning up and putting in recommendations for awards for the battle. Among these were Lieutenant Black, the Intelligence Officer, who in the course of his duties had had to wander for eighteen hours over the whole position captured by the Battalion, reporting situations, meeting crises as they arose, and keeping his head and his notes under continuous barrages. His right-hand man had been Sergeant Milligan, who "succeeded in establishing advanced Battalion Headquarters in the first objective five minutes after it had been captured, in spite of the fact that the barrage fell on that line for the next half-hour." He then found a Company, all of whose officers, save one, had been wounded, helped to "reorganize it" with a strong hand and a firm voice, went on with it, assisted in outflanking three machine-gun positions, and kept communication unbroken between the front and back of their attack. Be it remembered that the right sector over which the 2nd Irish Guards and the Scots Guards moved was much more blinded with houses, woods and the like than the left; and there was room for every sort of trouble if the sectors did not work together. But Greer's insistence that the men should know the model of the ground, and their officers the aeroplane maps of it, and his arrangements whereby all units could report lucidly at any moment where they were, had brought them success. So, with 50 per cent of their strength gone, and the dismal wet soaking the stiff survivors to the bone, they hobbled about, saying, "If *he* were only here now to see how he has pulled this off!"

Their work on the 2nd August was to take over from a 1st Brigade Battalion on the left of the Divisional front next to the French. The latter's front here ran several hundred yards in rear of the Guards, and since their centre was well forward again, the re-entrant angle was an awkward and unsafe pocket, which necessitated any Battalion that lay on the French right spending men and trouble in making a defensive left flank. The

About half-past five, Colonel Greer, while standing outside advanced Battalion Headquarters dug-out in the first objective line, was killed instantly by shrapnel or bullet... Men and officers together adored him for his justice... for the human natural fun of the man; for his knowledge of war... and for his gift of making hard life a thing delightful.

Major (Acting Lieut.-Colonel) Eric Greer, MC, killed in action 31st July 1917.

advance at this point had been carried forward to within a few hundred yards of the Steenbeek River. Indeed, on the right of the Divisional front the 2nd Grenadiers were across and established. The Battalion moved up in rain across the water-logged, shell-pitted ground at dusk, to be welcomed by news that the enemy were massing. The enemy would surely have stuck in the mud had they attempted any counter-attack, but the Thirty-eighth Division on the right seemed to see them advancing in battle-array and sent up urgent demands for a barrage, which at once brought the hostile barrage down all along the line. Under this quite uncalled-for demonstration the Companies floundered to their shallow trenches, which were a foot deep in mud. They had no particular idea where they or their rendezvous might be, but, obviously, the first thing was to get into touch with the French and beg them to straighten up their line where it nicked into ours. This was done in the dawn of the 3rd August, and before the end of the day our Allies had attended to the matter and advanced up to the line of the Steenbeek. Then they, in turn, asked us to supply a standing-patrol to link up their right to our left at Sentier Farm on the extreme edge of the ground won. It was not a locality, however, where any move could be attempted in daylight. The 3rd Coldstream had some men there, but these, for good reason, were lying low till we could relieve them. Captain Alexander and Lieutenant Hanbury had been sent down for a rest after their heavy work; and the Battalion, under Ferguson, was divided into two wings, the right commanded by Sassoon, with Lieutenants Van der Noot and Kane; the left by Captain Gunston, with Lieutenant Rea and, temporarily, Lieutenant Black. The 1st Coldstream turned up just on the edge of dusk to take over from the Battalion which was to relieve the 3rd Coldstream in the front line. Here, for once, efficiency did not pay. The handing-over was completed all too well before the light had gone, and as they moved forward a burst of shrapnel killed one man and seriously wounded Lieutenant Van der Noot and five men. They disposed two Companies in snipe-bogs at Signal Farm, and the other two, in like conditions, at Fourché Farm. There was practically no shelter against heavy shelling. Battalion Headquarters was an eight-by-four concrete dug-out with three inches of water on the floor, and the only people who kept warm seem to have been Lieutenant Rea and a couple of platoons who got into touch with the French and spent the night making a strong standing-patrol of two sections and a Lewis-gun at Sentier Farm, which was where the French wanted it. For the rest, "practically no shelter, incessant rain, continuous shell-fire, and mud half-way up the legs, but casualties comparatively few, and the spirit of all ranks excellent."

The Welsh Guards relieved them on the night of the 4th, and they got hot tea (the Adjutant had gone down on purpose to see to that) at Bleuet Farm, entrained at Elverdinghe for Proven, and at Porchester Camp, which they reached on the morning of the 5th, found a dry camp that had been pitched before the rain, more hot tea, a change of clothes, socks *and* rum waiting for them. They breakfasted "before retiring to bed." ("We was dead done, but ye'll understand, 'twas nothing more than that. Our hearts was light – except for Father Knapp an' Greer; but if they had not been taken that day 'twould have been later. That sort of men, they are not made to live. They do an' they die.")

The general impression at Porchester Camp was that the Guards Division would be out of the line for the next two weeks or so, while the Twenty-ninth Division took over their work and secured a jumping-off place on the far side of the Steenbeek, with a new advance, in which the Guards would take part, towards Houthulst Forest. Meantime, sufficient to the day was the camp's daily small beer – rows, for instance, with Company cooks about diet-sheets (this was a matter Greer had been deep in just before his death); an inspection which kept them standing-to for nearly a couple of hours and was then cancelled; a farmer who, meaning to be kind, cut his crops early so that they might have a nice stubbly parade-ground, which no one in the least wanted; a lecture on Boesinghe by the C.O. to Captains Ward and Redmond and Lieutenants FitzGerald and De Moleyns, and all the N.C.O.'s who had come up with the last drafts that were making good the Battalion losses and giving the old hands a deal of trouble. For the enemy had developed at Boesinghe a defensive system of shell-holes filled with a few men and a machine-gun, and further protected by modest flanking machine-gun pill-boxes, over a depth of fifteen hundred or two thousand yards before one got to his main-line system of triple trenches. It was wholly damnable because, as the Guards and the Twentieth and Twenty-ninth Divisions had found out, Artillery was not much use against holes in the ground, even when the field-guns could be brought close enough across the morasses to reach them. Warley knew little about the proper forms of attack of such positions, and the new hands had to be taught it under menace of the daring 'planes. The Hun never threw away an opportunity of doing evil to his enemy, and while they lay at Bedford Camp (August 13) a number of the A.S.C. horses died owing to steel shavings having been cunningly mixed in their baled hay by some pro-Boche agent in the far-off lands where it was purchased.

On the 18th August orders came to move up the line to a camp west of Bleuet Farm, where aeroplanes were more vicious than ever. There they had to construct the camp almost from the beginning, with tents and shelters as they could lay hands on them, while most of the Battalion was busy making and mending roads; and a draft of one hundred and fifty new men, under Lieutenant Manning, came in, so that nothing might be lacking to the activity of the days.

On the 20th August, owing to the aeroplanes, they had to spread out and camouflage the shelters for the men, which were too bunched together and made easy targets. Lieutenants D. FitzGerald, Dalton and Lysaght joined that afternoon, and in the evening there was a heavy air-raid along the east edge of the camp. Second Lieutenant Bellew, who had only joined with his draft ten days before, went to see the result, was hit and mortally wounded; and Lieutenant de Moleyns, who accompanied him, was also hit. The trouble was a couple of twelve-inch howitzers near our camp which were greatly annoying the enemy, and their machines rasped up and down like angry hornets hunting for them.

The 2nd Coldstream relieved the Battalion on the 21st August, when they returned to Elverdinghe, and were shifted to Paddington Camp – no improvement on its predecessor from the overhead point of view. Here the awards for Boesinghe came in: Captain Lees, who had been recommended for the V.C., getting the D.S.O. with Captain Alexander; Lieutenant Sassoon the M.C.; and Sergeant Milligan, that reorganizer of officerless Companies, the D.C.M.

On the 22nd August Father Browne, who had taken Father Knapp's place as Chaplain, held a short service over Lieutenant Bellew's grave, while the drums played the Last Post. His platoon, and a platoon has every opportunity for intimate knowledge, reported him "A grand little officer." ("There was so many came and went, and some they went so soon that 'tis hard to carry remembrance of them. And, d'ye see, a dead man's a dead man. But a platoon will remember some better than others. He'll have done something or said something amongst his own men the way his name'll last for a while in it.")

On the 25th of the month they were told that the Guards Division offensive was cancelled for the time being; that they would probably be used in the line till about the 20th September, and that the final attack on Houthulst Forest would be carried out by a couple of other Divisions. Meantime, they would be shifted from camp to camp, which they rather detested, and lectured and drilled. As an earnest of this blissful state they were forthwith shifted to Abingley Camp, in the Elverdinghe area and on the edge of trouble, in cold, driving wet, to find it very dirty and the tentage arrangements abominably muddled. Naturally, when complaints might have been expected, the men were wildly cheerful, and wrestled with flapping, sodden canvas in a half gale as merrily as sailors. The house-keeper's instinct, before mentioned, of primitive man always comes out best at the worst crisis, and, given but the prospect of a week's stay in one place, a Guards Battalion will build up a complete civilization on bog or bare rock. The squally weather was against aeroplane activity till the 2nd of September, when the neighbourhood of the camp was most thoroughly searched with bombs, but nothing actually landed on them. Next midnight, however, they had all to flee from their tents and take refuge in the "slits" provided in the ground. This is ever an undignified proceeding, but the complaint against it is not that it is bad for the men's nerves, but their discipline. The Irish appreciate too keenly the spectacle of a thick officer bolting, imperfectly clad, into a thin "slit." Hence, sometimes, unfortunate grins on parade next morning, which count as "laughing." Vastly more serious than the bombing, or even their occasional sports and cricket matches, was that their C.O. inspecting the Pipers "took exception to the hang of their kilts." It ended in his motoring over to the Gordons at Houbinghem and borrowing the Pipe-Major there to instruct them in this vital matter, as well as in the right time for march music. They were then sent to the Master Tailor to have some pleats taken out of the offending garments, and fetched up, finally, on parade wearing their gas-helmets as sporrans! But they looked undeniably smart and supplied endless material for inter-racial arguments at Mess.

These things and their sports and boxing competitions, where Drill-Sergeant Murphy and Private Conroy defeated two black N.C.O.'s of a West Indies Battalion, were interludes to nights of savage bombing; carrying and camouflage parties to the front line, where they met a new variety of mustard-gas; and the constant practice of the new form of attack. The real thing was set down now for the 14th September but was cancelled at the last moment, and the Battalion was warned for an ordinary trench tour on the night of the 12th–13th. Unluckily, just before that date Captain Sassoon and Lieutenant Kane and twenty-seven men of a big fatigue a day or two before, were badly burned and blistered by the new mustard-gas shells. It put them down two officers at a time when every head was needed.

They were to take over from the 3rd Coldstream on the 12th September on what was practically the old Boesinghe sector. That Battalion which lay next the French had just been raided, and lost nine men because their liaison officer had misunderstood the French language. Hence an order at the eleventh hour that each Battalion in the sector should attach a competent linguist to the liaison-post where the two armies joined. The advance across the Steenbeek, after Boesinghe, had only gone on a few hundred yards up the Staden railway line and was now halted three thousand yards sou'west of Houthulst Forest, facing a close and blind land of woods, copses, farms, mills and tree-screened roads cut, before any sure advance could be made, less than a quarter of a mile from the Guards Divisional Front, by the abominable Broembeek. This was more a sluit than a river. Its banks were marsh for the most part; and every yard was commanded by hostile fire of every kind. On the French right and our extreme left, was a lodgement of posts the far side of the Broembeek which the Coldstream had been holding when they were raided. These lay within a hundred yards of the enemy's line of strong posts (many lectures had been delivered lately on the difference between lines of trenches and lines of posts), and were backed by the stream, then waist-deep and its bed plentifully filled with barbed wire. Between Ney Copse and Ney Wood, say five hundred yards, they could be reached only by one stone bridge and a line of duck-boards like stepping-stones at the west corner of Ney Copse.

The Battalion went up in the afternoon of the 12th September, none the better for a terrific bombardment an hour or two before from a dozen low-flighting 'planes which sent every one to cover, inflicted twenty casualties on them out of two hundred in the neighbourhood, and fairly cut the local transport to bits. The relief too – and this was one of the few occasions when Guards' guides lost their way – lasted till midnight.

Six platoons had to be placed in the forward posts above mentioned, east of the little river whose western or home bank was pure swamp for thirty yards back. Says the Diary: "This position could be cut off by the enemy, as the line of the stream gives a definite barrage-line, and, if any rain sets in, the stone bridge would be the only possible means of crossing."

A Battalion seldom thinks outside of its orders, or some one might have remembered how a couple of Battalions on the wrong side of a stream, out Dunkirk way that very spring, had been mopped up in the sands, because they could neither get away nor get help. Our men settled down and were unmolested for three hours. Then a barrage fell, first on all the forward posts, next on the far bank of the stream, and our own front line. The instant it lifted, two companies of Würtembergers in body-armour rushed what the shells had left of the forward posts. Lieutenant Manning, on the right of Ney Wood, was seen for a moment surrounded and then was seen no more. All posts east of Ney Copse were blown up or bombed out, for the protected Würtembergers fought well. Captain Redmond commanding No. 2 Company was going the rounds when the barrage began. He dropped into the shell-hole that was No. 6 post, and when that went up, collected its survivors and those from the next hole, and made such a defence in the south edge of Ney Copse as prevented the enemy from turning us alto-gether out of it. Most of the time, too, he was suffering from a dislocated knee. Then the enemy finished the raid scientifically, with a hot barrage of three-quarters of an hour on all communications till the Würtembergers had comfortably withdrawn. It was an undeniable "knock," made worse by its insolent skill.

Losses had not yet been sorted out. The C.O. wished to withdraw what was left of his posts across the river – there were two still in Ney Copse – and not till he sent his reasons in writing was the sense of them admitted at Brigade Headquarters. Officer's patrols were then told off to search Ney Copse, find out where the enemy's new posts had been established, pick up what wounded they came across and cover the withdrawal of the posts there, while a new line was sited. In other words, the front had to fall back, and the patrols were to pick up the pieces. The bad luck of the affair cleaved, as it often does, to their subsequent efforts. By a series of errors and misapprehensions Ney Copse was not thoroughly searched and one platoon of No. 3 Company was left behind and reported as missing. By the time the patrols returned and the Battalion had started to dig in its new front line, it was too light to send out another party. The enemy shelled vigorously with big stuff all the night of the 13th till three in the morning; stopped for an hour and then barraged the whole of our sector with high explosives till six. During this, Lieutenant Gibson, our liaison officer with the French, was wounded, and at some time or another in a lull in the infernal din, Sergeant M'Guinness and Corporal Power, survivors of No. 2 Company, which had been mopped up, worked their way home in safety through the enemy posts.

The morning of the 14th brought their Brigadier who "seems to think that our patrol work was not well done," and had no difficulty whatever in conveying his impression to his hearers. Major Ward went down the line suffering from fever. There were one or two who envied him his trouble, for, with a missing platoon in front – if indeed any of it survived – and a displeased Brigadier in rear, life was not lovely, even though our guns were putting down barrages on what were delicately called our "discarded" posts. Out went another patrol that night under Lieutenant Bagot, with intent to reconnoitre "the river that wrought them all their woe." They discovered what every one guessed – that the enemy was holding both river-crossings, stone bridge and duckboards, with machine-guns. The Battalion finished the day in respirators under heavy gas-shellings.

Then came a piece of pure drama. They had passed the 15th September in the usual discomfort while waiting to be relieved by the 1st Coldstream. Captain Redmond with his dislocated knee had gone down and Lieutenants FitzGerald and Lysaght had come up. The talk was all about the arrangements for wiring in their new line and the like, when at 4.30, after a few hours' quiet, a terrific barrage fell on their front line followed by an S.O.S. from somewhere away to the left. A few minutes later five S.O.S. rockets rose on the right apparently in front of the 1st Scots Guards. Our guns on the Brigade front struck in, by request; the enemy plastered the landscape with H.E.; machine-guns along the whole sector helped with their barrages to which the enemy replied in kind, and with one searching crash we clamped a big-gun barrage on the far bank of the Broembeek, till it looked as if nothing there could live.

When things were at their loudest a wire came in from the Brigade to say that a Hun captured at St. Julien reported that a general advance of the enemy was timed for 6.30 that very morning! By five o'clock the hostile barrage seemed to have quieted down along our front, but the right of the Brigade sector seemed still to be at odds with some enemy; so the Brigadier kept our local barrage hard-on by way of distraction. And at half-past six, tired, very hungry, but otherwise in perfect order, turned up at Brigade Headquarters, Sergeant Moyney with the remainder of No. 3 Company's platoon which had been missing since the 12th. He had been left in command of an advanced shell-hole post in Ney Copse with orders neither to withdraw nor to let his men break into their iron ration. The Würtembergers' raid had cut off his little command altogether; and at the end of it he found a hostile machine-gun post well established between himself and the duckboard-bridge over the river. He had no desire to attract more attention than was necessary, and kept his men quiet. They had forty-eight hours' rations and a bottle of water apiece; but the Sergeant was perfectly definite as to their leaving their iron ration intact. So they lay in their shell-hole in the wood and speculated on life and death, and paid special attention to the commands of their superior officer in the execution of his duty. The enemy knew they were somewhere about, but not their strength nor their precise position, and having his own troubles in other directions, it was not till the dawn of the 16th that he sent out a full company to roll them up. The Sergeant allowed them to get within twenty-five yards and then ordered his men to "jump out and attack." It was quite a success. Their Lewis-gun came into action on their flank, and got off three drums into the brown of the host while the infantry expended four boxes of bombs at close quarters. "Sergeant Moyney then gave the order to charge through the Germans to the Broembeek." It was done and he sent his men across that foul water, bottomed here with curly barbed-wire coils while he covered their passage with his one rifle. They were bombed and machine-gunned as they floundered over to the swampy western bank; and it was here that Private Woodcock heard cries for help behind him, returned, waded into the water under bombs and bullets, fished out Private Hilley of No. 3 Company with a broken thigh and brought him safely away. The clamour of this fierce little running fight, the unmistakable crack and yells of the bombing and the sudden appearance of some of our men breaking out of the woods near the German machine-gun emplacement by the river, had given the impression to our front of something big in development. Hence the S.O.S. which woke up the whole touchy line, and hence our final barrage which had the blind good luck to catch the enemy as they were lining up on the banks of the Broembeek preparatory, perhaps, to the advance the St. Julien prisoner had reported. Their losses were said to be heavy, but there was great joy in the Battalion over the return of the missing platoon, less several good men, for whom a patrol went out to look that night in case they might be lying up in shell-holes. But no more were found. (" 'Twas a bad mix-up first to last. We ought never to have been that side the dam' river at that time at all. 'Twas not fit for it yet. And there's a lot to it that can't be told.... And *why* did Moyney not let the men break into their ration? Because, in a tight place, if you do *one* thing against orders ye'll do *annything*. An' 'twas a dam' tight place that that Moyney man walked them out of.")

They were relieved with only two casualties. The total losses of the tour had been – one officer missing (Lieutenant Manning), one (2nd Lieutenant Gibson) wounded; one man wounded and missing; eighty missing; fifty-nine wounded and seventeen killed. And the worst of it was that they were all trained hands being finished for the next big affair!

Dulwich Camp where they lay for a few days was, like the others, well within bombing and long gun-range. They consoled themselves with an inspection of the Drums and Pipes on the 17th, and received several six-inch shells from a naval gun, an old acquaintance; but though one shell landed within a few yards of a bivouac of No. 2 Company there were no further casualties, and the next day the Drums and Pipes went over to Proven to take part in a competition arranged by the Twenty-ninth Division (De Lisle's). They played beautifully – every one admitted that – but what chance had they of "marks for dress" against Line Battalions whose bands sported their full peace-time equipment – leopard skins, white buckskin gloves and all? So the 8th Essex won De Lisle's prize. But they bore no malice, for when, a few days later, a strayed officer and forty men of that Battalion cast up at their camp (it was Putney for the moment), they entertained them all hospitably.

They settled down to the business of intensive training of the new drafts that were coming in – 2nd Lieutenant Murphy with ninety-six men one day, and 2nd Lieutenants Dame and Close the next with a hundred and forty-six, all to be put through three weeks of a scheme that included "consolidation of shell-holes" in addition to everything else, and meant six hours a day of the hardest repetition-work. Sports and theatrical shows, such as the Coldstream Pierrots and their own rather Rabelaisian "Wild West Show," filled in time till the close of September when they were at Herzeele, warned that they would be "for it" on or about the 11th of the next month, and that their attack would not be preceded by any artillery registration. This did not cheer them; for experience had shown that the chances of surprising the enemy on that sector were few and remote.

The last day of September saw the cadres filled. Three 2nd Lieutenants, Anderson, Faulkner and O'Connor, and Lieutenant Levy arrived; and, last, Lieut.-Colonel the Hon. H. R. Alexander, who took over the command.

Rehearsals for the coming affair filled the next few days at Herzeele camp, and their final practice on the 4th before they moved over to Proven was passed as "entirely satisfactory." Scaled against the tremendous events in progress round them, the Broembeek was no more than a minor action in a big action intended to clear a cloudy front, ere the traitorous weather should make all work on the sector impossible, and, truly, by the time it was done, it cost the Division only two thousand casualties – say four battalions of a peace establishment.

The battle, they knew, would depend on the disposition of the little Broembeek. If that chose to flood it would be difficult to reach across its bogs and worse to cross; and, under any circumstances, mats and portable bridges (which meant men having to halt and bunch under fire) would be indispensable.

The existing line was to be held by the 3rd Guards Brigade till the 9th of October, when the attack would be put through by the 1st and 2nd Brigades on the right and left respectively. In Brigade disposition this would lay the 2nd Irish Guards next to the French on their left, and the 1st Scots Guards on their right. The usual three objectives were set for the Division; making an advance in all of rather more than three thousand yards from the Broembeek to the edge of the Houthulst Forest; and equally, as usual, when the leading Battalions had secured the first two objectives, the remaining battalions of each Brigade would go through them and take the final one.

With the idea of concealing the attack, no preliminary work was undertaken, but, on the morning of the 6th the light bridges and mats were issued, and the Battalion practised fixing and laying them over a piece of ground marked to represent the river. They moved from Putney Camp to the front line on the 7th, when Nos. 3 and 4 Companies relieved the 2nd Scots Guards who had been getting ready the mats and bridges for the real thing. The last day concerned itself with disposing the Companies in the trenches so that they should be able to have a good look at the ground ahead while it was yet light. No one could pretend that the sweeping of the small-featured, ill-looking and crowded landscape would be an easy job, and at the far end of the ominous perspectives lay the dull line of Houthulst Forest upon which rain shut down dismally as the day closed. The enemy made no signs beyond occasional shelling, in which Battalion Headquarters, a collection of three concrete block-houses, were hit once or twice with 5·9's, but no harm followed.

At dusk Nos. 3 and 4 Companies laid out the tapes parallel to the Broembeek that were to make forming-up easier. For some reason connected with the psychology of war, this detail has always a depressing influence on men's minds. An officer has observed that it reminded him of tennis-courts and girls playing on them at home. A man has explained that their white glimmer in the dusk suggests a road for ghosts, with reflections on the number of those who, after setting foot across on deadline, may return for their rum-ration.

The rain gave over in the night and was followed by a good drying wind. Zero of the 9th October was 5.20 a.m. which gave light enough to see a few hundred yards. An intense 18-pounder barrage was our signal to get away. Four barrages went on together – the creeping, a standing one, a back-barrage of six-inch howitzers and 60-pounders, and a distant barrage of the same metal, not to count the thrashing machine-gun barrages. They moved and halted with the precision of stage machinery or, as a man said, like water-hoses at a conflagration. Our two leading Companies (3 and 4) crossed the river without a hitch, met some small check for a few moments in Ney Wood where a nest of machine-guns had escaped the blasts of fire, and moved steadily behind the death-drum of the barrage to the first objective a thousand yards from their start. There the barrage hung like a wall from the French flank, across the north of Gruyterzaele Farm, over the Langemarck road and Koekuit, and up to Namur Crossing on the battered railway track, while the two leading Companies set to work consolidating till it should roll back and the rear Companies pass on behind it. The dreadful certainty of the job in itself masked all the details. One saw and realized nothing outside of one's own immediate task, and the business of keeping distances between lines and supports became a sort of absurd preoccupation. Occasionally a runner passed, very intent on his errand, a free man, it seemed, who could go where he chose at what pace suited his personal need to live; or the variously wounded would lurch by among the shell-holes; but the general impression in the midst of the din was of concentrated work. The barrage held still for three-quarters of an hour, and about half-past seven the 2nd Coldstream came up through our Nos. 3 and 4 Companies who were lying down, curiously unworried by casualties, to carry on the advance to the last objective which was timed to take place about eight. No. 3 Company was told to move up behind the Coldstream and dig in a couple of hundred yards behind Nos. 1 and 2 as a support to them, where they lay behind the second objective, in event of counter-attacks. Unluckily a French gun on the left began to fire short, and that Company had to be withdrawn with some speed, for a "seventy-five" that makes a mistake repeats it too often to be a pleasant neighbour. Battalion Headquarters came up as methodically as everything else, established themselves behind the first objective, strung their telephones and settled down to the day's work. So far as the Battalion was concerned they suffered no more henceforward than a few occasional shells that do not seem to have done any damage, and at six in the evening their two leading Companies were withdrawn, with the leading Companies of the 1st Scots Guards, and marched back to Dulwich Camp. The remaining two Companies of the Scots Guards passed under the Command of the C.O. of the Irish (Alexander), who had been slightly wounded in the course of the action. The four Companies then were in direct support of the troops at the third objective waiting on for counter-attacks which never came.

On the dawn of the 10th October Battalion Headquarters moved forward again to the second-objective line, but except for some low-flying enemy 'planes, the day passed quietly till the afternoon when the same French "seventy-five," which had been firing short the day before, took it into its misdirected head to shell No. 1 Company so savagely that that had to be shifted to the left in haste. There was no explanation, and while the Company was on the move the enemy put down a two hours' barrage just behind the second objective. It has often been remarked that when the Hun leads off on the wrong foot, so to say, at the beginning of a fray, he keeps on putting his foot into it throughout. Luckily, the barrage did not do much harm.

The Welsh Guards relieved in the late evening, and by eleven o'clock the whole Battalion was safe in Dulwich Camp with an amazingly small casualty list. The only officer killed had been Captain Hanbury. Lieutenants Close and Bagot were wounded and also Alexander and Father Browne, these last two so slightly that they still remained on duty. Of other ranks they had but twenty dead, eighty-nine wounded and two missing. The Würtembergers' raid had cost them more. And that, too, was the luck of war.

None of them knew particularly how the fight outside their limited vision had gone. The Scots Guards were comfortably on their right, keeping step for step; and the French on the left, barring their incontinent gun, had moved equally level. But they were all abominably stiff from negotiating the slippery-sided shell-holes and the mud, and it took them two days' hard work to clean up.

On the 13th October they relieved the 1st Scots Guards for fatigue-parties to the front, and lay in a camp of sand-bag and corrugated iron hovels where the men had to manufacture shelter for themselves, while a long-range German gun prevented that work from being too dull. But again, there was no damage. They were relieved on the 16th October from these duties by a Battalion of the Cheshires and marched to Elverdinghe, leaving the Pioneers behind for a little to put up crosses over the graves of the newly dead. That closed the chapter and they lapsed back to "the usual routine," of drill, inspections and sports. They were at Houlle Camp near Watten on the 21st when the 2nd Guards Brigade was inspected by H.R.H. the Duke of Connaught, and the Battalion, in walking-out order, lined the roads and cheered. Sir Douglas Haig, too, inspected them on the 25th October with the whole of their Division, dealt them all those compliments on past work which were their undeniable right, and congratulated them on their turn-out. The Battalion then was specially well set up and hard-bitten, running to largish men even in No. 2 Company. Their new drafts had all been worked up and worked down; the new C.O.'s hand and systems were firmly established; Company cooks and their satellites had been reformed, and – which puts a bloom on men as quickly as food – they were "happy" under a justice which allowed an immense amount of honest, intimate, domestic fun.

Of the tales which ran about at that period there is one perhaps worth recording. During the fatigues on the Boesinghe front it fell to them to relieve some Battalion or other which, after much manoeuvring in the mud, at last drew clear of its trenches to let in the wet and impatient Irish. The latter's C.O., wearied to the bone, was sitting in the drizzling dark beside the communication-trench, his head on his hand and on his wrist his campaign-watch with its luminous dial. Suddenly, as the relieved shadows dragged themselves by, he felt his wrist gently taken, slightly turned, and after an instant's inspection, loosed again. Naturally, he demanded by all the Gods of the Army what the unseen caitiff meant of his outrageous deed. To him, from the dark, in irresistible Cockney, "Beg pardon, Sir, but I thought it was a glow-worm," and the poor devil who had been cut off from all knowledge of earthly time for the past three days, shuffled on, leaving behind him a Lieut.-Colonel of the Brigade of Guards defeated and shaken with mirth.

Their rest lasted till the 9th November, during which time 2nd Lieutenants Cary-Elwes and A. F. Synge joined, and Captain Sassoon came up from the base and took over No. 3 Company. Lieut.-Colonel Pawlett of the Canadian Army was attached to the Battalion from the 6th of the month, and Captain the Hon. H. A. V. Harmsworth rejoined from the Staff where, like a brother-officer in the Entrenching Battalion, his heart was not. On the 9th, too, Lieutenant Lysaght and Sergeant R. Macfarlane were decorated with the Croix de Guerre by General Antoine commanding the First French Army.

On the 10th of November they were ordered out into the St. Pol area which, as a jumping-off place, offered as many possibilities as Charing Cross Station on a Bank Holiday. One knows from the record of the 1st Battalion that the whole Division now on the move were prepared for and given to believe anything – even that they might be despatched to Italy, to retrieve October's disaster of Caporetto. But it is known now that the long series of operations round The Salient – Messines, the two months' agony of the third Battle of Ypres and the rest – had drawn the enemy forces and held them more and more to the northward of our front; and that Sir Julian Byng had been entrusted to drive at the Hindenburg Line on the Somme with the Sixth, Fourth, Third and Seventh Army Corps, from Bullecourt southward to a little south of Gonnelieu.

It was to be a surprise without Artillery preparation, but very many tanks were to do the guns' work in rooting out trenches, barbed wire and machine-gun nests.

The main attack was on a front of six miles, and, as has been noted elsewhere, the official idea was not to make the capture of Cambrai, behind the Hindenburg Line, a main feature of the affair, but to get as far into the enemy's ground as could be, and above all, to secure a clean flank for ourselves to the north-east of Bourlon Wood near Cambrai where the lie of the Somme Downs gave vital observation and command. The Guards Division, as usual, would wait upon the results. If the thing was a success they would advance on Cambrai. If not, they would assist as requisite.

It was late in the year, and the weather was no treat as the 2nd Battalion Irish Guards marched out in the wet from Houlle on the 10th November to Ecques, and, in billets there, made its first acquaintance with a Battalion of Portuguese troops. Two days more brought them to Ostreville's bad billets and a draft of a hundred new hands with Lieutenant M. R. Hely-Hutchinson and 2nd Lieutenant F. C. Lynch-Blosse. Not a man had fallen out on the road, but they were glad of a four days' halt and clean-up, though that included instruction in outpost companies and positions.

On the 17th they continued their march south to Ambrines over the large untouched lands of the high watershed between the Scarpe and the little streams that feed the Authies river. The next day carried them no longer south, but east towards the noise of the unquiet Somme guns, and had they any doubts as to their future, it was settled by one significant gas-helmet drill. ("But we knew, or at least, *I* did, having done my trick here before, that we were for it. Ye could begin to smell the dam' Somme, as soon as ye was across that Arras railway.")

They heard the opening of Cambrai fight from Courcelles in the early morn of the 20th November – a sudden and immense grunt, rather than roar, of a barrage that lasted half an hour as the tanks rolled out through the morning mists, and for the first time the Hindenburg Line was broken.

BOURLON WOOD

They held on, under two hours' notice, through Achiet-le-Grand, Bapaume and Riencourt to Beaulencourt in icy rain and mud. The wreckage of battle was coming back to them now, as they moved in the wake of the Fifty-first Division that was pressing on towards Flesquières, and passed a number of prisoners taken round Noyelles and Marcoing. Here were rumours of vast captures, of Cambrai fallen, and of Cavalry pushing through beyond. The 24th November brought them, in continuous drizzle, to the smoking and ruined land between Trescault and Ribecourt, which was crowded with infantry and the Second Cavalry Division near by; and they lay out in a sound unoccupied trench, once part of the Hindenburg Line. Our tanks had left their trails everywhere, and the trodden-down breadths of wire-entanglements, studded here and there with crushed bodies, suggested to one beholder "the currants in the biscuits one used to buy at school." Suddenly, news of Cambrai fight began to change colour. They were told that it had "stuck" round Bourlon Wood, a sullen hundred-acre plantation, which commanded all the ground we had won north of Flesquières, and was the key to the whole position at the northern end of the field. Seldom had woodland and coppice cost more for a few days' rental, even at the expensive rates then current on the Somme. Here are some of the items in the account: On the 21st November the Fifty-first Division, supported by tanks, had captured Fontaine-Notre-Dame village which lay between Bourlon Wood and Cambrai, and, till beaten out again by the enemy, had worked into the Wood itself. Fontaine was lost on the 22nd, and attacked on the 23rd November by the Fifty-first Division again, but without definite result. The Fortieth Division were put in on the evening of the same day and managed to take the whole of the Wood, even reaching Bourlon village behind it. Here they held up a fierce counter-attack of German Grenadiers, but, in the long run, were pushed out and back to the lower ground, and by the evening of the 25th were very nearly exhausted. Five days of expensive fighting had gained everything except those vital positions necessary to security and command of gun-fire. Hence the employment of the Guards Division, to see what could be fished out of the deadlock. The decision was taken swiftly. The 1st and 3rd Guards Brigade had been sent up on the 23rd November to relieve two Brigades of the Fifty-first Division round Flesquières, and also to assist the Fortieth then battling in the Wood. It was understood that the whole of the Guards Division would now be employed, but no one knew for sure in which direction.

As far as the 2nd Guards Brigade was concerned, their Brigadier was not told of the intended attack on Bourlon till the afternoon of the 26th; the C.O.'s of battalions not till four o'clock, and Company Commanders not till midnight of that date. No one engaged had seen the ground before, or knew anything about the enemy's dispositions. Their instructions ran that they were to work with the 186th Brigade on their left "with the object of gaining the whole of Bourlon Wood, La Fontaine and the high ground behind it." As a matter of fact, they were to be brought up in the dark through utterly unknown surroundings; given a compass-bearing, and

155

despatched at dawn into a dense wood, on a front of seven hundred yards, to reach an objective a thousand yards ahead. This pleasing news was decanted upon them at Brigade Headquarters in the dusk of a November evening hailstorm, after the C.O., the Assistant Adjutant and all Company Commanders had spent the day reconnoitring the road from Trescault to the front line by Anneux and making arrangements for taking over from the 2nd Scots Guards, who were supporting the Fortieth Division outside the Wood.

The official idea of the Brigade's work was that, while the 3rd Grenadiers were attacking La Fontaine, the 2nd Irish Guards should sweep through Bourlon Wood and consolidate on its northern edge; the 1st Coldstream filling any gap between the Irish Guards and the Grenadiers. When all objectives had been reached, the 1st Scots Guards were to push up and get touch with the 3rd Grenadiers who should have captured La Fontaine. (It may be noted that the attack was to be a diverging one.) They would advance under a creeping barrage, that jumped back a hundred yards every five minutes, and they would be assisted by fourteen tanks. Above all, they were to be quick because the enemy seemed to be strong and growing stronger, both in and behind the Wood.

The Battalion spent the night of the 26th working its way up to the front line, through Flesquières where bombs were issued, two per man; then to La Justice by Graincourt; and thence, cross-country, by Companies through the dark to the Bapaume–Cambrai road, where they found the guides for their relief of the Scots Guards. Just as they reached the south edge of Bourlon Wood, the enemy put down a barrage which cost forty casualties. Next it was necessary for the C.O. (Alexander) to explain the details of the coming attack to his Company Commanders, who re-explained it to their N.C.O.'s, while the Companies dressed in attack-order, bombs were detonated and shovels issued. ("There was not any need to tell us we were for it. We knew that, and we knew we was to be quick. But that was all we *did* know – except we was to go dancin' into that great Wood in the wet, beyond the duckboards. The ground, ye'll understand, had been used by them that had gone before us – used and messed about; and at the back, outside Bourlon, all Jerry's guns was rangin' on it. A dirty an' a noisy business was Bourlon.")

"The ground, ye'll understand, had been used by them that had gone before us – used and messed about; and at the back, outside Bourlon, all Jerry's guns was rangin' on it. A dirty an' a noisy business was Bourlon."

By Bourlon Wood, November 1917.

156

By five in the morning, after a most wearing night, the Battalion was in position, the 2/5th West Riding of the 1st Brigade on its left and the 1st Coldstream on its right; and the Wood in front alive with concealed machine-guns and spattered with shells. They led off at 6.20 behind their own barrage, in two waves; No. 1 Company on the right, and No. 2 Company on the left, supported by No. 3 Company and No. 4. Everything was ready for them, and machine-guns opened on well-chosen and con-verging ranges. Almost at the outset they met a line of enemy posts held in strength, where many of the occupants had chosen to shelter themselves at the bottom of the trenches under oil-sheets, a protection hampering them equally in their efforts to fight or to surrender. Here there was some quick killing and a despatch of prisoners to the rear; but the Wood offered many chances of escape, and as our guards were necessarily few, for every rifle was needed, a number broke away and returned. Meantime, the Battalion took half-a-dozen machine-guns and lost more men at each blind step. In some respects Bourlon was like Villers-Cotterêts on a large scale, with the added handicap of severe and well-placed shelling. A man once down in the coppice, or bogged in a wood-pool, was as good as lost, and the in-and-out work through the trees and stumpage broke up the formations. Nor, when the affair was well launched, was there much help from "the officer with the compass" who was supposed to direct the outer flank of each Company. The ground on the right of the Battalion's attack, which the Coldstream were handling, was thick with undestroyed houses and buildings of all sorts that gave perfect shelter to the machine-guns; but it is questionable whether Bourlon Wood itself, in its lack of points to concen-trate upon, and in the confusion of forest rides all exactly like each other, was not, after all, the worst. Early in the advance, No. 2 Company lost touch on the left, while the rest of the Battalion, which was still somehow keeping together, managed to get forward through the Wood as far as its north-east corner, where they made touch with the 1st Coldstream. Not long after this, they tried to dig in among the wet tree-roots, just beyond the Wood's north edge. It seemed to them that the enemy had fallen back to the railway-line which skirted it, as well as to the north of La Fontaine village. Officially, the objective was reached, but our attacking strength had been used up, and there were no reserves. A barrage of big stuff, sup-plemented by field-guns, was steadily thrashing out the centre and north of the Wood, and, somewhere to the rear of the Battalion, a nest of machine-guns broke out viciously and unexpectedly. Then the whole fabric of the fight appeared to crumble, as, through one or other of the many gaps between the Battalions, the enemy thrust in, and the 2nd Irish Guards, hanging on to their thin front line, realized him suddenly at their backs. What remained of them split up into little fighting groups; sometimes taking prisoners, sometimes themselves being taken and again breaking away from their captors, dodging, turning and ducking in dripping coppices and over the slippery soil, while the shells impartially smote both parties. Such as had kept their sense of direction headed back by twos and threes to their original starting-point; but at noon Battalion Headquarters had lost all touch of the Battalion, and the patrols that got forward to investigate reported there was no sign of it. It looked like complete and unqualified disaster. But men say that the very blindness of the ground hid this fact to a certain extent both from us and the enemy, and the multiplied clamours in the wood supplied an additional blindage. As one man said: "If Jerry had only shut off his dam' guns and *listened* he'd ha' heard we was knocked out; but he kept on hammer – hammering an' rushin' his parties back and forth the Wood, and so, ye see, them that could of us, slipped back quiet in the height of the noise." Another observer compared it to the chopping of many foxes in cover – not pleasant, but diversified by some hideously comic incidents. All agreed that it was defeat for the Guards – the first complete one they had sustained; but the admitted fact that they had been turned on at a few hours' notice to achieve the impossible, did not spoil their tempers. The records say that the 2nd Guards Brigade with the rest of the Division "fell back to its original line." Unofficially: "We did – but I don't know how we did it. There wasn't any Battalion worth mentioning when the Welsh Guards relieved us in the dark, but stray men kept on casting up all night long." The losses were in proportion to the failure. Of officers, two were killed – Cary-Elwes, just as they reached their objective, by a bullet through the head, and A. F. Synge shot down at the beginning of the attack, both of them men without fear and with knowledge. Three were missing, which is to say, dead – 2nd Lieutenants N. D. Bayly of No. 2 Company, W. G. Rea of No. 3 and N. F. Durant of No. 4 who was also believed to have been wounded. Four were wounded – Captain the Hon. H. A. V. Harmsworth, No. 1; Captain Reford, No. 3, bullet through the shoulder; and Lieutenant S. S. Wordley, of the same company, in the head. Also 2nd Lieut. F. C. Lynch-Blosse of No. 2 blown up, but able to get back. The C.O. (Colonel the Hon. H. R. Alexander), the Second in Command (Captain the Hon. W. S. Alexander), Captain Nugent, Adjutant; 2nd Lieutenant W. D. Faulkner, Assistant Adjutant; Captain Sassoon and Lieutenant O'Connor, these last two being Company Officers in reserve who were kept with Battalion Headquarters, were unhurt. Twenty-five men were known to be dead on comrades' evidence; one hundred and forty-six were missing, of whom a number would naturally be dead; and one hundred and forty-two were wounded and brought back. Total, three hundred and twenty-two.

They came out of the Wood on the evening of the 27th one hundred and seventeen strong; lay, nominally in reserve, but actually finished for the time being, along the La Justice–Graincourt road till one company of the 2/5th Leicesters took over. Their losses seemed to be enough to justify their resting a little, which they did at Ribecourt and, next day, the 29th November, moved on to a camp, at Bertincourt, of Nissen huts, crowded but comfortable, where they thought to relax and take full stock of their hurts, and fill their ranks again from the Divisional Reserve. [It is to be remembered that Battalions went into action with only three officers per Company and platoons reduced to practically half strength.] They had been warned by prisoners that the enemy had at least three Battalions ready with which they intended to attack, but put the matter out of their collective minds as one to be attended to by their neighbours. All they desired were the decencies of a rest-billet far behind the infernal noise of the guns. But on the dawn of the 30th that irregular noise turned into the full-mouthed chorus which heralds a counter-attack. The Third Army Corps was being hammered somewhere towards Gonnelieu a few miles to the southward, and the orders were for the whole of the Guards Division to get thither with every speed, for it looked as though the bottom were all out of Cambrai fight. The 2nd Guards Brigade were away from Bertincourt ere noon, and, preceded by the 1st Scots Guards, moved in Artillery formation straight across the country-side to the ridge in front of Gouzeaucourt Wood – there are two ridges between Metz and Gouzeaucourt village – where they were told to dig in and lie up as reserve. They noticed in their progress that the landscape was fairly full of retiring troops to whom they occasionally addressed remarks of an encouraging nature. ("After what we had took in bloody Bourlon 'twas great comfort to see that there was others not making any picnic of it either.") But they also observed with satisfaction that the 1st and 3rd Guards Brigades were ahead of them, making almost a parade movement of their advance against the machine-guns of the village. It was abominably cold, they were without greatcoats for the most part, and they had to dig in in frozen chalk, and whenever there was a block on the road, the enemy shelled it. Occasionally, the shells got in among their own prisoners, of whom small detachments were already being gathered, and sent back. The Battalion had been made up to four hundred rifles at that time, and when on the evening of the 1st December they moved to the western outskirts of Gouzeaucourt they relieved one company of the 2nd Coldstream and a company of the 1st Battalion Irish Guards in the support-line beyond Gouzeaucourt railway station. Gouzeaucourt, and the situation, had been saved by the Guards Division. The 1st and 3rd Guards Brigade had attacked and, as we know, captured Gauche Wood to the east of Gouzeaucourt on the 1st, and the supporting Brigade was not called upon to do more than sit in its trenches and take a not too heavy overflow of enemy's shelling. Altogether the Battalion's casualties were under half-a-dozen. An attack, which they were told would be sprung on them on the 2nd, did not arrive, and on the 4th December the 1st South African Infantry Regiment relieved the whole of the 2nd Brigade without a hitch, and the men moved off to bivouac in Gouzeaucourt Wood. Their bitter cold shelters lay among our vociferous batteries, which worked all night. At three in the morning 4·2's began to fall among the officers' tents so that the disgusted inmates had to move. One officer's pillow was blown away almost immediately after he had quitted it, and it is reported that the C.O. and Adjutant "took refuge" behind a tent where they delivered their minds about the horrors of "sleeping with the guns." The incoming Brigade relieved them of their last responsibilities on the night of the 5th, and they would have rested at Fins, whose field railways they had helped to build in the pleasant summer days, but that a long-range gun was attending to the hutments there, and it was judged safer to push on several more weary miles to Etricourt which they reached at one in the morning.

Battles are like railway journeys in that the actual time of transit is as nothing compared to that wasted in getting from door to door. They were marched off to Etricourt Station at eight on the morning of their arrival, where they waited till eleven for a train that had run off the line, and it was late in the dark of the evening when, after passing Ginchy and the old battle-field of Transloy and Lesbœufs which they fought over on the 15th and the 26th of September the year before, and through Trônes Wood, of immortal and unhappy memories, they reached at last Beaumetz close to their billets at Simencourt where, with one day's rest, the Companies were "handed over to Company Commanders for reorganization, inspection, etc."

On review the last tour (everything between rests was a "tour" in those days) had not been very glorious, but there was no denying it was very much up to Somme pattern. One came out of line and was fatted up; one was "messed about," thrown in, used up and thrown out again, to be refatted for the next occasion with apparently small results, except, always, the saving of the situation at Gouzeaucourt. ("If that thing had happened one day later an' the Division in rest miles back instead of being on top of it, Saints know the whole line might have gone.") Otherwise the Somme seemed as large, as sticky and as well-populated with aggressive enemies as ever before. The bodies and the uniforms of the dead of past years had withered down somewhat on the clawed and raked fields; but to the mere soldier's eye, uninfluenced by statements of the Press, there was no reason under the grey heavens why their past performances should not be repeated, as part of the natural order of things, for ever and ever. Cambrai may have given hope and encouragement in England, but those who had been through it remained Sadducees.

161

There were those who said that that hour was the psychological one to have gone on and taken advantage of the moral effect of breaking the Hindenburg Line, but this theory was put forward after the event; and a total of eleven thousand prisoners and a hundred and forty-five German guns for three weeks' fighting seems small foundation for such large hopes. Everyone on the field seems to have been agreed as to the futility of trying to work with, and making arrangements for the keep of, masses of Cavalry on the chance that these might break through and overrun the enemy in the background.

That autumn Russia deliquesced and began to pass out of civilization, and the armed strength of Germany on that front was freed to return and rearrange itself on the Western border, ready for the fourth spring of the War. We are told with emphasis that that return-wave was foreseen, and to some extent provided for, by increasing the line for which our Armies were responsible, and by reorganizing those Armies so that Divisions stood on a ten-battalion as against a thirteen-battalion basis.[1] We may once more quote Sir Douglas Haig's despatches on this head. "An unfamiliar grouping of units was introduced thereby, necessitating new methods of tactical handling of the troops and the discarding of old methods to which subordinate Commanders had been accustomed." But the change was well supported in the home Press.

Meantime, as far as possible, the war stood still on both sides. The Battalion was encouraged to put on fat and to practise cleanliness, kit inspections and inter-regimental and Company football matches till the end of the year. During the month of December, at Simencourt, Captain the Hon. H. B. O'Brien arrived and took over No. 1 Company; Lieutenant B. Levy, M.C., joined from the 4th Army School, and 2nd Lieutenants J. C. Maher and T. Mathew also joined. The Christmas dinners were good and solid affairs of pork, plum-pudding, plum-dough (a filling and concrete-like dish), three bottles of Bass per throat and a litre of beer, plus cigars and tobacco. The C.O. had gone into Amiens to make sure of it and of the Headquarters' Christmas trees which, next day, were relighted and redecorated with small gifts and sweets for the benefit of the village children.

A moral victory over Eton crowned the year. The officers of the 2nd Battalion played the officers of the 1st Coldstream at Eton Football at Wanquetin. They lost by a goal to two goals and a rouge, but their consolation was that their C.O., an Harrovian, scored their goal and that half the Coldstream's goals were got by Harrow. It was a small thing but it made them very happy in their little idleness after "Bloody Bourlon."

[1] On this basis, as is noted in the history of the 1st Battalion, a 4th Brigade of the Guards Division was created by the lopped-off Battalions: viz. the 4th Grenadiers, 3rd Coldstream and 2nd Irish Guards, which as a Brigade was attached to the Thirty-first Division, Thirteenth Corps (Major-General Sir Charles Fergusson).

1918

ARRAS TO
THE END

ASSUMING that the information of our Intelligence Department was correct, the weight of the coming German attack would be delivered to the south of Arras; and that town would be the hinge on which it would turn. Elsewhere along the Somme front, ground might be given if required, but between Arras and Amiens the line, at all costs, must stand; and we are told that, months before the Spring of the year, attention was given to strengthening the systems of defence in the rear. It is difficult to discover how many of the precautions taken were made with serious expectation of trouble, and how many were, so to say, fitted into statements published after the events. Men who were on that front speak of most of the back-trenches and reserve lines as inadequate. The truth may be that no one believed the British collapse would be so swift or so catastrophic as it was.

On New Year's Day Colonel Alexander, commanding, went on leave, and was succeeded by Major R. H. Ferguson. The Battalion, reconstituted and replenished, marched to Arras Gaol, which was always regarded as a superior billet in cold weather, as the only shelling that mattered took the south-east end of the town. Their work for the next few weeks was to occupy and prevent the enemy from raiding into the system of trenches and posts on the Scarpe to the east of Arras at and round Fampoux and Rœux. Their experiences there were precisely the same as those of the 1st Battalion. It was, as we know, a variegated, swampy and in places over-looked, stretch of works which had been used as a front line almost since the beginning of the war, and was paved with odds and ends of ancient horrors as well as thoroughly soaked with remains of tear and other gas in the support-lines. Their first turn began on the 2nd January when they relieved a battalion of Gordon Highlanders in bitter cold weather, and settled down to the business of wiring and cleaning-up. A small excitement was the shelling of the left Company by trench-mortars, to which our guns replied but in their zeal cut our own wire. The frost so far kept the trenches standing up, but, as none of them were revetted, it was obvious that the next thaw would bring them all down. Then the duckboards froze and turned to ice, and the C.O., slipping on them, fell and strained himself so badly that he had to go to hospital. Food apart, there was little comfort or decency in that work of shovelling and firming dirt, and shivering day and night in their dry or sodden clothing. Their rests at Arras were complicated by the necessity of looking out for enemy aeroplanes, which forbade them drilling more than one Company at a time; and men grow vastly wearied of standing about and fiddling with small duties in a constricted town. The Battalion was so reduced in strength, too, that two Companies together made little more than an ordinary platoon. However, in spite of knowing each other to the limits of boredom, they found a certain amount of amusement in respirator drill for all cooks, Headquarters details and the like (one cannot afford to have cooks and storemen gassed) under the Company Gas N.C.O. At the end of it, the Sergeant-Major, without mask, drilled them where they stood, when their boomings and bellowings as they numbered off delighted every one. Gas was always a nuisance. Broadly speaking, a good scenting day would be good for gas, both old and new; but, without direct orders, the men loathed casing themselves in their masks, and Company Officers, sniffing the faint familiar flavour of ether or rotting leaves in Northumberland or Shaftesbury Avenue, had to chase them into the apparatus.

Then came a time when, on most of the sectors, the wet trenches went out of commission altogether, and both sides, if they wished to move about, had to climb out in full view of each other. At last, they practically abandoned the front line and fell back on the support. It made little difference, since the enemy was quiet except for occasional salvos of trench-mortar gas-bombs. Even when a dummy raid on their left caused him to put down a hot barrage for an hour, there were no casualties. The main trouble was the gas-shells in which the enemy, with an eye to the near future, specialized and experimented freely.

So passed January '18, and on the 10th February began the transfer of the newly formed 4th Guards Brigade, of three lean Battalions (2nd Irish Guards, 3rd Coldstream and 4th Grenadiers), to their new Division and companions.

The officers of the Brigade were conducted to Vimy Ridge that they might well look over the rear-line defences, in case it should be necessary to fall back there. It took them into the territory of the First Corps and a world where they were divorced from all their tried associates and had to learn the other ways that suited the other people among whom their lot would be cast. All Battalion Headquarters dined together at the Hôtel de l'Univers next day, after Brigadier-General Sergison-Brooke, commanding their old Brigade, had said good-bye and thanked them all for all they had done while they had been with him. They were played out of Barracks at Arras by the Regimental Band and the Drums of the Welsh Guards. "The

Battalion marched past our late Brigadier at the Rond Point in column of route. Thus we left the Guards Division." No one was over-elated at the change; and none could foresee that they were within a few weeks of their death as a Battalion.

Their first destination was Bray beneath the little hill above the Scarpe, south of the long pavé to Villers-au-Bois, and their first duty was rehearsal for ceremonial parade on St. Valentine's Day before their new Corps Commander. He complimented them on their looks and expressed his sense of the honour of having a Guards Brigade with him. After which came immediate conference on taking over the new ground assigned them, from strange troops of the Line. It was a sector of the line between Lens and Arras that had never shifted since the war was young – the Bailleul–Willerval stretch, about five miles north of their old sector at Fampoux, that ran up to Arleux-en-Gohelle and looked directly towards inaccessible Douai. It was worked on a different system from the old pattern – the Brigade front of 2000 yards being lightly held by widely spaced fortified posts; with a strong support-trench known as the Arleux Loop a thousand yards in the rear. Their Brigade went up in the night of the 17th, the 2nd Irish Guards in support. The enemy, quite aware there were new troops up, began to fish for samples. The 4th Grenadiers held the front line on the 19th February. The C.O. of the 2nd Irish Guards had been up that after-noon to look at the lie of the land as the Battalion were going to take over in a couple of days. Everything was quiet – too quiet to be healthy, indeed, till late in the evening when a heavy bombardment preluded a scientifically-thought-out German raid for identification purposes. It failed, for the Grenadiers dealt rudely with the raiders; but it lasted for a couple of hours from the time that the first S.O.S. was sent up, and served the Battalion, who stood to, but were not needed, as an excellent rehearsal for emergen-cies. Likewise, the enemy barrage knocked the front-line trenches about, and in the confusion of things an S.O.S. went up from too far on the left of the assaulted line, so that our protective barrage came down where there was no enemy and had to be shifted.

When the Battalion took over from the 4th Grenadiers (they could relieve all but two of the posts in daylight, thanks to the formation of the ground) Brigade Headquarters, in its turn, wanted samples from the German lines where had been recent reliefs. Nos. 1 and 2 Companies of the Battalion accordingly sent patrols unavailingly into No Man's Land to see if they could catch any one. By the sheer luck of the Irish, an enemy deserter in full uni-form must needs come and give himself up to our line in the afternoon. He was despatched at once to Brigade Headquarters with the single word: "Herewith." The quarter-mile of chaos between the lines was so convenient that they used quiet nights to train their young officers and N.C.O.'s in patrolling; and as the Brigades on their flanks were nearly half a mile away, the young also received much instruction in night-liaison work.

They were relieved, for the last time, in February by the 3rd Coldstream and sent into Brigade Reserve to their Division at Ecurie Camp till the 2nd March, when they were despatched to dig and improve a trench-line near Farbus under Vimy Ridge while the rest of their Brigade went into Divisional Reserve at Villers-Brulin. It cost a week of heavy work, after dark, under intermittent shell-fire, varied with fierce snow-storms, and ended in a return to the excellent billets of Villers-Brulin for half the Battalion, while the other half lay at Béthonsart near by – a dozen miles at the back of Arras. Here they were cleaned up, drilled and lectured while the great storm gathered along the fronts. St. Patrick's Day passed with the usual solemnities and sports, the extra good dinner and the distribution of the Shamrock. This last was almost superfluous as a large proportion of the Battalion had ceased to be Irish, and it was filled up with drafts from the Household Brigade and elsewhere.

On the 21st March they finished the finals in the Divisional sports – Tug-of-war and Boxing against the 15th West Yorkshires. At one o'clock in the morning came word that the Battalion would probably move by bus at eight directly into the battle, which promised to be hot. As a matter of fact, they and their Brigade found themselves on the outskirts of it almost as soon as they left billets. The enemy had begun a comprehensive shelling of all back-areas and they could hear the big stuff skying above them all round St. Pol. Their buses picked them up at St. Pol Fervent and headed for Beaumetz where they were met by a member of the General Staff who explained the local situation so far as they had been able to overtake it. Clearer information was supplied by the sight of the burning canteen stores at Boisleux-au-Mont, which, with vast food supplies, had been set alight as a precautionary measure, though the enemy did not arrive till some days later. There was no accurate news but any amount of rumour, none comforting. The upshot, however, was that the Thirty-first Division was to get into the line at once and hold the ground west of St. Léger, which village was already in the enemy's hands. There would be an Army Line in the neighbourhood dug to a depth of three feet – hardly what might be called a trench; but, such as it was, they would go forth into the night (it was now past 11 p.m.) and occupy it. The column departed with these instructions, marched through Hamelincourt, found the line, and settled down in the face of an agitated and noisy landscape under a sky illumined by strange lights and quivering to the passage of shell. The 4th Battalion Grenadiers was on their right and they themselves, with the 3rd Coldstream in support, held a thousand yards of front running down to the little Sensee River. Somewhere behind them was the Arras–Bapaume road being generously shelled; and somewhere in front and on the flank, felt to be all Germany with all its munitions. The shelling, moreover, was mixed, big and little stuff together, proving that the enemy field-guns were amazingly well forward. This orchestra was enlivened with blasts and rips of machine-gun fire from every unexpected quarter. All the 23rd of March was confusion, heavy shelling and contradictory orders from Brigades and Divisions that lay near them; and a certain amount of shelling from our own artillery, varied by direct attacks on the trenches themselves. In these the enemy failed, were cut down by our directed musketry, and left many dead. At the end of the day the Battalion was told to shift to the right of the 4th Grenadiers and so relieve the 13th Yorkshire and the 21st Middlesex who had suffered a good deal. They had hardly got into their new place when firing was heard from Mory on their right, and men were seen streaming down the road, with word that the enemy were through at Mory Copse and in full cry for Ervillers. This left the Battalion largely in the air and necessitated making some sort of flank to the southward, as well as collecting what remained of the Yorkshires and Headquarters details, and using them for the same purpose, much as it had been with the 1st Battalion at First Ypres, centuries ago. ("Yes, you may say that we made defensive flanks to every quarter of the world. We was *all* defensive flank and front line at one and the same time. But if any one tells you that any one knew what was done, or why 'twas done, in these days, ye will have strong reason to doubt them. We was anywhere and Jerry was everywhere, and our own guns was as big a nuisance as Jerry. When we had done all we could we fell back. We did not walk away by platoons.") They worked, then, at their poor little defensive flanks, and, between shellings, saw the enemy streaming down into the valley towards Béhagnies and Ervillers. Mory seemed to have gone altogether, and north and south of the cut and pitted hills they could hear the enemy's riot all over the forlorn Somme uplands. At evening came orders to fall back on the high ground from Courcelles to Moyenneville, three or four miles to their rear. This was none the less welcome because a battery of our own big guns had been dutifully shelling Battalion Headquarters and the Sensée valley at large for some hours past. Lieutenant Dalton and Captain the Hon. H. B. O'Brien were both wounded. There must have been a good deal of unnecessary slaughter on the Somme during those days. Gunners, of course, could not always tell whether our people had evacuated a position or were holding on; and at a few thousand yards range in failing lights, mistakes are bound to happen.

Their new position, on a front of three thousand yards, had no trenches. The C.O. himself sited for them and the men began digging at midnight on the 26th. At five in the morning they were ordered to move back at once to

. . . north and south of the cut and pitted hills they could hear the enemy's riot all over the forlorn Somme uplands. At evening came orders to fall back on the high ground from Courcelles to Moyenneville, three or four miles to their rear.

Courcelles, March 1918.

Ayette and leave what they had sketched out, for a couple of other Brigades to occupy. They next set about digging in at the southerly end of Ayette village, but as they were few, and their frontage was perilously long, could but hold the line in spots and trust to the massed fire of machine-guns on the slopes behind it, to dam back attacks.

On the afternoon of the 26th the enemy were in Moyenneville to the north-east of them; so a Company had to be despatched to dig in at the other end of Ayette and were badly machine-gunned while they worked, losing one officer and sixteen other ranks. At eleven o'clock on the morning of the 27th the enemy barraged two retiring Brigades in the trenches which the Battalion had so kindly begun for their use. At mid-day the enemy "attacked these two Brigades, who soon afterwards passed, leaving the 4th Guards Brigade once more in the line." Delicacy of diction could hardly go further. But the situation was very curious. The enemy came up; our battered troops went away. That was all there was to it. Panic and con-fusion broke out occasionally; but the general effect upon a beholder who was not withdrawing was that of the contagious "rot" that overtakes cricket and football teams. Effort ceased, but morale in some queer way persisted. The enemy after the "passing" of the two Brigades massed two Battalions by the aerodrome there, to press on the attack. Our guns had due word of it, waited till the force was well assembled, and destroyed it so utterly in a few minutes that there was no advance. Our line at Ayette was strengthened by the arrival of two Companies of Grenadier Guards and one hundred men of the East Lancashires, which were all that could be got hold of. Then – but nothing really seemed to matter in that scale of gigan-tic disaster – Colonel Alexander, their C.O., had to take command of the Brigade, as the Brigadier, Lord Ardee, had been gassed and forced to go sick. Major P. S. Long-Innes arrived at midnight of the 27th and took over command of the Battalion. On the 28th the enemy were well into Ayette and sniping viciously, and our line, intact here, be it remembered, drew back to the line of the Bucquoy–Ayette road while our howitzers from behind barraged Ayette into ruin. One Hun sniper in that confused coun-try of little dips and hollows and winding roads walked straight into our lines and was captured – to his intense annoyance, for he expected to go on to London at least.

On the 31st of March they were relieved and went to rest-billets. They had dug, wired, fought and fallen back as ordered, for ten days, and nights heavier than their days, under conditions that more than equalled the retreat from Mons. Like their 1st Battalion in those primeval days, they had lost most things except their spirits. Filthy, tired, hoarse and unshaven, they got into good billets at Chelers, just ripe for clean-up and "steady drills." The enemy rush on the Somme had outrun its own effective backing, and was for the while spent. Our line there had given to the last limits of concession and hung now on the west fringe of all that great cockpit which it had painfully won in the course of a year and lost in less than a fortnight. As far as the front could see, the game was now entirely in Hun hands. Our business, possibly too long neglected among our many political preoccupations, was to get more troops and guns into France. A draft of two hundred and twenty-four men reached the Battalion at Chelers on the 4th April, under Lieutenant Buller, who went on to join the 1st Battalion, and 2nd Lieutenant Kent. A further draft of sixty-two, nearly all English, came in on the 7th. Colonel Alexander resumed command after his turn as Brigadier, and Captain Charles Moore and Lieutenant Keenan also arrived. The former was posted to No. 1 Company for a time, pending acting as Second in Command, and the latter attached to Battalion Headquarters for the comprehensive duties of Sniping, Bombing and Intelligence. It was a hasty reorganization in readiness to be used again, as soon as the Battalion got its second wind.

VIEUX-BERQUIN

On the 9th April was a Brigade rehearsal of "ceremonial" parade for inspection by their Major-General next day. A philosopher of the barracks has observed: "When there's Ceremonial after rest and fat-up, it means the General tells you all you are a set of heroes, and you've done miracles and 'twill break his old hard heart to lose you; and *so* ye'll throt off at once, up the road and do it all again." On the afternoon of that next day, when the Brigade had been duly complimented on its appearance and achievements by its Major-General, a message came by motor-bicycle and it was "ordered to proceed to unknown destination forthwith." Buses would meet it on the Arras–Tinques road. But the Battalion found no buses there, and with the rest of its Brigade, spent the cool night on the roadside, unable to sleep or get proper breakfasts, as a prelude next morn to a twelve-hour excursion of sixty kilometres to Pradelles. Stripped of official language, the situation which the 4th Guards Brigade were invited to retrieve was a smallish but singularly complete debacle on Somme lines. Nine German Divisions had been thrown at our front between Armentières and La Bassée on the 9th April. They had encountered, among others, a Portuguese Division, which had evaporated, making a gap of unknown extent but infinite possibilities not far from Hazebrouck. If Hazebrouck went, it did not need to be told that the road would be clear for a straight drive at the Channel Ports. The 15th Division had been driven back from the established line we had held for so long in those parts, and was now on a front more or less between Merville and Vieux-Berquin south-east of Hazebrouck and the Forest of

Nieppe. Merville, men hoped, still held out, but the enemy had taken Neuf Berquin and was moving towards Vierhoek. Troops were being rushed up, and it was hoped the 1st Australian Division would be on hand pretty soon. In the meantime, the 4th Guards Brigade would discover and fill the nearest or widest gap they dropped into. It might also be as well for them to get into touch with the Divisions on their right and left, whose present whereabouts were rather doubtful.

These matters were realized fragmentarily, but with a national lightness of heart, by the time they had been debussed on the night of the 11th April into darkness somewhere near Paradis and its railway station, which lies on the line from the east into Hazebrouck. From Paradis, the long, level, almost straight road runs, lined with farm-houses, cottages and gardens, through the villages of Vieux-Berquin, La Couronne and Pont Rondin, which adjoin each other, to Neuf Berquin and Estaires, where, and in its suburb of La Gorgue, men used once to billet in peace. The whole country is dead flat, studded with small houses and cut up by ten-foot ditches and fences. When they halted they saw the horizon lit by distant villages and, nearer, single cottages ablaze. On the road itself fires of petrol sprang up where some vehicle had come to grief or a casual tin had ignited. As an interlude a private managed to set himself alight and was promptly rolled in some fresh plough. Delayed buses thumped in out of the night, and their men stumbled forth, stiff-legged, to join the shivering platoons. The night air to the east and southward felt singularly open and unwholesome. Of the other two Battalions of the Brigade there was no sign. The C.O. went off to see if he could discover what had happened to them, while the Battalion posted sentries and were told to get what rest they could. "Keep a good look-out, in case we find ourselves in the front line." It seemed very possible. They lay down to think it over till the C.O. returned, having met the Brigadier, who did not know whether the Guards Brigade was in the front line or not, but rather hoped there might be some troops in front of it. Battle order for the coming day would be the Battalion in Reserve, 4th Grenadiers on their left, and 3rd Coldstream on the right. But as these had not yet come up, No. 2 Company (Captain Bambridge) would walk down the Paradis–Vieux-Berquin road southward till they walked up, or into, the enemy, and would also find a possible line for the Brigade to take on arrival. It was something of a situation to explain to men half of whom had never heard a shot fired off the range, but the personality behind the words conveyed it, they say, almost seductively. No. 2 Company then split in two, and navigated down the Vieux–Berquin road through the dark, taking special care to avoid the crown of it. The houses alongside had been abandoned, except that here and there an old woman still whimpered among her furniture or distracted hens. Thus they prowled for an hour or so, when they were fired at down the middle of the road, providently left clear for that purpose. Next they walked into the remnants of one or two North Country Battalions lying in fresh-punched shell-holes, obviously trying to hold a line, who had no idea where they were but knew they were isolated and announced they were on the eve of departure. The enemy, a few hundred yards away, swept the road afresh with machine-gun fire, but made no move. No. 2 Company lay down in the shell-holes while Bambridge with a few men and an officer went on to find a position for the Brigade. He got it, and fell back with his Company just as light was breaking. By this time the rest of the Battalion was moving down towards Vieux-Berquin and No. 2 Company picked them up half an hour later. The Grenadiers and Coldstream appeared about half-past three, were met and guided back by Bambridge more or less into the position originally chosen. There had been some notion originally of holding a line from Vieux-Moulin on the swerve of the Vieux-Berquin road where it straightens for Estaires, and the College a little north of Merville; but Merville had gone by now, and the enemy seemed in full possession of the ground up to Vierhoek and were spreading, as their machine-gun fire showed, all round the horizon. The two Battalions adjusted themselves (they had hurried up in advance of their rations and most of their digging tools) on a line between the Le Cornet Perdu, a slight rise west of the main Vieux-Berquin road, and L'Epinette Farm. The 2nd Irish Guards lay behind them with Battalion Headquarters at Ferme Gombert – all, as has been said, in dead flat open country, without the haziest notion of what troops, if any, lay within touch.

The morning of April 12th broke hot and sunny, under a sky full of observation-balloons that seemed to hover directly above them. These passed word to the German guns, and the bombardment of heavies and shrapnel began – our own artillery not doing much to keep it down – with a careful searching of all houses and shelters, and specially for Battalion Headquarters. The Battalion, imperfectly dug in, or to the mere leeward of cottages and fences, suffered; for every movement was spotted by the balloons. The officers walking about between cottage and cottage went in even greater peril; and it was about this time that Lieutenant M. B. Levy was hit in the head by shrapnel and killed at once.

Meantime, the Coldstream on the right and the Grenadiers on the left, the former trying to work south towards Vierhoek and the latter towards Pont Rondin through the houses along the Vieux-Berquin road, were being hammered and machine-gunned to pieces. The Grenadiers in particular were enfiladed by a battery of field-guns firing with open sights at three hundred yards down the road. The Coldstream sent back word about ten o'clock that the 50th Division, which should have been on their right, was nowhere in view and that their right, like the Grenadiers' left, was in the air. Two Companies were then told off from the 2nd Irish Guards, No. 3 Company, under Captain Maurice FitzGerald, in support of the Grenadiers, and No. 2, Captain Bambridge, to the Coldstream. No. 3 Company at first lay a little in front of Ferme Gombert, one of the Battalion Headquarters. It was wiped out in the course of that day and the next, with the 4th Grenadiers, when, of that Battalion's nineteen officers, but two (wounded) survived and ninety per cent of the rank and file had gone.

No. 2 Company's road to the Coldstream lay across a couple of thousand yards of ploughed fields, studded with cottages. Their officer left his people behind in what cover offered and with a few men made a preliminary reconnaissance to see how the passage could be run. Returning to find his Company intact, he lectured them shortly on the situation and the neces- sity of "adopting an aggressive attitude"; but explained that the odds were against their reaching any destination unless they did exactly as they were told. So they advanced in four diamonds, working to word and whistle ("like sporting-dog trials") under and among and between shrapnel, whizz- bangs that trundled along the ground, bursts of machine-gun fire and stray sniping. Their only cover was a few willows by the bank of the Bourre River which made their right flank, an occasional hedge or furrow, and cottages from which they noticed one or two old women called out. They saw, in the intervals of their earnest death-dance ("It must have looked like children's games – only the sweat was dripping off us all"), cows and poultry at large, some peasants taking pitiful cover behind a fence, and a pair of plough-horses dead in their harness. At last the front was reached after only four killed and as many wounded, and they packed themselves in, a little behind the Coldstream.

The enemy all this while were well content with their artillery work, as they had good right to be; and when the Brigade tried to make an attack at eleven in the morning, checked it with machine-gun fire. One account of this period observes "there seemed to be nobody on the right or left of the Brigade, but all the morning we saw men from other Divisions streaming back." These headed, with the instinct of animals, for Nieppe Forest just behind the line, which, though searched by shell and drenched by gas, gave a semblance of shelter. Curiously enough, the men did not run. They walked, and before one could question them, would ask earnestly for the whereabouts of some Battalion or Division in which they seemed strangely interested. Then they would hold on towards cover.

("They told us the Huns were attacking. They weren't. We were. We told 'em to stop and help us. Lots of 'em did. No, they didn't panic a bit. They just seemed to have chucked it quietly.")

About two-thirty the enemy attacked, in fairly large numbers, the

Coldstream and the Division on its right, which latter gave – or had already given. No. 2 Company of the Irish Guards had made a defensive flank in view of this danger, and as the enemy pressed past punished them with Lewis-gun fire. (The German infantry nowhere seemed enthusiastic, but the audacity and bravery of their machine-gunners was very fine.) None the less they got into a little collection of houses called Arrewage, till a counter-attack, organized by Bambridge of the 2nd Irish Guards, and Foster of the Coldstream, cleared them out again. In this attack, Bambridge was wounded and Captain E. D. Dent was killed.

By dusk it would have puzzled any one in it to say where our line stood; but, such as it was, it had to be contracted, for there were not men enough for the fronts. Of No. 2 Company not more than fifty were on their feet. No. 3 Company with No. 4 were still in support of the 4th Grenadiers somewhere in front of Ferme Gombert (which had been Battalion H.Q. till shelled out) and the Vieux-Berquin road; and No. 1 Company, besides doing its own fighting, had to be feeding the others. Battalion Head-quarters had been shifted to a farm in Verte Rue a few hundred yards back; but was soon made untenable and a third resting-place had to be found – no easy matter with the enemy "all round everybody." There was a hope that the Fifth Division would that evening relieve the 2nd Irish Guards in the line, but the relief did not come; and Captain Moore, Second in Command of the Battalion, went out from Verte Rue to Arrewage to find that Division. Eventually, he seems to have commandeered an orderly from a near-by battalion and got its C.O. to put in a company next to the remnants of No. 2. All the records of that fight are beyond any hope of straightening, and no two statements of time or place agree. We know that Battalion Headquarters were shifted, for the third time, to a farm just out-side the village of Caudescure, whose intact church-spire luckily drew most of the enemy fire. No. 4 Company, under Heard, was ordered to line along the orchards of Caudescure facing east, and No. 1 Company lay on the extreme right of the line which, on the night of the 12th April, was sup-posed to run northward from Arrewage and easterly through Le Cornet Perdu, where the 4th Grenadiers were, to the Vieux-Berquin road. Whether, indeed, it so ran or whether any portion of it was held, no one knew. What is moderately certain is that on the morning of the 13th April, a message came to Battalion H.Q. that the enemy had broken through between the remnants of the Coldstream and the Grenadiers, somewhere in the direction of Le Cornet Perdu. Our No. 3 Company (Captain M. FitzGerald) was despatched at once with orders to counter-attack and fill the gap. No more was heard of them. They went into the morning fog and were either surrounded and wiped out before they reached the Grenadiers or, with them, utterly destroyed, as the enemy's line lapped round our left

175

from La Couronne to Verte Rue. The fighting of the previous day had given time, as was hoped, for the 1st Australian Division to come up, detrain and get into the Forest of Nieppe where they were holding the edge of the Bois d'Aval; but the position of the 4th Guards Brigade outside the Forest had been that of a crumbling sandbank thrust out into a sea whose every wave wore it away.

The enemy, after several minor attacks, came on in strength in the afternoon of the 13th, and our line broke for awhile at Arrewage, but was mended, while the Brigade Headquarters sent up a Trench Mortar Battery under a Coldstream officer, for the front line had only rifles. They were set between No. 4 and No. 2 Companies in the Irish Guards' line. Later the C.O. arrived with a company of D.C.L.I. and put them next the T.M.B. (It was a question of scraping together anything that one could lay hands on and pushing it into the nearest breach.) The shelling was not heavy, but machine-gun fire came from every quarter, and lack of bombs prevented our men from dealing with snipers in the cottages, just as lack of Véry lights prevented them from calling for Artillery in the night. The Australians were reported to be well provided with offensive accessories, and when Battalion Headquarters, seeing there was a very respectable chance of their being surrounded once more, inquired of Brigade Headquarters how things were going, they were told that they were in strength on the left. Later, the Australians lent the Battalion some smoke-bomb confections to clean out an annoying corner of the front. That night, Saturday 13th April, the men, dead tired, dug in as they could where they lay and the enemy – their rush to Hazebrouck and the sea barred by the dead of the Guards Brigade – left them alone.

Rations and ammunition came up into the line, and from time to time a few odds and ends of reinforcements. By the morning of April 14th the Australians were in touch with our left which had straightened itself against the flanks of the Forest of Nieppe, leaving most of the Brigade casualties, outside it. Those who could (they were not many) worked their way back to the Australian line in driblets. The Lewis-guns of the Battalion – and this was pre-eminently a battle of Lewis-guns – blazed all that morning from behind what cover they had, at the general movement of the enemy between La Couronne and Verte Rue which they had occupied. ("They was running about like ants, some one way, some the other – the way Jerry does when he's manoeuvrin' in the open. Ye can't mistake it; an' it means trouble.") It looked like a relief or a massing for an attack, and needed correction as it was too close to our thin flank. Telephones had broken down, so a runner was despatched to Brigade Headquarters to ask that the place should be thoroughly shelled. An hour, however, elapsed ere our guns came in, when the Germans were seen bolting out of the place in every direction. A little before noon they bombarded heavily all along our front and towards the Forest; then attacked the Guards' salient once more, were once more beaten off by our Lewis-guns; slacked fire for an hour, then re-bombarded and demonstrated, rather than attacked, till they were checked for the afternoon. They drew off and shelled till dusk when the shelling died down and the Australians and a Gloucester Regiment relieved what was left of the 2nd Irish Guards and the Coldstream, after three days and three nights of fighting and digging during most of which time they were practically surrounded. The Battalion's casualties were twenty-seven killed; a hundred missing and a hundred and twenty-three wounded; four officers killed (Captain E. D. Dent, Acting Captain M. B. Levy, Lieutenants J. C. Maher and M. R. FitzGerald); three wounded in the fighting (Captain Bambridge, 2nd Lieutenants F. S. L. Smith and A. A. Tindall) as well as Captain C. Moore on the 16th, and Lieutenant Lord Settrington and 2nd Lieutenant M. B. Cassidy among the missing.

Vieux-Berquin had been a battle, in the open, of utter fatigue and deep bewilderment, but with very little loss of morale or keenness, and interspersed with amazing interludes of quiet in which men found and played upon pianos in deserted houses, killed and prepared to eat stray chickens, and were driven forth from their music or their meal by shells or the sputter of indefatigable machine-guns. Our people did not attach much importance to the enemy infantry, but spoke with unqualified admiration of their machine-gunners. The method of attack was uniformly simple. Machine-guns working to a flank enfiladed our dug-in line, while field-guns hammered it flat frontally, sometimes even going up with the assaulting infantry. Meanwhile, individual machine-guns crept forward, using all shelters and covers, and turned up savagely in rear of our defence. Allowing for the fact that trench-trained men cannot at a moment's notice develop the instinct of open fighting and an eye for the lie of land; allowing also for our lack of preparation and sufficient material, liberties such as the enemy took would never have been possible in the face of organized and uniform opposition. Physically, those three days were a repetition, and, morally, a repercussion of the Somme crash. The Divisions concerned in it were tired, and "fed-up." Several of them had been bucketed up from the Somme to this front after punishing fights where they had seen nothing but failure, and heard nothing but talk of further withdrawals for three weeks past. The only marvel is that they retired in any effective shape at all, for they felt hopeless. The atmosphere of spent effort deepened and darkened through all the clearing-stations and anxious hospitals, till one reached the sea, where people talked of evacuating the whole British Force and concentrating on the Channel Ports. It does not help a wounded man, half-sunk in the coma of his first injection, to hear nurses, doctors and staff round him murmur: "Well, I suppose we shall have to clear out pretty soon." As one man said: "Twasn't bad at the front because we knew we were doing something, but the Hospitals were enough to depress a Tank. We kept *on* telling 'em that the line was holding all right, but, by Jove, instead of them comforting us with wounds all over us, we had to hold *their* hands an' comfort 'em!"

As far as the Guards Division was concerned, no reports of the fight – Company, Battalion or Brigade – tally. This is inevitable, since no company knew what the next was doing, and in a three days' endurance contest, hours and dates run into one. The essential fact remains. The 4th Guards Brigade stopped the German rush to the sea through a gap that other Divisions had left; and in doing so lost two-thirds at least of its effectives. Doubtless, had there been due forethought from the beginning, this battle need never have been waged at all. Doubtless it could have been waged on infinitely less expensive lines; but with a nation of amateurs abruptly committed to gigantic warfare and governed by persons long unused even to the contemplation of war, accidents must arise at every step of the game.

Sir Douglas Haig, in his despatches, wrote: "The performance of all the troops engaged in the most gallant stand," which was only an outlying detail of the Battle of the Lys, "and especially that of the 4th Guards Brigade on whose front of some 4000 yards the heaviest attacks fell, is worthy of the highest praise. No more brilliant exploit has taken place since the opening of the enemy's offensive, though gallant actions have been without number." He goes on to say – and the indictment is sufficiently damning – that practically the whole of the Divisions there had "been brought straight out of the Somme battle-field where they had suffered severely, and been subjected to great strain. All these Divisions, without adequate rest and filled with young reinforcements which they had had no time to assimilate, were again hurriedly thrown into the fight, and in spite of the great disadvantage under which they laboured, succeeded in holding up the advance of greatly superior forces of fresh troops. Such an accomplishment reflects the greatest credit on the youth of Great Britain as well as upon those responsible for the training of the young soldiers sent from home at the time." The young soldiers of the Battalion certainly came up to standard; they were keen throughout and – best of all – the A.P.M. and his subordinates who have, sometimes, unpleasant work to do at the rear, reported that throughout the fight "there were no stragglers." Unofficial history asserts that, afterwards, the Battalion was rather rude to men of other Divisions when discussing what had happened in the Forest.

On their relief (the night of the 14th–15th April) they moved away in

the direction of Hazebrouck to embus for their billets. There was a certain
amount of shelling from which the Coldstream suffered, but the Battalion
escaped with no further damage than losing a few of the buses. Consequently,
one wretched party, sleeping as it walked, had to trail on afoot in the direction of Borré, and those who were of it say that the trip exceeded anything
that had gone before. "We were all dead to the world – officers and men. I
don't know who kicked us along. Some one did – and I don't know who *I*
kicked, but it kept me awake. And when we thought we'd got to our billets
we were sent on another three miles. That was the final agony!"

What was left of the Brigade was next sorted out and reorganized. The
12th (Pioneer) Battalion of the K.O.Y.L.I., who had borne a good share of
the burden that fell upon our right, including being blown out of their
trenches at least once, were taken into it; the 4th Grenadiers and 3rd
Coldstream, of two weak Companies apiece, were, for a few days, made
into one attenuated Battalion. The 2nd Irish Guards, whose Companies
were almost forty strong, preserved its identity; and the enemy generously
shelled the whole of them and the back-areas behind the Forest on the
16th April till they were forced to move out into the fields and dig in where
they could in little bunches. Captain C. Moore, while riding round the
Companies with Colonel Alexander, was the only casualty here. He was
wounded by shrapnel while he was getting off his horse.

On the 17th and 18th April they took the place, in reserve, of the 3rd
Australian Brigade and worked at improving a reserve line close up to
Hazebrouck. The enemy pressure was still severe, no one knew at what
point our line might go next, while at the bases, where there was no digging to soothe and distract, the gloom had not lightened. The Australians
preserved a cheerful irreverence and disregard for sorrow, that was worth
much. The Battalion relieved two companies of them on the 19th in support-line on the east edge of the Forest of Nieppe (Bois d'Aval) which was
thick enough to require guides through its woodland rides. Here they lay
very quiet, looking out on the old ground of the Vieux-Berquin fight, and
lighting no fires for fear of betraying their position. The enemy at Ferme
Beaulieu, a collection of buildings at the west end of the Verte Rue–La
Couronne road and on the way to Caudescure, did precisely the same. But,
on the 21st April, they gassed them most of the night and made the wood
nearly uninhabitable. Nothing, be it noted once more, will make men put
on their masks without direct pressure, and new hands cannot see that the
innocent projectile that lands like a "dud" and lies softly hissing to itself,
carries death or slow disablement. Gassing was repeated on the 22nd
when they were trying to build up a post in the swampy woodlands where
the water lay a foot or two from the surface. They sent out Sergeant Bellew
and two men to see if samples could be gathered from Ferme Beaulieu. He

returned with one deaf man who, by reason of his deafness, had been sent to the Ersatz. The Sergeant had caught him in a listening-post!

Next night they raided Ferme Beaulieu with the full strength of Nos. 2 and 4 Companies (eighty men) under 2nd Lieutenants Mathew and Close. It seems to have been an impromptu affair, and their sole rehearsal was in the afternoon over a course laid down in the wood. But it was an unqualified success. Barrages, big and machine-gun, timings and precautions all worked without a hitch and the men were keen as terriers. They came, they saw and they got away with twenty-five unspoiled and identifiable captives, one of whom had been a North-German Lloyd steward and spoke good English. He told them tales of masses of reserves in training and of the determination of the enemy to finish the War that very summer. The other captives were profoundly tired of battle, but extremely polite and well disciplined. Among our own raiders (this came out at the distribution of honours later) was a young private, Neall, of the D.C.L.I. who had happened to lose his Battalion during the Vieux-Berquin fighting and had "attached himself" to the Battalion – an irregular method of transfer, which won him no small goodwill and, incidentally, the Military Medal for his share in the game.

Life began to return to the normal. The C.O. left, for a day or two, to command the Brigade, as the Brigadier was down with gas-poisoning, and on April the 25th a draft of fifty-nine men came in from home. Captain A. F. L. Gordon arrived as Second in Command, and Captain Law with him, from England on the 28th. On the 27th they were all taken out of D'Aval Wood and billeted in farms round Hondeghem, north of Hazebrouck on the Cassel road, to strengthen that side of the Hazebrouck defence systems. Continuous lines of parapet had to be raised across country, for all the soil here was water-logged. Of evenings, they would return to Hondeghem and amuse the inhabitants with their pipers and the massed Bands of the Brigade. Except for the last few days of their stay, they were under an hour's notice in Corps Reserve, while the final tremendous adjustments of masses and boundaries, losses and recoveries, ere our last surge forward began, troubled and kept awake all the fronts. They were inspected by General Plumer on the 15th for a distribution of medal-ribbons, and, having put in a thoroughly bad rehearsal the day before, achieved on parade a faultless full-dress ceremonial-drill, turn-out and appearance all excellent. ("The truth is, the way we were put through it at Warley, we knew *that* business blind, drunk, or asleep when it come to the day. But them dam' rehearsals, with the whole world an' all the young officers panickin', they're no refreshment to drilled men.")

On the 20th May, when the line of the Lys battle had come to a standstill, and the enemy troops in the Salient that they had won and crowded into were enjoying the full effect of our long-range artillery, there was a possibility that their restored armies in the south might put further pressure on the Arras-Amiens front, and a certain shifting of troops was undertaken on our side which brought the 4th Guards Brigade down from Hondeghem by train to Mondicourt on the Doullens–Arras line, where the Drums of the 1st Grenadiers played them out of the station, and, after a long hot march, to Barly between Bavincourt and Avesnes. Their orders were, if the enemy broke through along that front, they would man the G.H.Q. line of defence which ran to the east of Barly Wood, and, for a wonder, was already dug. There is an impenetrability about the Island temperament in the face of the worst which defies criticism. Whether the enemy broke through or not was in the hands of Providence and the valour of their brethren; but the Battalion's duty was plain. On the 22nd, therefore, they were lectured "on the various forms of salutes," and that afternoon selected, and ere evening had improved, "a suitable site in the camp for a cricket-pitch." Cricket, be it noted, is not a national game of the Irish; but the Battalion was now largely English. Next day Company Officers "reconnoitred" the G.H.Q. line. After which they opened a new school of instruction, on the most solid lines, for N.C.O.'s and men. Their numbers being so small, none could later boast that he had escaped attention. At the end of the month their 1st Battalion borrowed four Lieutenants (Close, Kent, Burke and Dagger) for duty, which showed them, if they had not guessed it before, that they were to be used as a feeding Battalion, and that the 4th Guards Brigade was, for further active use, extinct.

On the 9th June, after a week's work on the G.H.Q. line and their camp, Captain Nugent was transferred as Second in Command to the 1st Battalion, and 2nd Lieutenant W. D. Faulkner took over the duties of Acting Adjutant.

On the 11th they transferred to camp in the grounds of Bavincourt Château, a known and well-bombed area, where they hid their tents among the trees, and made little dug-outs and shelters inside them, when they were not working on the back defences. But for the spread of the "Spanish influenza" June was a delightful month, pleasantly balanced between digging and Divisional and Brigade sports, for they were all among their own people again, played cricket matches in combination with their sister Battalion, and wrote their names high on the list of prize-winners. Their serious business was the manufacture of new young N.C.O.'s for export to the 1st Battalion, and even to Caterham, "where they tame lions." Batches of these were made and drilled under the cold eye of the Sergeant-Major, and were, perhaps, the only men who did not thoroughly appreciate life on the edge of the Somme in that inconceivable early summer of '18.

The 14th July, the French celebration at Paris, fell just on the eve of Marshal Foch's historical first counter-attacks... the 2nd Irish Guards, entirely appreciating the comfort of their situation, despatched to Paris every member of their bureaucracy who could by any means hatch up passable excuses for helping to form the composite Battalion which should grace the festivities there.

The 2nd Battalion marching through Paris, July 1918.

The men, as men must be if they hope to live, were utterly unconcerned with events beyond their view. They comprehended generally that the German advance was stayed for the while, and that it was a race between the enemy and ourselves to prepare fresh armies and supplies; but they themselves had done what they were required to do. If asked, they would do it again, but not being afflicted with false heroisms, they were perfectly content that other battalions should now pass through the fire. ("We knew there was fighting all about an' about. We knew the French had borrowed four or five of our Divisions and they was being hammered on the Aisne all through May – that time we was learning to play cricket at Barly, an' *that'll* show you how many of us was English in those days! We heard about the old Fifth and Thirty-first Divisions retaking all our Vieux-Berquin ground at the end o' June (when we was having those sports at Bavincourt) an' we was dam' glad of it – those of us who had come through that fight. But no man can hold more than one thing at a time, an' a Battalion's own affairs are enough for one doings.... Now there was a man in those days, called Timoney – a runner – an' begad, at the one mile and the half mile there was no one could see him when he ran, etc. etc.")

The first little ripples of our own returning tide began to be felt along the Arras–Amiens line when on the 4th of July the Australians, under Lieutenant-General Monash, with four Companies of the Thirty-third American Division and many tanks, retook our lost positions round Hamel and by Villers-Bretonneux. The Battalion celebrated that same day by assisting the American troops with them (and the Guards Division) at their national game. Here the Second in Command narrowly escaped serious injury in the cause of international good-will, for a baseball, says the Diary most ungallantly, "luckily just missed him and struck a V.A.D. in the face." The views of the V.A.D. are not given.

The 14th July, the French celebration at Paris, fell just on the eve of Marshal Foch's historical first counter-attacks which, after the second Battle of the Marne, staggered the German front, when the same trees that had hidden the 1st Battalion's dead at Villers-Cotterêts, close on four years ago, covered and launched one of the armies that exacted repayment. And the 2nd Irish Guards, entirely appreciating the comfort of their situation, despatched to Paris every member of their bureaucracy who could by any means hatch up passable excuses for helping to form the composite Battalion which should grace the festivities there. The C.O. (the Second in Command had gone on already), the Adjutant, the Assistant-Adjutant, the Sergeant-Major, the M.O., the Sick Sergeant, the Orderly-room Clerk, the Signalling Sergeant, the Mess-Sergeant and all the Drums managed to get away. So Captain Nutting chaperoned the remainder down to the pleasant watering-place of Criel Plage, which is over against Dieppe. This time they were set up in business as a young officers' seminary for the benefit of newly commissioned officers who were to be taken in hand by the 4th Guards Brigade before passing on. Many of them had had considerable service in the ranks, which again required a special form of official education. They were distributed among the battalions to the number of twenty-five or thirty each, and drilled as companies. Whatever they learned, they were, beyond question, worked up to fit physical trim with the others, and, at the Guards Brigade Sports, the Battalion covered itself with glory. They won every single event that counted for points, and the Brigade Championship by an overwhelming aggregate. Next day, being the fourth anniversary of the war, they listened to a serious sermon on the matter – as they had listened to others – not much crediting that peace was in sight. Among the specialists who lectured them on their many businesses was an officer from the G.H.Q. Physical and Bayonet Training School, who spoke of "recreational training" – boxing for choice – and had a pretty taste in irony. For he told them how well some pugilists had done in the war; citing the case of an eminent professional who had been offered large purses to appear in the ring, but, feeling his country needed him, declined them all and, when the war had been going for rather more than two years, joined a select body of Cavalry, which, after another year, he discovered was not going to the Front. This so wrought on him that he forthwith gave his services to the G.H.Q. Bayonet School, where he had flourished ever since, heroically battling against stuffed gunny-bags. The Battalion held its breath at the record of such bravery; and a few days later professed loud horror at an indent which came in for a hundred and fifty men and four officers – a draft for their 1st Battalion. The Guards Division had been at work again since the 21st August on the thrice-fought-over Moyenneville–St. Léger-Mory ground, in our northern attack which had followed Rawlinson's blow round Amiens. The whole of the 4th Guards Brigade was drawn upon to help make good the wastage, and its draft of six hundred and seven men was one of the finest that had ever been furnished – trained to the last ounce, and taught to the limits of teaching. The young officers attached for instruction left after a joyous dinner that lasted till late in the dawn. And it may be that the draft had dined also; for, on the way to the station, one of our men who had lost his cap and had paraded in steel-helmet order was met by "a lady from out of a house," who solemnly presented him with the missing article. It was an omen of victory and of the days when steel helmets should become curios.

They returned to their depleted camps until more young officers came along for instruction, and in the last week of September their comrades, the 4th Grenadiers and the 3rd Coldstream, were called away to the moving front – "to fight" – as the horrified Diary puts it! Actually, the two Battalions merely followed the advance in the wake of the Cavalry Corps as mobile infantry on lorries, till the 26th of October. They then returned to their Brigade till the 14th November, when they joined the Guards Division for the march into Germany.

For the next six weeks or so, then, Criel Plage was all the Battalion's deserted own during the Autumn days that saw the German Armies driven back, but it is interesting to observe that, on the 10th of October, a special order of the day, issued by the G.O.C. Fourth Army, laid down that "all peace-talk must cease." As usual, they seemed to know more in the back-areas than at the front, where the 1st Battalion certainly did not believe in the chances of any immediate end.

On the 14th October their small world was shaken out of all its talk by the really serious news that their C.O. (Colonel the Hon. H. R. Alexander) was to transfer to command the 10th Army School. He left on the 18th, and the whole Battalion turned out to bid him good-bye with an affection few Commanding Officers have ever awakened. He wrote in orders (but he had spoken as well, straight from his heart): "I wish to express my sincere grief in leaving the Battalion I am so fond of. We have been through some hard times together, but the remembrance of those battles in which the 2nd Battalion has taken such a glorious part will always be a great pride to me. Remember the great name that this wonderful Battalion has made for itself in the war. Be proud of it and guard it jealously. I leave you with complete confidence that its reputation is safe in your hands. I thank you from the bottom of my heart for the loyalty that you have always shown me during the whole time that I have had the honour of commanding you. I wish you all and individually the best possible luck and success, and a safe return to your homes when the war is over."

It is undeniable that Colonel Alexander had the gift of handling the men on the lines to which they most readily responded; as the many tales in this connection testify. At the worst crises he was both inventive and cordial and, on such occasions as they all strove together in the gates of Death, would somehow contrive to dress the affair as high comedy. Moreover, when the blame for some incident of battle or fatigue was his, he confessed and took it upon his own shoulders in the presence of all. Consequently, his subordinates loved him, even when he fell upon them blisteringly for their shortcomings; and his men were all his own.

They wandered half round Northern France on that queer journey, halting for hours in a battered world just realizing that the weight of the past four years had lifted.

The 2nd Battalion halted in the valley of the Meuse, November 1918.

On the 26th October the 4th Grenadiers and the 3rd Coldstream returned from their adventures at the front with the Cavalry, full of their impressions that everything was over now except the shouting. Then there was more "peace-talk" than ever in the camp, and, three days after the Armistice was declared, the Battalion with the Brigade rolled statelily out of Criel for Cambrai by a "strategical" train, which is slower than a sundial. They were clean, polished and splendid to behold, and they instantly fought with Brigade Headquarters and their own Trench Mortar Battery, who had generous ideas as to the amount of truckage which they themselves required.

They wandered half round Northern France on that queer journey, halting for hours in a battered world just realizing that the weight of the past four years had lifted. Whereby everybody attended to everything except his proper job. At this distance one sees how all men were walking in a mild delirium of reaction, but it annoyed people at the time. Said one who had experienced it: "Ye would come on a man an' ask him for what ye wanted or where you was to go, an' the Frenchman, he'd say, ' Oui! Oui! Gare finnee,' an' smile an' rub his hands an' push off. The Englishman – some dam' back-area Sergeant-Clerk or ticket-collector that had been playin' ping-pong at Boulogne since '14 – he'd smile the same way an' ' 'Tis over! 'tis over!' he'd say, clean forgettin' everything for you that he hadn't done wrong-end-up. But we was all like that together – silly, foolish, an' goin' about grinnin'." At one of their many resting-places they found the 4th Grenadiers who had started four hours before them. The rail ahead was reported mined, and though the Battalion politely suggested that their friends might hurry on and test the truth of the rumour for themselves the Grenadiers declined. Men were beginning to set a value on their lives again. At ruined Cambrai, forty-eight hours after their start, they were warned to join the Guards Division, who were going to Cologne, and to travel light, as no further transport could be taken up. So they dumped surplus kit, including boots, which was a mistake, at Cambrai, and waited twenty-four hours till lorries should turn up, as guaranteed. When these at last appeared no destination was laid down, but the Guards Division was supposed to be somewhere near Maubeuge. They lost their way from Cambrai at the outset and managed to mislay no small portion of their lorries, all the Battalion, less Headquarters, and a good deal of the 3rd Coldstream, ere they reached Maubeuge, which was in the full swing of Armistice demonstrations. Their orders were to march with the 2nd Guards Brigade next day to Vieux Reng, which they did through a friendly and welcoming countryside, and on the 20th November to Charleroi through Marchienne where they were met by a mad brass band (entirely composed of men in bowler hats!). The roads filled as they went on, with returning prisoners even more compositely dressed than the natives – a general gaol-delivery of hidden, escaped, released, and all the flotsam and jetsam of violently arrested war. The customs of His Majesty's Armies were new to the world, and Charleroi did not in the least understand "saluting drill" with the Drums in the background, and when, to this marvel, was added the sight of a regiment of Grenadiers at physical drill, hopping on one foot, they assembled and shouted like the men of Ephesus.

The next move (November 24th) was to Presles on a frosty day, with billets for the officers in the superbly comfortable Château, with its pictures and wallpapers intact on the wall, handles to the doors, and roofs of flawless integrity. To wake up among surroundings that had altogether escaped the past four years was curious. ("Somehow or other, it felt like being in a shop where everything was free, and one could take down what one wanted. I remember looking at a ceiling with flowers painted on it one morning and wondering how it hadn't been cracked.") They were landed in the dull and cramped village of Lesves by November the 25th and rained upon in their utter boredom. Our national methods of conquest have nothing spectacular. They were neither talked to, sung to, nor lectured on their victory, nor encouraged to demonstrate their superiority over the rest of mankind. They marched and mourned that they had not brought spare boots. Company physical training and drills were kept up, and the sole thing approaching war was a football match of the right half-battalion against the left, which blossomed into an argument, which verged upon a free fight and, almost, the slaughter of the umpire. At Petit Han, in the remoter districts of the border where the people had accepted the Hun from the first, and had profited by his rule, the attitude of the civilians changed. Here they were prosperous pacifists who objected to militarism; even cursing and swearing and shaking their fists at the invaders. So one old lady had to be gently locked up in her own room for two hours while billets were being arranged and the officers patiently argued and entreated. Ouffey, another hamlet of a few sad houses, was of the same unaccommodating temper, and their transport turned up hours late after being delayed by traffic and bad roads. A halt was necessary here to sort out the general confusion of our brigades converging on Cologne. They were held, then, at Ouffey till the 10th December, another day at Aisomont, an unknown village, and at last on the 12th crossed into Germany from Stavelot at Pont Rucken with the Brigade. The Battalion, whose Staff never neglected their interests, had contrived to secure waterproof capes at some issue or other, which they wore under the approving eyes of the Corps Commander, who watched the march past in the unending rain. Honsfeld was their last journey afoot; there they got orders to go south to Burg and entrain for Cologne, and at Ehrenfeld, on the outskirts of that city, they dropped into the Pioneer Barracks, fitted with every luxury from electric light to drying-rooms and baths, and found the inhabitants both friendly and intensely curious.

Here some of our men noticed, first, how keenly curious were the natives to discover exactly what the strangers had in their minds, and, that point established, exactly how far they might presume upon their limitations. It was soon felt that our Armies boasted no tradition nor ritual of victory as the Germans understood it – that the utmost they could devise was some form of polite police-work and traffic regulation. So, as one observer put it – "There was Jerry takin' stock of us, under his hat-brim at the street-corners in the wet; and there was those little steamers with some of our officers in charge (an' the Irish flag flyin' at the bows of course) convoyin' prisoners an' refugees an' details an' all, up an' down that Rhine river, like pirates play-actin'! An' there was the Jerry Frowlines so polite an' anxious for to please, playin' the 'Marseillaise' an' 'God Save the King' to the officers in the evenin', an' every Jerry willin' to sell us everything he thought we'd like to buy. An' there was us Micks mountin' guard on the dumps, an' patrollin' the streets an' sittin' on machine-guns acrost bridges in that wet an' cold an' – an' 'twas all like play-actin'. Nothin' real to it at all, except the long waitin' an' we crazy to get home. Maybe the new hands an' the Cease Fire drafts liked the victoriousness of it, but for us, the old birds, that had come through great doin's for so long, 'twas not in nature, ye'll understand. All false-like, except the dam' ceremonials."

The last was quite true. The "smartening-up" that overtook both Battalions in Cologne was of a thoroughness new even to the extended experience of the "old birds." Sergeants, sickened by long months of gritty and dusty hutments that ruin the bloom and port of the ideal "soldier," with officers on the rebound from service requirements to a desperate interest in the haberdashery and appurtenances of real, and possible, life, fell upon them from either flank; while Colonels in the background and Generals on far heights proclaimed the iniquity of deviating by one hair's breadth from the highest standards of propriety in kit, conduct and bearing while they were among the late enemy. So they said, with justice, that Jerry managed to give them as much trouble when they occupied him as when he was occupying them on the Somme.

...An' there was us Micks mountin' guard on the dumps, an' patrollin' the streets an' sittin' on machine-guns acrost bridges in that wet an' cold an' – an' 'twas all like play-actin'. Nothin' real to it at all, except the long waitin' an' we crazy to get home.

2nd Battalion sentries on the Bavai Gate, Maubeuge, November 1918.

It was an insane interval of waiting, as the world did in those days, for the immediate demobilization of democratic hosts, all units of which were convinced that they had the right to go home before all others. "The prisoner at the Bar," as men then styled Germany, being entirely at home, was saving himself to continue the War underground when time, occasion and dissension among his conquerors should show him his chance. But of this there was no foreknowledge. The hearts of the men who had borne the burden were still pulsing to the thud of the guns; their minds still obsessed in their leisure by the return of horrors seen and heard; their souls crying out for something that should veil them from themselves; and at the hour when the spent world, like a spent battalion, most needed a few low-voiced, wholly unsentimental orders and an orderly return to light but continuous mechanical work, when, above all, it was in no shape to be talked at or to or over, it was delivered to whirlwinds and avalanches of allocutions, exhortations, and strenuously conflicting "ideals" that would have shaken the sanity of the gods themselves. Thus the barren months passed. The most fortunate people were those who had their hands full of necessary and obvious work – mere detail to be put through for immediate needs. "We cursed it enough at the time, but we would have given a good deal for it afterwards. You see, it kept one from thinking."

And in the Spring of '19 came the release, and the return of the Guards to England, and, on a grey March day, the Division, for the last time, was massed and moved through London, their wounded accompanying them on foot, or in the crowded lorries, while their mascots walked statelily in the intervals.

To see the actual weapons with which great works have been done is always astonishing. The stream of troops seemed scanty between the multitudes that banked it. Their faces, too, told nothing, and least of all the faces of the veterans – the Sergeants of twenty-three, and the Commanding Officers of twenty-eight, who, by miracle or the mercy of severe wounds, had come through it all since that first hot August evening, at the milestone near Harmignies, when the first bullet fell on the turf, and men said, "This is The War!" The wounded, in civil kit, having no more fear of their superior officers before their eyes, occasionally, when they shouted to a friend, gave away by unguarded tone, or change of countenance, a hint of the hells which they had shared together. And London, solid on its pavements, looked, counted over, compared, hailed, but never too loudly, some known face in the ranks or figure on horseback, and rejoiced or grieved as the fortune of war had dealt with its men. For the Guards belong to London, and, by that time, even the Irish Guards were half London recruits.

The 2nd Battalion of the Irish Guards was marked to be disbanded later, with thousands of others. Their loyalty, their long endurance, their bravery – the ceaseless labour, love and example that had gone to their making and upholding, in which work men had died as directly as any killed by gas or shell – had done all that was called for. They made no claim to have accomplished or suffered more than others. They knew what load had been laid upon all.

They were the younger Battalion, born in Warley, officered from the first by Special Reserve Officers, always most intimately bound up with their sister Battalion, yet always most strictly themselves. They had been a "happy" Battalion throughout, and, on the admission of those whose good opinion they most valued, one that had "done as well as any" in a War that had made mere glory ridiculous. Of all these things nothing but the memory would remain. And, as they moved – little more than a Company strong – in the wake of their seniors, one saw, here and there among the wounded in civil kit, young men with eyes which did not match their age, shaken beyond speech or tears by the splendour and the grief of that memory.

COMMANDING OFFICERS
2ND BATTALION

From August 16, 1915

Rank	Name	From	To
Lt.-Col.	Hon. L. J. P. Butler, c.m.g., d.s.o.	16.8.15	5.5.16
Lt.-Col.	P. L. Reid, o.b.e.	12.5.16	12.1.17
Lt.-Col.	E. B. Greer, m.c.	13.1.17	31.7.17
Major	R. H. Ferguson	1.8.17	1.10.17
Lt.-Col.	H. R. Alexander, d.s.o., m.c.	2.10.17	3.11.18
Lt.-Col.	A. F. L. Gordon, d.s.o., m.c.	6.11.18	To return to England.

OFFICERS: KILLED IN ACTION OR DIED OF WOUNDS WOUNDED IN ACTION · MISSING REWARDS

KILLED IN ACTION OR DIED OF WOUNDS

Major E. B. Greer, M.C. (Acting Lieut.-Colonel), 31.7.17
Major R. A. French Brewster (died), 17.2.17

CAPTAINS

E.D. Dent, 12.4.18

C. E. R. Hanbury, 9.10.17

The Hon H. A. V. St. G. Harmsworth, M.C., 12.2.18

LIEUTENANTS

C. H. Brew, 12.10.16
B. S. Close, 27.9.18
M. R. Fitzgerald, 19.4.18
R. H. W. Heard, M.C. (died), 3.3.19
C. G. H. C. Hyne, 21.11.16
J. Kipling, 27.9.15
J. C. Maher, 14.4.18
E. L. Mylne, M.C., 15.9.16
C. F. Purcell, 15.9.16
F. L. M. Pym, 2.7.16
G. Y. L. Walters, 15.9.16

W. G. Cary-Elwes, 27.11.17
J. W. M. Dame, 27.11.17
F. St. L. Greer, M.C., 1.2.17
D. D. Hudson-Kinahan, 9.4.16
G. L. B. James, 18.7.17
M. B. Levy, M.C., (Acting Captain), 12.4.18
H. Montgomery, 13.9.16
D. C. Parsons (Temp. Captain), 15.9.16
C. J. Pym, 27.3.17
A. J. Rowan-Hamilton, 21.10.15
F. P. H. Synge, M.C. (Acting Captain), 29.7.17
C. D. Wynter, 5.10.15

A. F. Synge, 27.11.17

2ND LIEUTENANTS

A. S. Armfield, 31.7.17
R. C. Bellew, 21.8.17
M. B. Cassidy, 13.4.18
G. V. B. Hine, 6.10.15
T. Pakenham-Law, 27.9.15
K. C. Vaughan, 13.9.16

N. D. Bayly, 27.11.17
T. A. Carey, 5.12.17
W. F. J. Clifford, 27.9.15
A. H. O'Farrell, 27.9.18
A. G. Tomkins, 13.9.16
T. B. Wilson, 18.7.17

OFFICERS ATTACHED TO 2ND BATTALION

Captain Rev. S. S. Knapp, D.S.O., M.C., 31.7.17

IRISH GUARDS OFFICERS WITH OTHER REGIMENTS

Lieut. J. N. Marshall, V.C., M.C. (Acting Lieut.-Colonel, attached Lancs. Fusiliers), 4.11.18
2nd Lieut. C. H. Eiloart (Guards Machine-Gun Regiment), 27.9.18
2nd Lieut. E. H. Fallows (att. Guards Machine-Gun Regiment), 25.3.18
2nd Lieut. A. G. Hunt (Guards Machine-Gun Regiment), 4.11.18
2nd Lieut. N. King (att. Guards Machine-Gun Regiment), 26.5.18
Lieut. C. H. Lord Settrington (died of wounds received in action with the Russian Relief Force), 24.8.19
Lieut. J. C. Zigomala, M.B.E. (killed whilst serving with the Russian Relief Force), 25.8.19

WOUNDED IN ACTION

Lieut.-Col. E. B. Greer, M.C.	28.10.14
Major R. H. Ferguson (twice w.)	31.10.14; 23.6.17
Lieut.-Col. Hon. H. Alexander, D.S.O., M.C. L. OF H. (twice w.)	1.11.14; Oct. 1917
Lieut.-Col. Hon. T. Vesey (twice w.)	31.10.14; 27.9.15
Col. Lord Ardee, C.B.	7.11.14; gassed 4.4.18
Capt. F. H. Witts, M.C. (three times w.)	25.12.14; Oct. 1917; 25.5.18
Major P. S. Long-Innes, M.C. (twice w.)	1.2.15; 15.9.16
Capt. Hon. H. A. V. St. G. Harmsworth (twice w.)	11.2.15; 2.8.15
Capt. T. E. G. Nugent (accidentally) (twice w.)	24.3.15; 3.3.16
Lieut.-Col. P. L. Reid	18.5.15
Capt. R. S. G. Paget (twice w.)	18.5.15; 18.7.17
Major G. E. S. Young (twice w.)	18.5.15; 16.3.17
Capt. Hon. W. S. P. Alexander, D.S.O.	18.5.15
Capt. A. W. L. Paget (twice w.)	19.5.15; 27.7.17
Brig.-Gen. R. J. Cooper, C.B., C.V.O. (M.E.F.)	16.8.15
W. B. Stevens	27.9.15
Capt. R. E. Sassoon M.C. (twice w.)	27.9.15; (slight) 8.9.17
R. H. S. Grayson (twice w.)	27.9.15; Oct. 1917
R. H. W. Heard	7.10.15; gassed 26.4.18
Lieut.-Col. G. H. C. Madden	11.10.15
Capt. F. P. H. Synge, M.C. (twice w.)	21.10.15; July 1916
T. F. Tallents, M.C. (twice w.)	21.10.15; Oct. 1917
Capt. G. N. Hubbard	16.11.15
H. R. Hordern (severely)	3.8.16
Capt. D. C. Parsons	13.9.16
J. C. Zigomala (twice w.)	13.9.16; 30.3.18
Capt. R. Rankin	15.9.16
Major C. E. A. Rocke, D.S.O.	15.9.16
C. H. Brew	15.9.16
M. R. FitzGerald	15.9.16
C. G. H. C. Hyne	15.9.16
T. C. Gibson (twice w.)	25.9.16; 13.9.17
Rev. F. M. Browne, M.C. (attached) (twice w.)	25.9.16; Oct. 1917
P. G. Denson	1.1.17
C. E. R. Hanbury	Jan. 1917
Capt. J. W. Dalton (twice w.)	25.3.17; 7.4.18
H. J. Lofting	18.7.17
Capt. J. B. Keenan (twice w.)	21.7.17; 21.10.18
R. L. Dagger	29.7.17
R. Hannay	29.7.17
Lieut. G. E. C. Vaughan-Morgan	July 1917
N. M. Buller (twice w.)	31.7.17; 24.5.18
G. L. Crawford	31.7.17
Capt. H. F. d'A. S. Law, M.C.	1.8.17
A. R. S. Nutting, M.C.	17.8.17
A. F. D. de Moleyns	20.8.17
J. J. Kane (slight)	8.9.17
C. E. Bagot	Oct. 1917
B. S. Close	Oct. 1917
Capt. R. B. S. Reford, M.C.	Oct. 1917
Capt. Hon. H. V. Harmsworth, M.C.	27.11.17
F. C. Lynch-Blosse	27.11.17
S. S. Wordley	30.11.17

A. F. L. Gordon, M.C.	19.1.18
S. S. Harrison	24.3.18
Capt. the Hon. H. B. O'Brien	26.3.18
D. J. B. Fitzgerald	27.3.18
C. W. Brisley	3.4.18
J. A. S. Gatti, M.C.	3.4.18
Lieut. F. S. L. Smith, M.C. (twice w.)	12.4.18; 4.11.18
Capt. G. L. Bambridge	14.4.18
G. J. S. Repton	15.4.18
A. A. Tindall	15.4.18
Capt. C. Moore	17.4.18
E. O. Mackwood (gassed)	24.4.18
P. F. O'Driscoll	25.4.18
Lieut. K. E. Schweder (gassed)	14.8.18
H. M. Henderson	10.10.18

OFFICERS MISSING

Capt. Viscount Castlerosse (wounded and since found)	1.9.14
Brig.-Gen. Hon. L. J. P. Butler, C.M.G., D.S.O. (since found)	8.9.14
J. Kipling (killed in action)	27.9.15
F. L. M. Pym (killed in action)	3.7.16
B. O. D. Manning	13.9.17
W. G. Rea	27.11.17
N. D. Bayly (killed in action)	27.11.17
M. R. FitzGerald	13.4.18
Lord Settrington	13.4.18
M. B. Cassidy	13.4.18

REWARDS

C.B.E.

Brig.-General R. Le N. Lord Ardee (Base Comdt.)	3.6.19
Colonel Sir J. Hall, Bart.	3.6.19

D.S.O.

Major H. R. L. G. Alexander	1.1.16
Captain W. S. P. Alexander	20.8.17
Colonel Hon. L. J. P. Butler	Jan. 1916
Major Hon. A. C. S. Chichester (Staff)	3.6.18
Captain A. F. L. Gordon	12.12.19
Captain W. A. Redmond	28.9.17
Lieut.-Colonel C. E. A. S. Rocke	28.12.17
Captain F. H. Witts (Staff)	2.6.19

O.B.E

Major Hon. A. C. S. Chichester (Staff)	3.6.19
Captain T. C. Gibson (Staff)	–
Lieut.-Colonel P. L. Reid (Staff)	4.6.18
Captain B. B. Watson (Staff)	10.6.20

M.B.E.

Captain J. S. N. FitzGerald (Staff)	–

MILITARY CROSS

Major H. R. L. G. Alexander	1.1.16
Lieut. E. E. Anderson	30.10.17
Captain G. L. St. C. Bambridge	13.9.18
Lieut. J. Black	30.10.17
Lieut. E. Budd	7.4.17
Lieut. W. D. Faulkner	1.1.19
Captain J. S. N. FitzGerald	—
2nd Lieut. R. Gamble	1.1.17
Lieut. J. A. S. Gatti	26.7.18
Captain A. F. L. Gordon	1.1.17
Lieut.-Colonel E. B.Greer	22.6.15
Lieut. F. St. L. Greer	14.11.16
Captain D. W. Gunston	28.10.17
Captain H. A. V. St. G. Harmsworth	1.1.18
Lieut. S. S. Harrison	3.1.18
Lieut. M. R. Hely-Hutchinson	5.6.17
Captain H. F. d'A. S. Law	5.6.17
Lieut. M. B. Levy	30.10.17
Major P. S. Long-Innes	14.11.16
Lieut. (Acting Lieut.-Col.) J. N. Marshall	7.11.18
Lieut. T. Mathew	28.9.18
Captain C. J. O'Hara Moore	26.9.18
Lieut. L. D. Murphy	10.11.18
Lieut. E. L. Mylne	14.11.16
Captain T. E. G. Nugent	30.9.18
Captain A. R. S. Nutting	31.10.17
Captain Hon. H. B. O'Brien (Staff)	26.7.18
Captain A. W. L. Paget	15.10.18
Lieut. R. H. M. Park	5.11.17
Lieut. R. B. S. Redford	23.4.18
Captain R. E. Sassoon	20.8.17
Lieut. F. S. L. Smith	26.7.18
Lieut. F. P. H. Synge	3.6.16
Captain T. F. Tallents	3.6.16
Captain F. H. Witts	1.1.17

CROIX DE GUERRE

Major Hon. C. A. S. Chichester (Staff)	16.5.19
Lieut. J. L. Lysaght	6.11.17
Lieut.-Colonel T. E. Vesey	17.8.18

APPENDIX B

REWARDS TO OFFICERS OF
THE FIRST AND SECOND BATTALIONS
Extracts from the *London Gazette*

The compiler gives below as many of the accounts of acts of bravery that won decoration, as he understands were published in the London Gazette *on various dates. These are what were known as "immediate rewards." The details of services acknowledged by decorations which did not come under this category were not given in the* Gazette.

10th March 1915	M.C. to Second Lieutenant A. C. W. Innes, 1st Battalion, Irish Guards: 'For conspicuous gallantry and ability at Cuinchy on 1st February 1915. When all the officers of the attacking company had been put out of action, this officer was sent forward to take command. Leading his men he captured the enemy's post, and then advancing a further 60 yards captured another.'
10th March 1915	M.C. to Lieutenant R. St. J. Blacker-Douglass, late 1st Battalion, Irish Guards: 'For conspicuous gallantry and devotion to duty in continuing to lead an attack after he had been wounded. He was killed in this attack.'
6th September 1915	M.C. to Lieutenant (Temp. Captain) Montague Vernon Gore-Langton, 1st Battalion, Irish Guards: 'For conspicuous gallantry on the night of l0th August 1915, at Cuinchy, when, with an orderly and one bomber, he carried out a successful and daring reconnaissance. He crawled out across a crater and discovered another crater reaching to within a few yards of the enemy's trenches. Here he was seen by a German on patrol, who came within 8 yards, when he was killed by the orderly. He still lay out, aided by Véry's pistol lights fired from his own trenches for the purpose; he examined carefully the whole of the enemy' s wire entanglements and trenches hidden behind the craters.'
31st May 1916	M.C. to Temporary Captain Philip Randal Woodhouse, M.B., R.A.M.C. (attached 1st Battalion, Irish Guards): 'For conspicuous gallantry and devotion to duty. He tended the wounded under heavy shell fire, and, though himself wounded, continued his work. On another occasion he went across the open under shell fire to attend to the wounded.'
24th June 1916	M.C. to Lieutenant Charles Richard Tisdall, Special Reserve (attached 1st Battalion, Irish Guards): 'For conspicuous gallantry. When on patrol with two men he discovered a strong enemy patrol, who evidently intended to rush an isolated post. With great determination he dispersed the enemy patrol with one of his men, after sending the other for reinforcements. His promptness in all probability saved the post.'
20th October 1916	D.S.O. to Captain the Hon. Harold Rupert Leofric George Alexander, M.C., 2nd Battalion, Irish Guards: 'For conspicuous gallantry in action. He was the life and soul of the attack, and throughout the day led forward not only his own men but men of all regiments. He held the trenches gained in spite of heavy machine-gun fire.'
11th May 1917	M.C. to Lieutenant Edward Budd, Irish Guards, Special Reserve (attached 1st Battalion): 'For conspicuous gallantry and devotion to duty. He carried out a dangerous reconnaissance under very heavy fire, and brought back most valuable information. He has on many occasions done fine work.'
8th January 1918	D.S.O. to Lieutenant (Acting Captain) the Hon. William Sigismund Patrick Alexander, Irish Guards: 'For conspicuous gallantry and

devotion to duty. Whilst leading his company in an attack he came under heavy machine-gun fire from a concrete emplacement. He immediately led a successful attack through a gap in our barrage, and outflanked three gun positions, capturing three machine-guns and fourteen men. He then continued the attack, and seized his objective within the scheduled time, in spite of having to pass through our own barrage as well as that of the enemy. He set a splendid example of fearlessness and resource.'

8th January 1918

Bar to M.C. to Lieutenant Edward Budd, M.C., Irish Guards, Special Reserve: 'For conspicuous gallantry and devotion to duty. After a personal reconnaissance of an enemy blockhouse which was harassing his front line, he made sound and skilful dispositions for its capture which was effectively carried out. The capture of the blockhouse not only relieved the front line from annoyance and loss, but enabled the whole line in this vicinity to be advanced about 200 yards. He showed very great initiative and military skill.' (M.C. gazetted 11th May 1917.)

8th January 1918

M.C. to Lieutenant Reginald Ellice Sassoon, Irish Guards, Special Reserve: 'For conspicuous gallantry and devotion to duty. During an attack, when his company was held up by hostile machine-gun fire, he organized and led a party to the capture of a concrete strong point and of a machine-gun and trench mortar. He was then subjected to machine-fire from another strong point, which he promptly and successfully attacked from the flank, capturing another machine-gun and killing and capturing several of the enemy. His dash and initiative at a critical moment were worthy of the highest praise.'

7th March 1918

D.S.O. to Captain William Archer Redmond, Irish Guards, Special Reserve: 'For conspicuous gallantry and devotion to duty when in command of a company holding a line of posts. When, following a heavy barrage, the enemy attacked in strength and a bomb fell in his post, knocking out half the occupants, he immediately led the survivors out and drove the enemy back, which enabled him to establish a new defensive line and to hold it against repeated attacks until day broke.'

6th April 1918

M.C. to Lieutenant Arthur Ronald Stansmore Nutting, Irish Guards: 'For conspicuous gallantry and devotion to duty. In spite of heavy shell fire at night he brought up the rations to battalion headquarters in the second objective, and remained there until his duty was finished. He has never failed to supply his battalion with rations in most dangerous situations.'

6th April 1918

M.C. to Second Lieutenant Eric Edwin Anderson, Irish Guards, Special Reserve: 'For conspicuous gallantry and devotion to duty when in command of his platoon. He attacked a machine-gun position, capturing the two guns, and killed all the garrison. He was responsible for capturing two more machine-guns at the first objective. He had previously carried out a very valuable reconnaissance.'

6th April 1918

M.C. to Lieutenant James Black, Irish Guards, Special Reserve: 'For conspicuous gallantry and devotion to duty as Adjutant during three days' operations. When the trenches of one of the support companies were being blown to pieces he went from Battalion Headquarters and led the company forward into a new position.'

23rd April 1918

M.C. to Second Lieutenant Ronald Hubert Mungo Park, Irish Guards, Special Reserve, attached M.G. Corps: 'For conspicuous gallantry and devotion to duty when in charge of a section of machine-guns which he established in a well-chosen position from which to bring in direct fire upon the enemy's approaches. He worked untiringly to establish a large reserve of ammunition, and when the enemy counter-attacked they were twice subjected to a heavy fire from his guns.'

23rd April 1918	M.C. to Lieutenant (Acting Captain) Robert Bruce Stephen Reford, Irish Guards: 'For conspicuous gallantry and devotion to duty. He was in command of the right flank company in an attack, and maintained the direction of the battalion under very difficult conditions. Though encountering many 'pill-boxes' and strong points, he reached his final objective.'
23rd April 1918	M.C. to Second Lieutenant Edward Murray Harvey, Irish Guards, Special Reserve: 'For conspicuous gallantry and devotion to duty when in charge of the platoon guides and the marking out of the assembly areas, which he successfully carried out under shell fire and the most trying weather conditions. He led his platoon with skill and judgement in the attack, until wounded at the final objective.'
5th July 1918	M.C. to Lieutenant Stewart Sandbach Harrison, Irish Guards, Special Reserve, attached M.G. Corps: 'For conspicuous gallantry and devotion to duty in an attack. Whilst he was in charge of a section of forward machine-guns the right flank of the line was held up by a party of enemy with several machine-guns. He rushed forward with one of his guns in front of the leading infantry under very heavy rifle and machine-gun fire and enfiladed the enemy, thus enabling the line to go forward again.'
5th July 1918	M.C. to Second Lieutenant Donald Arthur Birbeck Moodie, Irish Guards, Special Reserve: 'For conspicuous gallantry and devotion to duty. On the company commander becoming a casualty, he took command and successfully checked several enemy attempts to get round the flank of his company, which was for some hours critically situated. Later, when the trenches held by his company were attacked and entered by the enemy he directed his men with great skill and judgement, and himself fought with splendid courage and determination. '
5th July 1918	Second Bar to M.C. to Lieutenant (Acting Captain) Edward Budd, M.C., Irish Guards, Special Reserve: 'For conspicuous gallantry and devotion to duty. He led his company with great skill and judgement, and during the subsequent consolidation displayed marked ability and disregard of danger, reorganizing his own company and rendering great assistance to neighbouring company commanders. Later, when, during an enemy attack, all communications were cut, he volunteered to go up to the front line and clear up the situation. He successfully accomplished this task, in spite of continuous sniping and machine-gun fire. Throughout the operations his coolness was most marked, and his sound judgement was of the greatest help to his battalion commander.'
5th July 1918	M.C. to Second Lieutenant Cyril Elmore Hammond, Irish Guards, Special Reserve: 'For conspicuous gallantry and devotion to duty. During an attack, at a time when the position was most obscure, he was sent forward on patrol. Though under fire the whole time, and in spite of suffering several casualties, he kept his battalion commander in touch with the situation, furnishing accurate and valuable information.'
18th July 1918	M.C. to Captain the Hon. Harold Alfred Vyvyan St. George Harmsworth, Irish Guards, Special Reserve: 'For conspicuous gallantry and devotion to duty in an attack. He led his company forward under heavy fire, and himself put out of action two enemy machine-guns. It was entirely due to his splendid example that his company reached their objective.'
26th July 1918	M.C. to Captain the Hon. Henry Barnaby O'Brien, 2nd Battalion, Irish Guards: 'For conspicuous gallantry and devotion to duty. When the enemy broke the line on the right, this officer, collecting all the available men, formed a defensive flank under heavy machine-gun and rifle fire, saving the situation.'

26th July 1918	M.C. to Lieutenant Frederick Sydney Leslie Smith, 2nd Battalion, Irish Guards: 'For conspicuous gallantry and devotion to duty. Whilst in process of relief the enemy broke through on his right. Promptly realizing the situation, this officer formed a defensive flank, supervising the placing of his men under heavy machine-gun fire.'
26th July 1918	M.C. to Second Lieutenant John Augustin Stephano Gatti, 2nd Battalion, Irish Guards: 'For conspicuous gallantry and devotion to duty. After an attack by his platoon, this officer walked along the line within 200 yards of the enemy, encouraging his men in their work of consolidation, under very heavy fire, until he was wounded.'
26th July 1918	M.C. to Lieutenant Robert Henry Warren Heard, 2nd Battalion, Irish Guards: 'For conspicuous gallantry and devotion to duty. Whilst he was relieving another unit in the front line, the enemy attacked and broke through on the right, leaving the flank of this officer's company exposed. He immediately placed the men himself, under heavy machine-gun fire, to form a defensive flank, and rectified the situation.'
26th July 1918	M.C. to Captain Joseph Illingworth Lawson, R.A.M.C. (Scottish Rifles), attached 2nd Battalion, Irish Guards: 'For conspicuous gallantry and devotion to duty in bringing in wounded under heavy shell-fire, with no one between him and the enemy, thereby saving them from being made prisoners.'
16th September 1918	M.C. to 2nd Lieutenant Theobald Mathew, Irish Guards: 'For conspicuous gallantry and devotion to duty. This officer led a raid with dash and ability, its success being largely due to his leadership and example. When one of his sections was held up by a machine-gun he rushed it from a flank, putting the gun out of action and killing the gunner.'
16th September 1918	M.C. to Lieutenant (Acting Captain) George Louis St. Clair Bambridge, Irish Guards, Special Reserve: 'For conspicuous gallantry and devotion to duty. When the enemy, attacking in great strength, succeeded in driving a wedge into our line, this officer immediately led a counter-attack which was entirely successful, the enemy being driven back with loss and the line re-established. It was entirely due to his initiative and dash that the line was maintained.'
16th September 1918	M.C. to Captain Charles Joseph Henry O'Hara Moore, Irish Guards: 'For conspicuous gallantry and devotion to duty. In a situation of extreme gravity, when the troops on the right had been forced out of their trenches by the intensity of the fire, this officer collected them, leading them back through a heavy barrage to the original line, when he stayed with them, walking down the line under sniping and machine-gun fire, until their confidence had returned. His courage and coolness were an example to all.'
16th September 1918	M.C. to Captain Terence Edmund Gascoigne Nugent, Irish Guards: 'For conspicuous gallantry and devotion to duty, in going forward into the open through an extremely heavy barrage to rally some men who were falling back. He led them back into the line, and by his fearless example encouraged the troops to stiffen their resistance. His conduct throughout the operations was of a high order.'
16th September 1918	M.C. to Second Lieutenant Charles Stuart O'Brien, Irish Guards: 'For conspicuous gallantry and devotion to duty in charge of a raiding party. When the party was formed up he found that the barrage that came down at zero hour was for the greater part just beyond the enemy post. He therefore ordered his party to crawl forward until they were quite close to the post and then to charge exactly as the barrage lifted, with the result that every man of the garrison was captured without much resistance. Had he not noticed that the barrage was a little too far, and remained where he was, his party would not have arrived at exactly the right moment, and the success of the raid entirely depended upon this.'

7th November 1918	Bar to M.C. to Lieutenant (Acting Major) John Neville Marshall, M.C., Irish Guards, Special Reserve: 'For conspicuous gallantry and devotion to duty during an advance. He was ordered to take a company and two platoons and fill a gap and capture a position in the hands of the enemy. He succeeded splendidly, and, advancing further than the unit on his left, he formed a defensive flank and beat off a hostile attack. Though wounded early in the attack, his courage and fine leadership were chiefly responsible for the success of the operation.' (M.C. gazetted 1st January 1917.)
2nd December 1918	Bar to M.C. to Lieutenant (Acting Major) Thomas Francis Tallents, M.C., Irish Guards, Special Reserve, attached 4th Guards M.G.C.: 'For conspicuous gallantry and devotion to duty. When part of the line was held up and troops were finally obliged to retire to avoid being cut off, this officer carried out, at great risk, a reconnaissance, which enabled the machine-gunners to move forward with their guns and equipment. The result was that the hostile fire against the infantry was much neutralized, and a movement to cut them off stopped, with heavy loss to the enemy.' (M.C. gazetted 3rd June 1916.)
11th January 1919	M.C. to Lieutenant (Acting Captain) Daniel Joseph Hegarty, 1st Battalion, Irish Guards: 'For conspicuous gallantry in an attack. He led his company with great determination through intense artillery barrage and machine-gun fire, and finding the leading battalion held up he established and consolidated posts, thus protecting their flanks. Throughout the operations he showed marked courage and devotion to duty.'
11th January 1919	M.C. to Second Lieutenant Alan Edward Hutchinson, Irish Guards, Special Reserve, attached 1st Battalion: 'For conspicuous gallantry and devotion to duty. He reconnoitred and occupied with his platoon an enemy trench, which was to be the battalion's objective the next morning, thus assisting a tank which had to cross the railway at zero hour. Later, in an attack, he led his platoon skilfully in face of intense machine-gun fire, and although wounded gained his objective and remained during consolidation. He set a fine example of courage and cheerfulness to all under him.'
11th January 1919	M.C. to Second Lieutenant John Alexander Mulloy Faraday, Irish Guards, Special Reserve, attached 1st Battalion: 'For conspicuous gallantry and devotion to duty. He led a patrol forward some 800 yards, gained touch with the enemy, and, after pushing on a little further, consolidated his position. Two platoons were sent to support him, but were later ordered to withdraw. Under heavy artillery and machine-gun fire he maintained his position for some hours, and covered the withdrawal of the platoons before withdrawing his own party in perfect order. Though the enemy tried to cut him off, and he was badly wounded, he got his party safely back to his lines, together with four prisoners. Throughout he showed fine courage and leadership under most difficult circumstances.'
11th January 1919	M.C. to Rev. Francis Stanislaus du Moulin Browne, Army Chaplain Department, attached 1st Battalion Irish Guards: 'For conspicuous gallantry and devotion to duty during an attack. He went forward with the battalion under very heavy fire and spent the whole day tending wounded and helping stretcher-bearers to find them under machine-gun fire. He showed splendid zeal and disregard of danger.'
11th January 1919	M.C. to Captain Arthur Wyndham Louis Paget, Irish Guards, Special Reserve, attached 1st Battalion: 'For conspicuous gallantry during an attack. He led his company to their objective through intense artillery barrage, showing great courage and coolness under heavy machine-gun fire while organizing his company and consolidating his position. He also went out and helped in a wounded officer. He set a very fine example to his men.'

11th January 1919	M.C. to Captain Cuthbert Avenal John Vernon, Irish Guards, Special Reserve, attached 1st Battalion: 'For conspicuous gallantry and devotion to duty on 26th to 27th September 1918, during the attack on Flesquières. In the evening he laid the tapes to mark out the assembly positions for the battalion, only 250 yards from the front line, and directed the companies in the dark to their places. The next morning when some confusion was caused by the intense hostile barrage, he collected stragglers and reorganized the battalion on its objective.'
1st February 1919	M.C. to Second Lieutenant Patrick Redmond Joseph Barry, 1st Battalion, Irish Guards: 'For conspicuous gallantry and devotion to duty on 27th September 1918, near St. Léger. Throughout the fighting he was calm and collected, acting as Adjutant, making all arrangements and assisting in the reorganization. The next day, when there was some confusion owing to the hostile barrage at the crossing of the Hindenburg line, he did fine work in reorganizing the men and giving them the right direction.'
1st February 1919	M.C. to Lieutenant Henry Archibald Arthur Collett, 1st Battalion, Irish Guards: 'For conspicuous gallantry and devotion to duty on 27th September 1918. At the attack on Flesquières he commanded his company with skill and dash. The start was over difficult ground, the Hindenburg line having to be crossed under a heavy barrage. Although it was barely light he steadied his men and gave them the right direction, capturing the objective in spite of strong opposition.'
1st February 1919	M.C. to Lieutenant Lawrence Derek Murphy, 1st Battalion, Irish Guards: 'For conspicuous gallantry and devotion to duty on 27th September 1918, during the attack on Flesquières. Very soon after the start he was the only officer left with his company, but grasping the situation he led the men on to their objective, where he reorganized at once under deadly shell fire, and established touch with the enemy on his right. He then collected stragglers and reorganized them, showing great coolness and disregard of danger.'
1st February 1919	M.C. to Lieutenant (Acting Captain) the Hon. Bruce Arthur Ashley Ogilvy, 1st Battalion, Irish Guards: 'For conspicuous gallantry and devotion to duty, on 27th September 1918, during the capture of Flesquières and the ridge beyond. He was in command of the company that had to take the furthest objective, and got across both the Hindenburg lines and the canal without losing direction or getting behind time. He was in front the whole time, personally reconnoitring a machine-gun position and organizing its capture. He was wounded while working forward with a few men against a machine-gun nest in the Sugar Factory.'
13th February 1919	V.C. to Lieutenant (Acting Lieut.-Colonel) John Neville Marshall, M.C., late Irish Guards, Special Reserve, attached 16th Battalion, Lancashire Fusiliers: 'For most conspicuous bravery, determination and leadership in the attack on the Sambre-Oise Canal, near Catillon, on the 4th November 1918, when a partly constructed bridge came under concentrated fire and was broken before the advanced troops of his battalion could cross. Lieut.-Colonel Marshall at once went forward and organized parties to repair the bridge. 'The first party were soon killed or wounded, but by personal example he inspired his command and volunteers were instantly forthcoming. Under intense fire and with complete disregard of his own safety, he stood on the bank encouraging his men and assisting in the work, and when the bridge was repaired attempted to rush across at the head of his battalion and was killed while so doing. 'The passage of the canal was of vital importance, and the gallantry displayed by all ranks was largely due to the inspiring example set by Lieut.-Colonel Marshall.'

APPENDIX C

W.O.s, N.C.O.s AND MEN
KILLED IN ACTION OR DIED
OF WOUNDS OR DISEASE

Agnew, Charles, 7890, Pte., *k. in a. 13.9.16*
Ahern, Joseph, 6728, Pte., *k. in a. 31.7.17*
Akerman, Fred A., 12350, Pte., *k. in a. 14.4.18*
Ardick, Daniel, 4942, Pte., *d. of w. 27.11.17*
Arkins, Bernard, 3931, Pte., *d. of w. 1.8.17*
Armstrong, James H., 6882, Pte., *d. of w. 2.10.15*
Armstrong, William, 6157, Pte., M.M., *k. in a. 3.5.18*
Artes, George, 8800, Pte., *d. 9.1.19*
Ashmore, Luke, 8815, Pte., *d. 3.9.15*
Attridge, Bart, 8614, Pte., *k. in a. 13.9.16*
Aylward, Edward, 2255, Pte., *d. 28.10.18*
Baines, James, 12235, Pte., *k. in a. 12.4.18*
Bannon, John, 9809, Pte., *k. in a. 27.11.17*
Bannon, Michael, 6880, Pte., *k. in a. 27.9.15*
Barran, Herbert P., 12620, Pte., *d. of w. 29.3.18*
Barry, John, 7579, Pte., *k. in a. 17.3.17*
Barry, Patrick, 7125, Pte., *d. of w. 9.10.15*
Barter, Richard W., 7463, Pte., *k. in. a. 8.10.15*
Beglan, Michael, 7108, Pte., *k. in a. 14.10.15*
Bell, George R., 6270, Pte., *k. in a. 21.1.18*
Bell, Henry, 8628, Pte., *k. in a. 15.9.16*
Bell, James, 8003, Pte., *k. in a. 25.6.17*
Benn, Arthur, 9254, Pte., *d. of w. 26.9.16*
Bennett, Edward, 12334, Pte., *d. of w. 8.5.18*
Bennett, William, 12813, Pte., *d. of w. 28.4.18*
Benson, John, 8161, L.-Cpl., *k. in a. 13.4.18*
Birmingham, Thomas, 10811, Pte., *k. in a. 31.7.17*
Blackwood, Joseph, 8021, Pte., *d. of w. 30.3.18*
Bodie, Thomas, 8200, Pte., *k. in a. 15.9.16*
Boland, John, 7310, L.-Sgt., *k. in a. 31.7.17*
Boulton, Percy, 10658, Pte., *k. in a. 27.11.17*
Boyd, John, 2641, Pte., *d. 3.3.18*
Boyd, William, 6453, L.-Sgt., *d. of w. 6.10.15*
Boyle, Thomas J., 6666, Pte., *k. in a. 13.9.16*
Boyton, Robert, 7967, Pte., M.M. and bar, *k. in a. 23.4.18*
Bradley, John, 6454, L.-Sgt., *d. of w. 4.10.15*
Brady, James, 3881, L.-Sgt., *d. 10.10.18*
Brady, Michael, 9219, Pte., *k. in a. 27.11.17*
Brady, Simon, 5255, Pte., *k. in a. 17.3.17*
Branagan, Eugene, 10041, Pte., *k. in a. 25.7.17*
Branigan, Henry, 4633, *d. 15.12.15*
Bransfield, Richard, 8918, Pte., *k. in a. 27.11.17*
Bridges, William D., 7368, L.-Cpl., *k. in a. 28.9.15*
Brien, John J., 6268, Pte., *k. in a. 29.3.18*
Brien, John, 7028, Pte., *d. of w. 8.9.17*
Brophy, James, 7212, Pte., *k. in a. 21.10.15*
Brown, James, 5589, Pte., *d. of w. 23.10.15*
Browne, Michael, 7171, Pte., *k. in a. 16.4.18*

Buckley, Jeremiah, 8293, Pte., *d. of w. 17.9.16*
Bullen, Robert, 6341, Pte., *k. in a. 30.9.15*
Burchill, George T., 12650, Pte., *d. of w. 14.4.18*
Burke, Edward, 9315, Pte., *k. in a. 15.9.16*
Burke, John, 6039, Pte., *k. in a. 30.9.15*
Burke, Peter, 9186, Pte., *d. of w. 10.8.17*
Burney, Daniel J., 8015, Pte., *k. in a. 13.9.17*
Butler, William, 7404, Pte., *k. in a. 15.9.16*
Buttimer, William, 10455, L.-Cpl., *d. of w. 30.6.17*
Byers, Thomas, 7207, Pte., *d. of w. 24.11.15*
Byrne, John M., 6374, Pte., *k. in a. 28.9.16*
Byrne, John, 8789, Pte., *k. in a. 23.3.18*
Byrne, John, 11192, Pte., *d. of w. 2.8.17*
Byrne, John, 11664, Pte., *k. in a. 31.7.17*
Byrne, Peter, 6723, L.-Cpl., *k. in a. 20.6.16*
Byrne, Robert, 7033, L.-Cpl., *k. in a. 27.9.16*
Cafferty, Patrick, 6553, L.-Cpl., *k. in a. 15.9.16*
Cagney, Cornelius, 8084, Pte., *k. in a. 15.9.16*
Cahill, Maurice, 6494, Pte., *k. in a. 5.11.15*
Cahill, Michael, 6950, Pte., *k. in a. 27.9.15*
Caldwell, Stephen, 6175, Pte., *d. of w. 17.9.16*
Callaghan, John, 7422, Pte., *k. in a. 18.10.15*
Callaghan, Thomas, 7711, Pte., *k. in a. 15.9.17*
Callaghan, Thomas, 9914, Pte., *k. in a. 22.5.18*
Callaghan, William, 11167, Pte., *k. in a. 12.4.18*
Cantwell, Henry, 9438, Pte., *k. in a. 9.10.17*
Carley, Joseph, 6380, Pte., *d. 3.10.16*
Carolan, Terence, 5531, L.-Cpl., *k. in a. 31.7.17*
Carr, Edmund H., 6098, L.-Cpl., *k. in a. 27.11.17*
Carroll, Edward F., 6495, Pte., *k. in a. 15.9.16*
Carroll, Edward 7178, Pte., *d. of w. 1.10.16*
Carson, John, 7170, Pte., *k. in a. 27.9.16*
Casey, John, 2810, Pte., *d. of w. 3.7.16*
Casey, John E., 5225, L.-Sgt., *k. in a. 30.9.15*
Casey, Thomas, 3267, Pte., *k. in a. 14.9.16*
Cassidy, Thomas, 4990, Pte., *k. in a. 2.7.16*
Cavanagh, John, 8159, Pte., *k. in a. 15.9.16*
Cavanagh, John H., 10578, Pte., *d. of w. 23.7.17*
Cawley, John, 3659, Pte., M.M., *k. in a. 27.11.17*
Cawley, Michael, 11266, Pte., *k. in a. 27.3.18*
Cawley, Patrick, 9708, Pte., *k. in a. 31.7.17*
Chapman, William, 11680, Pte., *k. in a. 27.11.17*
Childs, James, 9912, Pte., *k. in a. 27.9.16*
Chism, Patrick, 4800, Pte., *k. in a. 27.11.17*
Clarke, John, 6870, Pte., *k. in a. 13.9.16*
Clarke, John, 7811, Pte., *k. in a. 13.9.16*
Clarke, Michael, 8473, Pte., *k. in a. 27.11.17*
Clarke, Thomas, 7114, Pte., *k. in a. 30.9.15*
Clarke, Thomas, 9125, Pte., *d. 13.6.17*
Clarkin, Patrick, 6719, Pte., *k. in a. 30.9.15*

Clyne, James, 8043, Pte., *k. in a. 19.10.15*
Coghlin, Michael, 7546, L.-Cpl., *k. in a. 14.3.17*
Colclough, Henry W., 5768, Pte., *k. in a. 14.9.17*
Colclough, Michael, 6908, L.-Cpl., *d. of w.
1.10.15*
Collins, Thomas, 9724, Pte., *d. of w. 1.8.17*
Collis, John, 7885, Pte., *d. of w. 22.9.16*
Coman, Michael, 10460, Pte., *k. in a. 25.6.17*
Conachy. Thomas, 12199, Pte., *k. in a. 26.3.18*
Connell, Lawrence, 6948, Pte., *k. in a. 27.9.15*
Connolly, James, 6452, L.-Sgt., *k. in a. 23.3.18*
Connolly, James, 9035, Pte., *k. in a. 10.4.16*
Connolly, Peter, 11622, Pte., *k. in a. 12.4.16*
Connolly, Peter, 11974, Pte., *k. in a. 27.11.17*
Connor, Thomas, 6679, Pte., *k. in a. 15.9.16*
Conroy, Michael, 7313, Pte., *k. in a. 31.7.17*
Conroy, Michael, 7322, Pte., *k. in a. 14.4.18*
Conway, Martin, 541, Pte., *k. in a. 30.9.15*
Cooke, John, 5445, Pte., *d. of w. 31.7.17*
Corbett, James, 10386, Pte., *k. in a. 31.7.17*
Corcoran, Richard, 10735, Pte., *d. of w. 28.9.16*
Corcoran, Thomas, 6687, Pte., *k. in a. 9.10.17*
Corcoran, Thomas, 10189, L.-Cpl., *d. of w.
28.11.17*
Corhill, Robert H., 11817, Pte., *k. in a. 27.11.17*
Corr, Simon, 9079, Pte., *k. in a. 27.11.17*
Corrigan, John, 4590, Sgt., *k. in a. 15.9.16*
Costello, Hugh, 8870, Pte., *k. in a. 9.10.17*
Costello, John, 9034, Pte., *k. in a. 13.9.16*
Costley, Edmund, 8594, Pte., *k. in a. 9.4.16*
Cotter, Harry, 7268, Pte., *d. of w. 11.10.15*
Coulter, Alexander, 3473, Pte., *k. in a. 21.7.17*
Courtney, Patrick, 11902, Pte., *k. in a. 12.4.18*
Cox, Eugene, 11519, Pte., *d. of w. 15.12.17*
Cox, Frank, 11845, Pte., *k. in a. 27.11.17*
Cronin, John, 5011, Pte., *k. in a. 13.9.16*
Cronin, John, 7505, Pte., *k. in a. 7.10.15*
Cryan, Patrick, 2679, Pte., *k. in a. 13.9.16*
Culhane, Timothy, 10532, Pte., *k. in a. 31.7.17*
Cullen, John, 10711, Pte., *d. of w. 11.10.17*
Cullen, John, 2670, Pte., *k. in a. 27.11.17*
Cullen, Sidney H., 7703, Pte., *k. in a. 15.9.16*
Culver, Joseph, 10601, Pte., *k. in a. 9.10.17*
Cummins, Denis, 5492, L.-Cpl., *k. in a. 15.9.16*
Cummins, John, 8139, Pte., *k. in a. 13.9.16*
Cunningham, John, 8309, Pte., *k. in a. 5.11.15*
Cunningham, William, 10917, Pte., *k. in a.
23.3.18*
Curran, Lawrence, 9372, Pte., *k. in a. 31.7.17*
Curran, Michael, 6619, Pte., *d. of w. 15.9.16*
Curtayne, Richard, 7649, Pte., *k. in a. 15.9.16*
Curtin, Lawrence, 8510, Pte., *d. of w. 27.11.17*
Cusack, Patrick J., 10220, Pte., *d. of w. 17.10.17*
Daley, Thomas J., 11635, Pte., *k. in a. 31.7.17*
Dalkin, William H., 8521, Pte., *k. in a. 15.9.16*
Daly, James, 6523, Pte., M.M, *d. of w. 30.3.18*
Daly, Michael, 6623, L.-Cpl., *d. 2.1.17*
Daly, Michael, 8291, Pte., *d. of w. 29.5.18*
Daly, Michael, 8984, L.-Sgt., *k. in a. 16.3.17*
Daly, Patrick, 8857, Pte., *k. in a. 13.9.17*
Dannaher, William, 7529, Pte., *d. 19.7.17*
Darmody, Jeremiah, 7329, L.-Sgt., *k. in a.
13.9.16*

Davin, Thomas, 10568, Pte., *k. in a. 31.7.17*
Davis, John G., 11640, Pte., *k. in a. 9.10.17*
Delahunty, John, 8073, Pte., *k. in a. 15.9.16*
Delahunty, John, 10793, Pte., *k. in a. 9.10.17*
Delaney, Morgan, 7197, L.-Cpl., *k. in a. 18.5.16*
Dempsey, Michael, 1818, Pte., *k. in a. 30.7.17*
Dempsey, Patrick, 9548, Pte., *k. in a. 15.9.16*
De Renzy, Richard, 8804, Pte., *k. in a. 12.9.17*
Devine, William, 10607, Pte., *k. in a. 27.9.16*
Deviney, William, 7824, Pte., *k. in a. 27.11.17*
Devlin, James, 8683, Pte., *k. in a. 12.9.17*
Diamond, James, 12139, Pte., *k. in a. 27.11.17*
Docherty, Michael, 6491, L.-Cpl., *k. in a. 27.9.15*
Docherty, Rodger, 6721, L.-Cpl., *k. in a. 15.9.16*
Docherty, William, 6388, Pte., *d. of w. 19.9.17*
Doherty, James, 6918, L.-Cpl., *k. in a. 12.4.18*
Doherty, William J., 8449, Pte., *k. in a. 15.9.17*
Donnellan, John, 8489, Pte., *k. in a. 31.7.17*
Donnelly, Miles, 10844, Pte., *k. in a. 12.4.18*
Donohoe, Francis, 8379, Pte., *k. in a. 6.3.17*
Donohoe, John, 11253, Pte., *k. in a. 21.7.17*
Donohoe, Thomas, 11353, Pte., *d. of w. 7.8.17*
Donohue, John J., 10741, Pte., *k. in a. 22.11.17*
Donovan, Michael, 2646, L.-Cpl., *k. in a. 13.9.16*
Donovan, Patrick, 8879, Pte., *k. in a. 2.7.16*
Doonan, James L., 6896, L.-Sgt., *k. in a. 13.9.16*
Dooley, James, 9075, L.-Cpl., *k. in a. 9.10.17*
Dooley, John, 2331, L.-Cpl., *k. in a. 31.7.17*
Dooley, John, 10479, Pte., *k. in a. 31.7.17*
Dowd, Patrick, 5102, L.-Cpl., *d. 29.7.16*
Dowling, Albert M., 10130, L.-Cpl., *k. in a.
9.10.17*
Dowling, Edward, 7077, Pte., *k. in a. 15.9.16*
Dowling, Michael, 6221, Pte., *d. 10.12.17*
Doyle, John, 5907, Pte., *k. in a. 26.9.16*
Doyle, Martin, 6547, Pte., *k. in a. 28.9.15*
Doyle, Michael, 7793, Pte., *k. in a. 27.9.16*
Doyle, Thomas, 6622, Pte., *k. in a. 8.10.15*
Dreeling, Nicholas, 7071, Pte., *k. in a. 9.10.17*
Drennan, Joseph, 9795, Pte., *k. in a. 24.7.19*
Duffy, Patrick, 8849, Pte., *k. in a. 24.3.18*
Duffy, Patrick, 10814, Pte., *k. in a. 15.9.17*
Duffy, Thomas, 5965, Pte., *k. in a. 27.11.17*
Duggan, Patrick, 11662, Pte., *k. in a. 13.9.17*
Duncan, Kiernan, 8329, Pte., *d. of w. 20.6.17*
Dunlea, John, 8531, Pte., *k. in a. 28.3.18*
Dunleavy, Patrick, 10664, Pte., *k. in a. 27.11.17*
Dunne, Edward, 11574, Pte., *k. in a. 13.9.17*
Dunne, James, 6353, Pte., *k. in a. 27.9.18*
Dunne, John, 7180, Pte., *k. in a. 31.7.17*
Dunne, Thomas, 9506, Pte., *k. in a. 31.7.17*
Dwyer, Edward, 9508, Pte., *k. in a. 20.11.16*
Dyra, John, 6765, Pte., *k. in a. 15.9.16*
Early, John J., 10355, Pte., *k. in a. 27.11.17*
Eagleton, Thomas, 6379, L.-Cpl., *d. of w.
5.12.17*
Edney, Bernard, 4878, L.-Sgt., *k. in a. 30.9.15*
Egan, Thomas, 6399, L.-Cpl., *k. in a. 27.11.17*
Egan, William C., 7462, L.-Cpl., *k. in a.
27.11.17*
Egan, William, 7884, Pte., *d. of w. 21.10.15*
Elliott, Andrew, 11205, Pte., *k. in a. 7.3.17*
Elliott, John B., 12628, Pte., *k. in a. 27.3.18*

Ellis, Thomas, 6438, Pte., *k. in a. 15.9.16*
Ennis, James, 7470, Pte., *k. in a. 19.10 15*
Ennis, Patrick, 4983, L.-Cpl., *k. in a. 15.9.16*
Eustace, Robert, 8608, Pte., *k. in a. 14.9.16*
Evans, John, 6031, Pte., *k. in a. 27.11.17*
Fagan, John, 8124, Pte., *k. in a. 16.9.16*
Fanning, James, 4075, Pte., *k. in a. 14.4.18*
Fanning, William, 10868, Pte., *k. in a. 31.7.17*
Farrell, Francis, 6698, Sgt., M.M., *d. of w. 19.4.18*
Feenick, James, 10261, Pte., *d. of w. 25.4.18*
Ferguson, William, 7480, Pte., *k. in a. 15.9.16*
Finlay, Owen M., 10182, L.-Cpl., *k. in a. 13.4.18*
Fitzgerald, John, 9824, Pte., *k. in a. 27.6.17*
Fitzgerald, Michael, 7556, Pte., *d. of w. 21.10.15*
Fitzhenry, Thomas, 7110, Pte., *d. 18.8.18*
Fitzpatrick, Christopher, 6961, Pte., *d. of w. 30.9.15*
Fitzpatrick, James, 7601, Pte., *k. in a. 15.9.16*
Fitzpatrick, Peter, 7146, L.-Cpl., *k. in a. 27.11.17*
Flanders, Walter, 12751, Pte., *k. in a. 12.4.18*
Fleming, Patrick C., 10912, Pte., *k. in a. 12.1.17*
Flood, Thomas, 10901, L.-Cpl., *k. in a. 31.7.17*
Flynn, Joseph, 6257, Pte., *d. of w. 24.10.15*
Flynn, James, 11257, Pte., *d. of w. 4.12.17*
Flynn, Michael, 7080, Pte., *d. of w. 2.3.16*
Flynn, Patrick, 6923, L.-Cpl., *k. in a. 14.9.16*
Flynn, Thomas, 10278, Pte., *d. of w. 13.8.17*
Fogarty, John, 8863, Pte., *d. of w. 25.10.16*
Foley, Timothy, 8218, L.-Sgt., *k. in a. 13.4.18*
Foster, Thomas M., 10205, Pte., *k. in a. 27.6.17*
Fox, Thomas, 6520, Pte., *d. of w. 21.10.15*
Freeman, James, 1962, Pte., *k. in a. 13.9.16*
Freyne, Patrick, 8236, Pte., *k. in a. 27.9.16*
Frizelle, William R., 9573, L.-Cpl., *k. in a. 13.4.18*
Gallagher, George, 9128, Pte., *k. in a. 22.6.17*
Gallagher, Thomas, 7595, Pte., *k. in a. 31.7.17*
Gannon, Thomas, 9898, Pte., *k. in a. 22.6.17*
Garven, Peter, 8450, Pte., *d. 1.3.17*
Garner, Hugh, 8518, Pte., *k. in a. 15 9.16*
Gaughan, John, 8610, Pte., *k. in a. 27.3.18*
Gault, Hugh, 6142, Pte., *k. in a. 28.3.18*
Gennoy, Michael, 9727, Pte., *k. in a. 25.6.17*
Gibbie, Robert, 9245, Pte., *k. in a. 9.10.17*
Gilbert, Charles, 6422, Pte., *d. 18.3.16*
Gilbert, Henry N., 9763, L.-Cpl., *d. of w. 16.4.18*
Gilmore, Boyce, M., 6770, L.-Cpl., *k. in a. 30.9.15*
Gilroy, James, 12393, Pte., *k. in a. 13.4.18*
Glennon, Thomas H., 6771, Sgt., *k. in a. 20.11.16*
Glynn, John J., 3303, Sgt., D.C.M., *k. in a. 16.9.16*
Goggan, James, 12219, Pte., *k. in a. 12.4.18*
Goggin, Michael, 8649, Pte., *k. in a. 15.9.16*
Golding, William, 10946, Pte., *d. of w. 27.3.18*
Gooding, John S., 5194, Pte., *k. in a. 19.7.17*
Gordon, John, 6996, Pte., *k. in a. 8.10.15*
Gorham, Owen, 10387, Pte., *k. in a. 31.7.17*
Gould, Patrick, 6949, Pte., *k. in a. 29.9.15*
Grace, James, 4794, Pte., *d. 20.7.17*

Graham, Andrew, 11524, Pte., *d. of w. 1.5.18*
Grainger, Maurice J., 7972, Pte., *k. in a. 21.10.15*
Grant, Patrick, 7482, Pte., *k. in a. 15.9.16*
Gray, Thomas, 8583, Pte., *d. 2.12.18*
Green, James, 6677, Pte., *k. in a. 27.9.15*
Green, John, 5838, L.-Cpl., *k. in a. 13.9.16*
Griffin, John, 3644, L.-Sgt., *k. in a. 5.9.16*
Grimwood, William, 3081, C.S.M., *k. in a. 20.7.17*
Guilfoyle, John, 6691, Pte., *k. in a. 27.9.15*
Guy, William, 11691, Pte., *k. in a. 9.10.17*
Hagan, Edward, 5119, Pte., *k. in a. 31.7.17*
Hagerty, James, 8197, Pte., *d. of w. 14.9.16*
Hain, Robert, 12057, Pte., *k. in a. 12.4.18*
Halliday, John, 6866, L.-Cpl., *d. of w. 5.4.16*
Hamilton, Charles, 11393, Pte., *d. of w. 4.4.18*
Hamilton, James, 4372, Pte., *d. of w. 6.10.15*
Hanley, John, 9665, L.-Cpl., *k. in a. 29.1.18*
Hannon, Frank, 6984, Pte., *k. in a. 13.9.17*
Hanrahan, John, 11002, Pte., *k. in a. 31.7.17*
Harfitt, Henry, 11302, Pte., *d. 1.8.17*
Harrold, William, 6772, Pte., *k. in a. 30.9.15*
Harte, John J., 6773, L.-Sgt., *k. in a. 19.11.15*
Harty, John, 7469, Pte., *k. in a. 30.7.17*
Haughey, John, 8890, Pte., *k. in a. 13.4.18*
Hawe, Michael, 4730, Sgt., *k. in a. 27.11.17*
Hayes, James, 7818, L.-Cpl., *d. of w. 1.3.17*
Hayes, Patrick, 6245, L.-Sgt., *k. in a. 15.9.16*
Hays, Archibald, 8204, L.-Sgt., *k. in a. 31.7.17*
Healey, Francis, 11093, Pte., *k. in a. 27.11.17*
Healey, Joseph, 4742, Pte., *d. of w. 21.4.16*
Healy, Michael J., 7970, Pte., *k. in a. 13.9.16*
Heaphy, William H., 3236, Pte., *d. of w. 7.5.16*
Henaghan, Patrick, 10158, Pte., *k. in a. 3.8.17*
Heneghan, Simon, 8306, L.-Cpl., *k. in a. 9.10.17*
Henry, John, 4906, Pte., D.C.M., *d. of w. 27.11.17*
Henry, Peter, 8227, Pte., *d. of w. 1.8.17*
Heydon, Aloysius, 8453, Pte., *k. in a. 27.11.17*
Hickey, John, 8427, Pte., *d. of w. 9.7.17*
Higgins, Michael, 7493, L.-Cpl., M.M., *k. in a. 15.9.16*
Higgins, William, 2445, Sgt., *k. in a. 21.10.15*
Hill, Joseph L. F., 7780, L.-Sgt., *d. of w. 13.4.18*
Hill, William, 6900, Pte., *k. in a. 7.10.15*
Hilley, Patrick, 6015, Pte., *d. 7.11.18*
Hinds, John J., 11153, Pte., *d. of w. 1.8.17*
Hoban, Gregory, 11671, Pte., *k. in a. 13.9.17*
Hogan, Frank, 7269, Pte., *k. in a. 15.9.16*
Hogan, William, 10396, Pte., *k. in a. 27.11.17*
Holden, Henry, 12786, Pte., *k. in a. 13.4.18*
Horan, William, 6924, Pte., *k. in a. 2.7.16*
Horgan, William, 6391, Pte., *k. in a. 16.11.15*
Houlihan, Michael, 7835, Pte., *d. of w. 18.9.16*
Howard, William, 12753, Pte., *k. in a. 12.4.18*
Howlett, Martin, 9142, Pte., *k. in a. 31.7.17*
Hudson, George, 12591, Pte., *k. in a. 27.3.18*
Hughes, Patrick, 6555, L.-Cpl., *k. in a. 19.10.15*
Hughes, Patrick, 9297, Pte., *k. in a. 13.9.16*
Hughes, William, 8445, Pte., *k. in a. 27.11.17*
Humphreys, James, 8818, Pte., *k. in a. 13.4.18*
Hurley, Patrick, 6722, L.-Cpl., *k. in a. 30.9.15*

Hussey, John, 7863, Pte., *k. in a. 13.9.16*
Hutchinson, Martin, 6982, Pte., *k. in a. 13.9.16*
Hutchinson, William, 6778, L.-Cpl., *d. of w. 27.9.15*
Hutton, John, 10886, Pte., *k. in a. 27.11.17*
Hyde, John, 7600, L.-Cpl., *d. 5.11.15*
Irwin, Thomas, 5595, Pte., *k. in a. 3.8.17*
Jeffs, Arthur, 12085, Pte., *d. of w. 25.4.18*
Jennings, Thomas, 8010, L.-Cpl., *k. in a. 15.9.16*
Jolly, Thomas, 7116, Pte., *k. in a. 27.9.15*
Jordan, Stephen, 8248, Pte., *k. in a. 31.7.17*
Joyce, Michael, 9296, Pte., *k. in a. 13.9.16*
Keaney, Terence, 9694, Pte., *k. in a. 27.9.16*
Kearney, John, 9384, Pte., *d. of w. 1.8.17*
Kearns, John, 7816, Pte., *d. of w. 15.9.16*
Keating, Arthur, 6289, Pte., *k. in a. 28.9.15*
Keating, John, 6316, Pte., *k. in a. 30.9.15*
Keaveny, Patrick, 11495, Pte., *k. in a. 27.11.17*
Keegan, John, 9801, Pte., *k. in a. 13.4.18*
Keelan, Joseph, 11545, Pte., *k. in a. 28.3.18*
Kelleher, Denis, 5103, Pte., *k. in a. 12.1.16*
Kelleher, Denis, 8323, Pte., *d. 24.3.16*
Kelleher, Mortimer, 7545, Pte., *k. in a. 2.7.16*
Kelly, Edward, 11034, L.-Cpl., *k. in a. 12.4.18*
Kelly, Henry, 5457, Pte., *k. in a. 31.7.17*
Kelly, Joseph, 11522, Pte., *d. of w. 31.3.18*
Kelly, Martin, 8905, Pte., *k. in a. 27.11.17*
Kelly, Patrick J., 10266, L.-Cpl., *k. in a. 27.6.17*
Kelly, Simon, 10703, Pte., *k. in a. 26.9.16*
Kelly Thomas, 4084, Pte., *k. in a. 28.9.15*
Kelly Thomas, 8407, Pte., *k. in a. 15.9.16*
Kelly, William, 7405, Pte., *k. in a. 30.9.15*
Kenefick, Edward, 8110, Pte., *d. of w. 25.12.16*
Keniry, John, 2746, Sgt., M.M., *k. in a. 27.11.17*
Kennedy, Michael, 12362, Pte., *k. in a. 12.4.18*
Kenny, Cornelius, 8320, Pte., *d. of w. 15.9.17*
Kenny, John, 4955, Pte., *k. in a. 12.9.17*
Keogan, Horace J., 6998, Pte., *k. in a. 27.9.15*
Keogh, James 6542, Pte., *k. in a. 20.5.16*
Keogh, James 7384, Pte., *k. in a. 13.9.16*
Keogh, Joseph, 7518, Pte., *k. in a. 19.5.16*
Keppel, Edward, 9095, Pte., *k. in a. 15.9.17*
Kerr, Thomas, 2323, Pte., *k. in a. 27.11.17*
Kerrigan, Francis, 8596, L.-Sgt., *k. in a. 27.3.18*
Kerslake, Walter G., 12593, Pte., *k. in a. 26.3.18*
Kiernan, James, 6884, Pte., *d. of w. 8.9.17*
Kilgallon, William O., 7755, Pte., *k. in a. 1.7.16*
Killerlane, Patrick, 10333, L.-Cpl., *k. in a. 13.4.18*
Kinahan, Edward, 8278, Pte., *k. in a. 23.12.15*
King, John, 9972, Pte., *k. in a. 31.7.17*
King, Peter, 10429, Pte., *k. in a. 13.4.18*
Kinsella, James, 11303, Pte., *k. in a. 13.4.18*
Kinsella, Michael, 10558, Pte., *d. of w. 13.9.17*
Kirwan, John T., 6954, Pte., *k. in a. 30.9.15*
Kirwin, Matthew, 7230, Pte., *d. of w. 19.5.16*
Kirwan, William, 7661, Pte., *k. in a. 27.11.17*
Kivlan, Patrick, 6564, Pte., *k. in a. 15.9.16*
Lally, Thomas, 9455, Sgt., *d. 27. 10.18*
Larkin, Patrick, 6971, Pte., *k. in a. 26.9.16*
Larkin, Peter, 6842, Pte., *k. in a. 30.9.15*
Lawrence, Lewis, 10117, Pte., *k. in a. 28.9.16*

Lawson, Horace L. M., 7219, L.-Cpl., *k. in a. 27.9.15*
Leahy, Daniel, 7425, L.-Sgt., *k. in a. 27.11.17*
Leahy, Denis F., 7591, Pte., *k. in a. 8.10.15*
Leahy, James, 7426, Pte., *k. in a. 17.10.15*
Leech, James, 10292, Pte., *k. in a. 20.7.17*
Leggett, Robert, 10804, Pte., *d. of w. 31.7.17*
Leitch, William, 1909, L.-Cpl., *k. in a. 27.11.17*
Lenihan, Edward, 6820, Pte., *k. in a. 30.9.15*
Lennon, Daniel, 8331, Pte., *k. in a. 31.7.17*
Lennon, Patrick, 8904, Pte., *d. of w. 2.12.16*
Lennon, Philip, 4636, Pte., *k. in a. 20.6.16*
Leonard, William, 9390, Pte., *d. of w. 27.6.17*
Lewis, Charles, 6404, Pte., *k. in a. 27.9.15*
Lewis, George, 2902, L.-Sgt., *k. in a. 27.9.15*
Lewis, George, 8313, Pte., *k. in a. 15.9.16*
Lewis, Michael, 6891, Pte., *k. in a. 21.10.15*
Linehan, Charles, 6727, Pte., *k. in a. 15.9.16*
Little, Michael, 3563, Sgt., *d. of w. 29.9.15*
Lockington, William, 3113, L.-Cpl., *k. in a. 27.9.16*
Lonergan, John F., 10682, Pte., *d. of w. 2.8.17*
Long, Frank H., 7948, L.-Cpl., *d. of w. 15.9.16*
Lowe, Arthur, 7157, Pte., *k. in a. 30.9.15*
Lucas, Albert J., 6684, Sgt., *k. in a. 20.11.16*
Lynch, Michael J., 7655, L.-Cpl., *k. in a. 13.9.16*
Lynn, Charles F. C., 11920, Pte., k. in a. 28.3.18
Lyons, Daniel, 7090, Pte., *k. in a. 15.9.16*
Mackay, Thomas, 7553, Pte., *k. in a. 11.7.16*
Madgwick, Percival J., 7135, Pte., *k. in a. 13.4.18*
Magee, James, 10545, Pte., *k. in a. 27.11.17*
Magill, John, 3586, Pte., *k. in a. 14.4.18*
Maguire, Dominic, 9358, Pte., *k. in a. 12.9.17*
Maguire, Redmond, 6308, L.-Cpl., *d. of w. 15.10.17*
Maguire, Thomas, 10089, Pte., *k. in a. 30.3.18*
Maher, Matthew, 7323, Pte., *k. in a. 2.7.16*
Mahon, Henry, 7508, Pte., *k. in a. 15.9.16*
Mahon, Matthew J., 12151, Pte., *k. in a. 23.3.18*
Mahoney, William, 11078, Pte., *d. 16.6.18*
Maloney, Michael, 8396, Pte., *k. in a. 15.9.16*
Manning, Francis, 8437, Pte., *k. in a. 15.9.16*
Mara, Daniel, 4638, Pte., *k. in a. 23.3.18*
Marcham, James F., 12717, Pte., *d. of w. 15.4.18*
Martin, Denis, 8167, Pte., *k. in a. 15.9.17*
Martin, David, 8794, Pte., *k. in a. 15.9.16*
Martin, Edward, 6709, Pte., *k. in a. 30.9.15*
Martin, Joseph, 8886, Pte., *k. in a. 2.7.16*
Martin, Michael, 6188, Pte., *d. of w. 28.1.16*
Marsh, Albert J., 10377, Pte., *k. in a. 13.4.18*
Matear, Henry, 6939, Pte., M.M., *k. in a. 27.11.17*
Mathers, Samuel G., 8293, Pte., *d. of w. 18.9.16*
Matthews, James I., 8520, Pte., *d. of w. 14.4.18*
Mawhenny, Andrew, 8841, L.-Cpl., *k. in a. 31.7.17*
Maye, John, 10064, Pte., *k. in a. 13.9.17*
Meehan, Bernard, 8016, Pte., *k. in a. 13.9.16*
Merryweather, James, 11402, Pte., *k. in a. 1.3.17*
Millsopp, James, 6572, Pte., *k. in a. 30.9.15*

Moan, Hugh, 4521, Pte., *k. in a. 23.12.16*
Mohan, Andrew, 6655, Pte., *k. in a. 26.7.17*
Molloy, Martin, 6649, Pte., *k. in a. 13.9.16*
Moloney, Martin, 11243, Pte., *d. of w. 1.8.17*
Monahan, John, 7395, Pte., *k. in a. 7.10.15*
Moody, Thomas, 10156, L.-Cpl., *d. 27.11.17*
Moore, Arthur, 12614, Pte., *k. in a. 23.4.18*
Moore, George, 6295, L.-Cpl., *k. in a. 29.9.15*
Moore, John, 10202, Pte., *d. of w. 13.10.17*
Moran Patrick 6665 Pte., *d. of w. 22.10.15*
Morley, John E., 10990, Pte., *k. in a. 9.10.17*
Morrow, Alexander, 3035, Pte., *k. in a. 27.9.15*
Moss, David, 6671, Pte., *k. in a. 23.3.18*
Moss, James, 11358, Pte., *k. in a. 27.11.17*
Moynan, Alfred, 8057, Pte., *k. in a. 5.5.16*
Muir, Albert, 6481, Pte., *k. in a. 16.9.16*
Mulhearn, John, 10548, Pte., *d. of w. 14.10.17*
Mulhill, Arthur, 10304, Pte., k. in a. *15.3.17*
Mullaly, Miles, 9733, Pte., k. in a. *8.10.17*
Mullaney, Laurence, 11546, Pte., *d. of w. 3.8.17*
Mullen, Albert C., 7117, Pte., *k. in a. 30.9.15*
Mulligan, Christopher, 11270, L.-Cpl., *k. in a. 8.10.17*
Mullin, John, 12161, Pte., *d. 2.8.19*
Mulvehill, Dennis, 10517, Pte., *k. in a. 31.7.17*
Mulvihill, Edward, 9289, Pte., *k. in a. 13.9.16*
Murphy, Cornelius, 7660, Pte., *k. in a. 31.7.17*
Murphy, James, 4985, Pte., *k. in a. 18.10.15*
Murphy, Martin, 7618, Pte., *k. in a. 21.10.15*
Murphy, Patrick, 9488, Pte., *k. in a. 15.9.16*
Murphy, Stephen, 7901, L.-Cpl., *k. in a. 14.9.16*
Murray, John V., 6865, Pte., *k. in a. 27.9.15*
Murray, Patrick, 6497, Pte., *k. in a. 27.9.15*
Murray, Patrick, 8868, Pte., *d. of w. 16.9.16*
Murray, Philip, 11342, Pte., *k. in a. 14.4.18*
Murray, William, 7437, Pte., *k. in a. 21.10.15*
McAnany, John, 11649, L.-Cpl., *k. in a. 27.11.17*
McAteer, John, 10443, L.-Cpl., M.M., *k. in a. 13.4.18*
McAughley, John, 8511, Pte., *k. in a. 13.9.17*
McAuley, Archibald, 11695, Pte., *k. in a. 9.10.17*
McAuley, John, 6711, Pte., *d. of w. 28.9.15*
McAuley, John, 7411, Pte., *k. in a. 15.9.16*
McAuliffe, Peter, 8318, L.-Cpl., *k. in a. 15.3.17*
McBride, Charles, 10487, Pte., *d. of w. 22.10.17*
McBride, Charles, 11657, Pte., *d. of w. 1.10.17*
McCabe, Daniel, 7432, Pte., *k. in a. 30.9.15*
McCaffrey, Thomas, 12202, *k. in a. 14.4.18*
McCallum, John, 6739, Pte., *k. in a. 27.9.15*
McCann, John, 7577, Pte., *d. of w. 29.3.18*
McCann, Joseph, 8956, Pte., *k. in a. 15.9.16*
McCarthy, James, 9288, Pte., *k. in a. 15.9.16*
McCarthy, Patrick, 8045, Pte., *k. in a. 15.9.16*
McCarthy, Robert, 6528, Sgt., M.M., *k. in a. 15.9.16*
McClennan, James, 5376, Pte., *k. in a. 27.9.15*
McCole, Daniel, 5988, Pte., *k. in a. 13.4.18*
McConnell, Henry, 9015, Pte., *k. in a. 27.9.16*
McConnell, Patrick, 4796, Pte., *k. in a. 31.7.17*
McCormack, John, 6707, Pte., *k. in a. 30.9.15*
McCourt, John, 2694, Pte., *d. of w. 13.7.17*
McCoy, Arthur, 11436, Pte., *k. in a. 27.11.17*
McDaid, William, 9810, Pte., *k. in a. 27.11.17*

McDermott, Philip, 3234, Pte., *k. in a. 15.9.16*
McDonagh, James, 7115, Pte., *d. of w. 18.9.16*
McDonald, Peter, 6493, Pte., *k. in a. 9.10.17*
MacDonald, Patrick J., 11639, Pte., *k. in a. 29.1.18*
McEnery, Thomas D., 10922, Pte., *k. in a. 27.11.17*
McEnroe, John, 4221, Pte., *k. in a. 30.9.15*
McEvoy, Edward, 11208, Pte., *d. of w. 21.9.17*
McEvoy, Patrick, 6397, L.-Cpl., *k. in a. 16.10.15*
McEvoy, Patrick J., 7849, Pte., *d. of w. 19.10.15*
McFadden, William, 12032, Pte., *k. in a. 14.4.18*
MacFarlane, Patrick, 8094, Pte., *k. in a. 15.9.16*
McGeeney, Peter, 12140, Pte., *d. of w. 29.2.18*
McGeough, John, 11357, Pte., *k. in a. 13.4.18*
McGiff, Peter, 7994, Pte., *k. in a. 7.10.15*
McGinnis, Charles, 5532, Pte., M.M., *d. of w. 13.10.17*
McGladdery, Thomas, 8833, Pte., *k. in a. 15.3.17*
McGlinchy, Francis, 5529, Pte., *k. in a. 21.10.15*
McGlone, Edward, 10756, Pte., *k. in a. 31.7.17*
McGoldrick, Michael, 8301, Pte., *k. in a. 13.9.16*
McGookin, Thomas J., 9117, Pte., *k. in a. 13.9.16*
McGowan, Charles, 11396, Pte., *k. in a. 9.10.17*
McGregor, James, 4929, Pte., *d. of w. 1.10.17*
McGrorty, Patrick, 7208, Pte., *k. in a. 30.9.15*
McGuinn, John F., 5097, Sgt., *d. of w. 27.3.16*
McGuire, Charles J., 6521, Pte., *d. of w. 17.10.15*
McGuire, Francis, 6745, Pte., *k. in a. 2.7.16*
McGuire, John, 9635, Pte., *k. in a. 13.9.17*
McHale, Michael, 8944, Pte., *k. in a. 2.7.16*
McHugh, James J., 11899, Pte., *k. in a. 9.10.17*
McHugh, Patrick, 7106, Pte., *k. in a. 27.9.15*
McKay, James, 8087, Pte., *k. in a. 15.9.16*
McKenna, John, 8013, Pte., *k. in a. 13.9.16*
McKenna, John, 9249, Pte., *k. in a. 15.9.16*
McKeon, James, 8472, Pte., *k. in a. 13.9.17*
McKeown, William, 6607, Pte., *d. of w. 17.4.18*
McKernin, Frank, 11326, Pte., *k. in a. 31.7.17*
McKnight, Thomas, 3198, Sgt., *k. in a. 13.9.16*
McLeish, Peter, 10195, Pte., *k. in a. 22.1.18*
McLoughlin, James, 9427, Pte., *k. in a. 13.4.18*
McMahon, James, 6650, Pte., *k. in a. 27.9.15*
McManus, William, 2785, Pte., *k. in a. 30.9.15*
McMenamy, Thomas S., 8419, Pte., *k. in a. 12.9.17*
McMullan, Daniel, 8444, Pte., *d. of w. 29.9.16*
McMullan, William, 10271, Pte., *d. of w. 22.7.17*
McNamara, Joseph, 7259, Pte., *k. in a. 15.9.16*
McNamee, Patrick, 6613, Pte., *k. in a. 30.9.15*
McNicholas, Michael, 11181, Pte., *k. in a. 31.7.17*
McPartland, Matthew, 7985, Pte., *k. in a. 18.10.15*
McPartland, Peter, 10094, Pte., *k. in a. 31.7.17*
McPete, James M., 813, Pte., *d. of w. 30.9.15*
McQuiggan, Henry, 5931, Pte., *k. in a. 21.10.15*
McQuinn, Patrick J., 6914, L.-Cpl., *k. in a. 2.7.16*
Nash, 7416, Pte., *d. of w. 14.10.17*

Neafsy, Patrick, 6534, Pte., *k. in a. 27.9.15*
Nealon, Daniel, 6785, L.-Cpl., *k. in a. 15.9.16*
Nealon, Patrick J., 11350, L.-Cpl., *k. in a. 27.11.17*
Neary, Peter, 6225, Pte., *k. in a. 15.9.16*
Neill, Robert, 8123, Pte., *d. of w. 24.9.16*
Nelson, Andrew, 8877, Pte., *k. in a. 13.9.16*
Newton, Richard, 12639, Pte., *d. of w. 13.4.18*
Nicholson, William, 7710, Pte., *k. in a. 13.9.17*
Niland, Joseph, 6224, Pte., *d. of w. 19.7.17*
Nolan, Patrick, 8541, Pte., *k. in a. 2.7.16*
Nolan, Peter, 6484, Sgt., D.C.M., M.M. and bar, *k. in a. 27.11.17*
Nolan, Peter, 7298, Pte., *k. in a. 13.9.16*
Nolan, Philip, 6786, L.-Sgt., *k. in a. 20.6.16*
Noonan, Patrick, 9425, Pte., *k. in a. 15.9.16*
Nowlan, William, 7232, Pte., *k. in a. 17.10.15*
O'Beirne, William, 11564, Pte., *k. in a. 13.4.18*
O'Brien, James J., 199, Pte., *k. in a. 30.9.15*
O'Brien, James, 11720, Pte., *k. in a. 9.10.17*
O'Brien, Michael, 4656, Pte., *d. 26.12.17*
O'Brien, Peter, 9338, Pte., *k. in a. 15.9.16*
O'Brien, Peter, 10048, Pte., *k. in a. 27.11.17*
O'Brien, William, 6229, Pte., M.M., *k. in a. 27.11.17*
O'Brien, William, 7815, Pte., *k. in a. 15.9.16*
O'Brien, William, 7831, L.-Cpl., *k. in a. 13.9.16*
O'Connell, Jeremiah, 7671, Pte., *k. in a. 2.7.16*
O'Connell, Timothy, 7589, Pte., *k. in a. 30.9.15*
O'Connor, Fergus, 9769, L.-Cpl., *d. of w. 26.11.16*
O'Connor, Hugh, 6999, Pte., *k. in a. 21.10.15*
O'Connor, James, 4424, Pte., *k. in a. 30.9.15*
O'Connor, James, 6845, Pte., *k. in a. 15.9.16*
O'Connor, James, 10164, L.-Cpl., *k. in a. 27.11.17*
O'Connor, John, 7771, Pte., *d. of w. 22.10.17*
O'Connor, Patrick, 4936, L.-Sgt., *k. in a. 17.10.15*
O'Connor, William, 10572, Pte., *d. of w. 16.4.18*
O'Dea, Timothy, 10231, L.-Cpl., M.M., *k. in a. 27.11.17*
Odlum, William, 6378, Pte., *k. in a. 9.10.17*
O'Donnell, Charles, 6516, Pte., *k. in a. 15.9.16*
O'Donnell, Denis, 5846, Pte., *k. in a. 15.9.16*
O'Donnell, Peter, 9326, Pte., *k. in a. 15.3.17*
O'Donnell, Peter, 11554, Pte., *d. of w. 27.4.18*
O'Donohue, John, 11158, Pte., *k. in a. 13.4.18*
O Donovan, Martin, 8059, Pte., *k. in a. 27.3.18*
O'Driscoll, John, 11075, L.-Cpl., *d. of w. 23.7.17*
O'Farrell, Patrick, 7716, Pte., *d. 16.1.18*
O'Grady, James, 11229, Pte., *k. in a. 31.7.17*
O'Hagan, John J. C. F., 11121, Pte., *k. in a. 22.6.17*
O'Kane, Darby, 6695, Pte., *k. in a. 31.7.17*
O'Mahony, John, 7790, Pte., *k. in a. 15.9.16*
O'Neil, Owen, 12238, Pte., *k. in a. 13.4.18*
O'Neill, Edward F., 6805, Pte., *k. in a. 30 9.15*
O'Neill, Patrick, 10562, Pte., *k. in a. 27 6.17*
O'Neill, Thomas, 10063, Pte., *k. in a. 3.12.17*
O'Regan, John, 9151, Pte., *d. of w. 31.3 18*
O'Regan, Terence, 7649, L.-Cpl., *d. of w. 26.10.17*

O'Rourke, Peter, 2811, L.-Cpl., *k. in a. 27.9.15*
Orr, John, 11670, Pte., *k. in a. 31.7.17*
Orr, William, 8481, Pte., *d. 1.10.16*
O'Shea, Patrick, 3501, Pte., *d. 14.11.17*
O'Sullivan, Daniel J., 11000, Pte., *k. in a. 27.6.17*
O'Sullivan, Denis, 7458, Pte., *k. in a. 23.12.16*
O'Sullivan, John, 9735, L.-Cpl., *d. of w. 2.8.17*
O'Sullivan, Patrick, 6699, Pte., *k. in a. 2.7.16*
O'Sullivan, Patrick, 9236, Pte., *d. of w. 30.9.16*
O'Sullivan, Thomas, 11752, L.-Cpl., *k. in a. 23.3.18*
O'Toole, Joseph, 11643, Pte., *k. in a. 13.9.17*
Palmer, Joseph M., 6922, L.-Cpl., *k. in a. 13.9.16*
Parkinson, Thomas, 6867, Pte., *k. in a. 28.9.15*
Parker, Thomas, 4595, Pte., *k. in a. 13.4.18*
Pender, Andrew J., 2267, Pte., *k. in a. 31.7.17*
Peoples, William, 9253, Pte., *d. of w. 19.9.16*
Peppard, Joseph, 10785, Pte., *d. of w. 3.8.17*
Phelan, Edward, 7765, Pte., *k. in a. 31.7.17*
Phelan, Lawrence, 6676, Pte., *k. in a. 30.9.15*
Phillips, John, 8166, Pte., *d. of w. 21.1.17*
Pickett, William, 11176, Pte., *d. of w. 2.8.17*
Plunkett, Hugh, 10860, Pte., *k. in a. 27.11.17*
Pope, Edward, 9251, Pte., *d. of w. 25.4.18*
Potter, Charles, 5941, Pte., *k. in a. 27.11 17*
Power, Joseph, 7626, Pte., *d. of w. 27.9.16*
Power, Michael, 5824, Pte., *d. of w. 23.10.15*
Quigley, William, 11620, Pte., *k. in a. 9.10.17*
Quinlan, .Joseph, 10215, Pte., *k. in a. 27.9.16*
Quinn, James P., 11828, Pte., *k. in a. 13.4.18*
Quinn, Jeremiah, 10391, Pte., *k. in a. 9.10.17*
Quinn, Patrick J., 6232, Pte., *k. in a. 27.11.17*
Quinn, Patrick, 9107, Pte., *k. in a. 16.9.16*
Quinn Peter, 6552, Pte., *k. in a. 30.9.15*
Quirke, James, 11727, L.-Cpl., *k. in a. 31.3.18*
Quirke, Michael, 11530, Pte., *k. in a. 12.9.17*
Rafferty, Owen, 6596, Pte., *k. in a. 21.10.15*
Rainey, William J., 9482, L.-Cpl., *d. of w. 4.5.16*
Reddy, Joseph, 8091, L.-Sgt., *k. in a. 31.7.17*
Redmond, Joseph, 3836, L.-Sgt., M.M., *d. of w. 8.9.17*
Redmond, Nicholas, 10648, Pte., *d. of w. 19.8.17*
Redmond, Thomas, 3795, Pte., *d. of w. 18.9.16*
Regan, Edward, 12377, Pte., *k. in a. 13.4.18*
Reid, Edgar, 7111, Pte., *d. of w. 8.10.15*
Reilly, James, 6804, Pte., *k. in a. 30.9.15*
Reilly, John, 6886, Pte., *k. in a. 17.9.16*
Reilly, John, 7409, Pte., *k. in a. 15.9.16*
Reilly, Joseph, 10752, Pte., *k. in a. 31.7.17*
Reilly, Patrick, 8624, Pte., *k. in a. 13.9.16*
Reilly, Thomas, 11532, Pte., *d. of w. 20.4.18*
Renney, Thomas, 8678, Pte., *d. of w. 27.12.16*
Rice, Joseph, 3426, Pte., *d. 9.2.16*
Richmond, Leo C., 8855, Pte., *k. in a. 19.11.16*
Riley, Patrick, 8048, Pte., *d. of w. 23.10.15*
Rivill, Patrick, 6736, Pte., *k. in a. 15.9.16*
Robertshaw, Harry, 7159, Pte., *d. of w. 28.3.18*
Robinson, James, 7378, Pte., *k. in a. 15.9.16*
Roche, John, 6334, L.-Cpl., *d. of w. 7.12 15*
Rogers, James, 4265, Pte., *k. in a. 27.9.15*
Rogers, Patrick, 6976, Pte., *d. of w. 10.10.15*

Roland, Frederick, 7725, L.-Cpl., *d. of w. 14.1.17*
Rooney, Bernard, 11989, Pte., *k. in a. 13.4.18*
Ross, Robert H., 8892, Pte., *d. of w. 29.9.17*
Rossiter, James, 6846, L.-Cpl., *d. of w. 21.10.15*
Rowan, Patrick, 9503, Pte., *k. in a. 27.9.16*
Rowe, Oliver A., 6436, Pte., *k. in a. 31.7.17*
Rowe, Michael, 11050, Pte., *k. in a. 27.11.17*
Royle, Andrew, 11884, Pte., *k. in a. 27.11.17*
Ryan, Denis, 4817, Pte., M.M., *k. in a. 15.9.16*
Ryan, John, 5472, Pte., *k. in a. 15.9.16*
Ryan, John P., 7804, Pte., *k. in a. 21.10.15*
Ryan, Michael, 6652, L.-Cpl., *k. in a. 27.11.17*
Ryan, Patrick, 3074, Pte., *k. in a. 5.10.15*
Ryan, Patrick, 7326, L.-Cpl., *k. in a. 2.5.16*
Ryan, Patrick, 10318, Pte., *k. in a. 28.3.18*
Rynard, James, 10843, Pte., *k. in a. 12.9.17*
Rynn, Myles, 11164, Pte., *d. of w. 16.8.17*
Saich, Charles M., 9316, L.-Sgt., *k. in a. 27.11.17*
Sanders, James, 9749, Pte., *d. of w. 18.7.18*
Sarsfield, Timothy, 8821, Pte., *k. in a. 13.4.18*
Savage, Hugh, 9783, Pte., M.M., *k. in a. 14.4.18*
Savage, William, 7204, L.-Sgt., *k. in a. 9.4.16*
Seaney, Archibald, 8284, Pte., *k. in a. 15.9.16*
Shanks, Charles, 8492, L.-Cpl., *d. of w. 5.7.16*
Shannon, John Francis, 3327, Pte., *d. of w. 15.9.17*
Sharkey, Charles, 5956, Pte., *k. in a. 30.9.15*
Sharkey, Edward, 7283, Pte., *d. of w. 20.9.16*
Sharkey, Edward, 7764, L.-Cpl., *k. in a. 27.11.17*
Shawlin, Anthony, 11886, Pte., *k. in a. 27.3.18*
Shea, Patrick, 7430, Pte., *k. in a. 29.4.16*
Sheehy, James, 7653, Cpl., *k. in a. 16.9.16*
Sheerin, Thomas, 9483, Pte., *k. in a. 9.10.17*
Sherwood, William H., 6791, Pte., *k. in a. 27.9.15*
Shine, Peter, 6792, Pte., *k. in a. 27.11.17*
Sholdis, Thomas, 5507, Pte., *d. of w. 29.5.18*
Smith, Christopher, 10782, Pte., *k. in a. 31.7.17*
Smith, Lewis, 12247, Pte., *k. in a. 14.4.18*
Smith, Michael J., 11722, L.-Cpl., *k. in a. 13.4.18*
Smith, Patrick, 10641, Pte., *k. in a. 23.3.18*
Smith, Thomas, 4992, Pte., *k. in a. 17.9.16*
Smith, Thomas, 6856, Pte., *k. in a. 30.9.15*
Smyth, Alexander, 9351, Pte., *d. of w. 31.7.17*
Smythe, Robert, 10501, Pte., *k. in a. 13.4.18*
Smyth, William, 7827, L.-Sgt., *k. in a. 15.3.17*
Somers, Daniel, 7256, Pte., *d. of w. 28.10.15*
Somers, Lawrence, 8112, Pte., M.M., *d. of w. 28.10.16*
Somers, Patrick, 10426, Pte., *k. in a. 26.9.16*
Southren, John, 12604, Pte., *d. 22.4.18*
Speakman, James, 9161, Pte., *k. in a. 15.9.17*
Spiby, Thomas, 12715, Pte., *k. in a. 13.4.18*
Spring, Harry, 3672, Pte., *k. in a. 27.11.17*
Staddon, Arthur, 11892, Pte., *k. in a. 13.4.18*
Stanley, Edward, 10441, Pte., *k. in a. 23.3.18*
Staunton, John, 10294, Pte., *d. of w. 5.12.17*
Stephenson, George, 8569, Pte., *k. in a. 12.9.17*
Stevens, Frank, 12749, Pte., *k. in a. 13.4.18*

Stewart, William, 7365, Pte., *d. of w. 15.11.15*
Sullivan, Eugene, 7504, Pte., *k. in a. 27.9.15*
Sullivan, James, 6176, Pte., *d. 26.8.17*
Sullivan, James, 7734, Pte., *k. in a. 30.9.15*
Sullivan, James, 9111, Pte., *k. in a. 27.11.17*
Sullivan, John, 7574, Pte., *k. in a. 14.2.16*
Sutton, Elijah, 2054, Pte., *k. in a. 30.9.15*
Sutton, Geoffrey A., 11686, L.-Cpl., *k. in a. 27.11.17*
Sutton, Michael, 7258, Pte., *k. in a. 27.9.15*
Sweeney, Michael J., 10951, Pte., *k. in a. 25.3.18*
Sweeney, William H., 7066, Pte., *d. of w. 15.4.18*
Sweetland, Michael, 3109, Pte., *k. in a. 27.9.15*
Talbot, Joseph, 6533, Pte., *k. in a. 27.9.16*
Talbot, William, 12059, Pte., *k. in a. 27.11.17*
Thompson, Joseph, 7039, Pte., *k. in a. 30.9.16*
Thompson, William J., 2537, Pte., *k. in a. 27.3.18*
Tierney, Bernard, 10244, Pte., *d. 12.2.17*
Toher, Martin, 6958, Pte., *k. in a. 13.9.16*
Torpey, Frank, 12179, Pte., *k. in a. 27.3.18*
Torsney, Thomas, 7882, L.-Sgt., *d. of w. 13.9.18*
Towey, Martin, 8973, Pte., *k. in a. 31.7.17*
Towland, Edward, 3861, L.-Cpl., *k. in a. 27.11.17*
Tracey, Henry, 12608, Pte., *k. in a. 27.3.18*
Tudenham, Maurice, 6898, Pte., *k. in a. 30.9.15*
Twomey, Humphrey, 7247, Pte., *k. in a. 15.9.16*
Walkden, Albert, 8187, Pte., *d. of w. 1.8.17*
Walker, Christopher, 10307, Pte., *d. of w. 24.4.18*
Walker, John, 11403, Pte., *k. in a. 31.7.17*
Wall, John, 6396, Pte., *k. in a. 27.9.16*
Wall, Patrick, 2726, Pte., *k. in a. 10.10.17*
Wallace, Michael J., 9757, Pte., *d. of w. 27.11.17*
Wallace, Richard C., 7722, Pte., *k. in a. 13.9.17*
Walsh, Hugh, 6194, L.-Cpl., *k. in a. 3.8.17*
Walsh, James, 7561, Pte., *k. in a. 15.9.16*
Walsh, John, 11190, L.-Cpl., *d. of w. 27.11.17*
Walsh, Michael, 6056, Pte., *k. in a. 15.9.16*
Walsh, Thomas, 9649, Pte., *d. of w. 17.4.18*
Walsh, Thomas, 12821, Pte., *d. of w. 28.3.18*
Walsh, William, 7532, Pte., *k. in a. 15.9.16*
Walshe, Richard, 7748, Pte., *k. in a. 9.10.17*
Walshe, Thomas, 7074, Pte., *k. in a. 7.10.15*
Ward, Simon, 9732, Pte., *k. in a. 9.10.17*
Ward, William H., 12822, Cpl., *k. in a. 13.4.18*
Warlow, Andrew, 10284, Pte., *d. of w. 11.10.17*
Waters, Denis, 11098, Pte., *k. in a. 31.7.17*
Watson, William H., 8083, Pte., *k. in a. 13.4.18*
Watson, William, 9256, L.-Sgt., *k. in a. 27.11.17*
Watt, Herbert, 11772, Pte., *k. in a. 27.11.17*
Wellwood, Samuel, 12044, Pte., *k. in a. 27.11.17*
Whelan, Nicholas, 7736, Pte., *d. 19.12.16*
Whelan, Peter, 6965, Pte., *k. in a. 15.9.16*
Whelan, Richard, 9356, Pte., *k. in a. 12.9.17*
Whelehan, Patrick, 10078, Pte., *k. in a. 10.3.17*
Whelton, John, 11555, Pte., *k. in a. 29.1.18*
White, John, 6658, Pte., *k. in a. 30.9.15*
White, Joseph, 8843, Pte., *d. of w. 15.4.18*
Whyte, Valentine, 9897, Pte., *k. in a. 13.4.18*

Wiggall, John H., 9024, L.-Cpl., *k. in a. 13.9.17*
Williams, William J., 9487, L.-Cpl., *k. in a.*
    10.10.17
Wilson, James, 8769, Pte., *k. in a. 12.9.17*
Wilson, Thomas, 8289, L.-Cpl., *k. in a. 31.7.17*
Wilson, William, 9986, Pte., *d. of w. 14.9.17*
Woodcock, Thomas, 8387, L.-Cpl., v.c., *k. in a.*
    27.3.18

Woods, Thomas, 12178, Pte., *d. of w. 13.10.18*
Woore, Frederick, 11822, Pte., *k. in a. 13.4.18*
Worthington, Hugh, 6980, Pte., *k. in a 27.9.16*
Wren, Edward, 6797, Pte., *k. in a. 27.11.17*
Wright, James, 7953, Pte., *k. in a. 9.2.16*
Wright, William J., 6489, L.-Cpl., *k. in a. 4.9.17*
Yabsley, Richard, 7133, Pte., *k. in a. 27.9.15*
Younger, Robert, 12206, Pte., *d. of w. 25.4.18*

RESERVE BATTALION IRISH GUARDS

Barry, Edward, 9218, Pte., *d. 8.8.15*
Byrne, James F., 7011, Pte., *d. 29.4.15*
Carroll, Owen, 3907, Pte., *d. 20.2.15*
Cleary, James, Pte., m.m., *d. 28.7.17*
Cooke, Michael, 6279, L.-Sgt., *d. 10.10.18*
Deasy, Timothy, 6811, Pte., *d. 26.3.15*
Doyle, Dominick, 6834, *d. 9.1.16*
Doyle, James, 9243, Pte., *d. 17.10.15*
Doyle, John, 9311, Pte., *d. 7.9.15*
Duggan, Bernard, 8277, Pte., *d. 8.1.16*
Dunne, John, 9785, Pte., *d. 3.9.16*
Farrell, Michael J., 4145, L.-Sgt., *d. 18.5.17*
Flaherty, Martin, 6040, Pte., *d. 10.10.18*
Foreman, John H., 5716, *d. 12.5.17*
Halligan, Patrick, 7938, Pte., *d. 10.10.18*
Hogan, Francis J., 8623, Pte., *d. 27.3.18*
Jay, Harry, 5814, Pte., *d. 9.12.15*
Joyce, Frank J., 6598, Pte., *d. 3.3.17*
Kenna, Robert A., 6290, Pte., *d. 3.11.16*

Kilduff, Michael, 7265, Pte., *d. 11.11.18*
Longhurst, James, 5650, Pte., *d. 8.6.16*
Lyons, Joseph, 11481, Pte., *d. 10.10.18*
Moore, Louis, 8364, Pte., *d. 24.4.16*
Murphy, Edward, 9255, Pte., *d. 23.2.18*
Murphy, William, 14116, Pte., *d. 10.10.18*
Murray, John, 56, Pte., *d. 6.8.15*
McEvoy, Richard, 9396, Pte., *d. 8.1.16*
McMichael, William, 6070, Pte., *d. 31.1.17*
Nolan, Michael, 4953, Pte., *d. 17.11.14*
Nunan, James, 9723, L.-Cpl., *d. 13.5.16*
O'Donnell, Anthony, 5968, Pte., *d. 3.12.14*
O'Rourke, Francis, 1339, Sgt., *d. 8.6.16*
Pentleton, Joseph, 14103, Pte., *d. 10.10.18*
Plunkett, Thomas, 7119, Pte., *d. 17.5.17*
Rowe, John, 3668, Pte., *d. 1.9.17*
Scully, Patrick, 5343, Pte., *d. 1.8.16*
Sheerin, Hugh, 12284, Pte., *d. 10.10.18*
Wallace, James, 4226, Pte., *d. 17.9.16*

APPENDIX D

W.O.s, N.C.O.s, AND MEN
FIRST AND SECOND BATTALIONS
REWARDS

VICTORIA CROSS
7708 L.-Sgt. Moyney, J.
3556 L.-Cpl. O'Leary, M.
8387 L.-Cpl. Woodcock, T.

MILITARY CROSS
3578 C.S.M. Kennedy, M
108 S.M. Kirk, J.

DISTINGUISHED CONDUCT MEDAL

No.	Rank	Name	No.	Rank	Name
7218	Sgt.	Anstey, C. E.	8384	Sgt.	McGuinness, J.
5722	Pte.	Barry, H.	5741	Pte.	McKendry, W.
12501	Sgt.	Bishop, T.	7830	Pte.	McKinney, P.
5841	Pte.	Boyd, J.	4432	L.-Sgt.	McMullen, T.
10133	L.-Sgt.	Bray, H.	2112	C.S.M.	McVeigh, H.
3975	Pte.	Brine, M.	3567	Pte.	Meagher, W.
3221	Sgt.	Burling, D.	3235	Sgt.	Milligan, J.
7321	L.-Sgt.	Butler, T.	7683	L.-Sgt.	Mohide, P.
918	S.M.	Cahill, T.	4015	Pte.	Moore, W.
525	Pte.	Cannon, J.	3632	C.S.M.	Moran, M.
10161	Pte.	Cooper, W.	1664	Sgt.	Moran, C.
2384	C.S.M.	Corry, T.	9500	Pte.	Morrison, P.
3507	Sgt.	Curtin, J.	552	C.S.M.	Munns, A.
4455	Sgt.	Daly, P.	3655	C.S.M.	Murphy, G.
2195	L.-Cpl.	Deacons, J.	3006	Sgt.	Murphy, F.
2853	L.-Cpl.	Delaney, W.	8828	Sgt.	Murray, T.
4039	Pte.	Dempsey, B.	6484	Sgt.	Nolan, P.
4116	L.-Sgt.	Dignan, J.	5743	Pte.	O'Brien, D.
6193	Sgt.	Dolan, P.	2760	Pte.	O'Connor, J.
2372	Sgt.	Feighery, W.	4389	Sgt.	O'Hare, E.
9210	Pte.	Finnegan, J.	4612	Sgt.	Pearce, W.
11712	L.-Cpl.	Flanagan, M.	10757	Pte.	Priesty, J.
1226	Sgt.	Foley, J.	6311	L.-Cpl.	Quinn, P.
7570	L.-Sgt.	Frawley, J.	6301	Pte.	Regan, J.
12124	Pte.	Gallagher, M.	2506	Sgt.	Reilly, T.
2793	Pte.	Geon, R.	2618	Sgt.	Riordan, M.
3303	Sgt.	Glynn, J.	5446	Pte.	Roche, J.
2535	C.S.M.	Harradine, C.	5279	Pte.	Rochford, J.
4613	Pte.	Hennigan, P.	3072	Pte.	Russell, W. G.
4906	Pte.	Henry, J.	8255	L.-Cpl.	Smith, R.
1155	Sgt.	Hiscock, H.	2623	Sgt.	Spicer, W.
55	C.S.M.	Holmes, W.	2303	Sgt.	Usher, W.
2807	Sgt.	Keown, F.	2767	Sgt.	Voyles, D.
10210	L.-Cpl.	Lecky, W.	5910	Sgt.	Wain, F.
5973	Pte.	Lynch, M.	1033	C.S.M.	Walsh, J.
2845	Pte.	Mansfield, J.	8050	Sgt.	Walsh, W.
8149	Pte.	McCarthy, T.	3987	Sgt.	Wilkinson, J.
2385	Sgt.	McClelland, T.	4182	Pte.	Younge, A.
3726	Sgt.	McGoldrick, P.			

BAR TO DISTINGUISHED CONDUCT MEDAL

No.	Rank	Name	No.	Rank	Name
4432	L.-Sgt.	McMullen, T.	6301	Pte.	Regan, J
2760	Pte.	O'Connor, J.	2618	Sgt.	Riordan, M.
4389	Sgt.	O'Hare, E.	2303	Sgt.	Usher, W.

MILITARY MEDAL

No.	Rank	Name	No.	Rank	Name
7218	Sgt.	Anstey, C. E.	5752	Pte.	Docherty, G.
6157	Pte.	Armstrong, W.	11271	L.-Cpl.	Doherty, C. M.
8922	Pte.	Arthor, S.	9376	L.-Cpl.	Dollar, W.
9093	L.-Sgt.	Baker, C.	2922	Sgt.	Donnelly, J.
4512	Sgt.	Balfe, J.	3056	Sgt.	Donohoe, P.
5132	Sgt.	Barrett, J.	2786	Pte.	Doolan, J.
6351	Pte.	Barry, P.	2867	Sgt.	Doolan, P.
11794	L.-Cpl.	Bishop, M.	8046	L.-Cpl.	Dooney, E.
6276	L.-Sgt.	Black, P.	7750	Pte.	Driscoll, T.
6402	L.-Cpl.	Bonham, J.	3003	L.-Cpl.	Duff, J.
6273	L.-Cpl.	Boyle, F.	4488	Pte.	Dunne, D.
10732	Pte.	Boyle, P.	4658	Cpl.	Dunne, J.
7967	Pte.	Boyton, R.	4944	Pte.	Durkin, J.
4751	Pte.	Brabston, M.	11858	L.-Sgt.	English, S.
6332	Sgt.	Brennan, J.	10521	Pte.	Erwin, R.
6202	L.-Cpl	Brien, P.	8773	Pte.	Evans, T.
6271	L.-Sgt	Browne, M.	9794	Pte.	Farley, P.
5115	Pte.	Bruton, P.	6698	Sgt.	Farrell, F.
9632	Pte.	Buckley, S.	4166	Sgt.	Fawcett, J.
8106	Pte.	Byrne, J.	2372	Sgt.	Feighery, W.
1730	Sgt.	Byrne, J. G.	4993	L.-Cpl.	Fitzgerald, M.
6186	Pte.	Byrnes, P.	6768	L.-Sgt.	Flaherty, J.
6457	Sgt.	Cahill, T.	11712	L.-Cpl.	Flanagan, M.
9309	Pte.	Callaghan, P.	5797	Sgt.	Flynn, J.
1985	Cpl.	Campbell, D.	6266	Pte.	Fox, A.
4435	Pte.	Carberry, M.	10358	Pte.	Furlong, M.
4009	Pte.	Carroll, J.	8743	L.-Cpl.	Galbraith, J.
3483	Pte.	Carroll, J.	11985	Pte.	Gardiner, H.
3132	Sgt.	Carton, H.	10436	Pte.	Gault, J.
7043	Pte.	Caulfield, W.	7954	Pte.	Glacken, C.
3659	Pte.	Cawley, J.	6970	Pte.	Gorbey, R.
1579	Pte.	Cleary, J.	8229	Pte.	Gowan, F.
8395	L.-Cpl.	Coard, J.	3972	C.Q.M.S.	Grady, R.
6196	Sgt.	Cole, M.	3847	Sgt.	Greany, M.
11099	L.-Sgt.	Collins, M.	2858	L.-Cpl.	Green, A.
12234	Pte.	Collins, R.	7032	Pte.	Greene, L.
6277	L.-Sgt.	Comesky, J.	7695	Sgt.	Griffin, J.
3515	Sgt.	Connor, G.	3477	Cpl.	Gunning, M.
9014	L.-Cpl.	Conroy, M.	12958	Sgt.	Hamill, R.
7109	Pte.	Corliss, J.	6632	Cpl.	Hanlon, W.
6044	L.-Cpl.	Cousins, A.	5004	Pte.	Hannan, J.
6583	Pte.	Courtney, J.	10449	L.-Cpl.	Hannan, L.
3146	Pte.	Coyne, F.	6135	L.-Sgt.	Harris, T.
6509	L.-Cpl.	Cronin, J.	7739	Pte.	Hawthorne, J.
9349	Pte.	Cunnane, J.	8572	L.-Cpl.	Heaney, J.
11321	Pte.	Curley, M.	7493	L.-Cpl.	Higgins, M.
3507	Sgt.	Curtin, J.	6471	Sgt.	Hillock, E.
4529	L.-Cpl.	Daly, J.	4068	Sgt.	Hodgson, W.
6523	Pte.	Daly, J.	4632	Pte.	Horan, J.
1999	Sgt.	Denn, A.	7475	Pte.	Horton, A.
7958	Pte.	Devine, J.	10848	L.-Cpl.	Hunt, J.

No.	Rank	Name	No.	Rank	Name
10059	Pte.	Hurley, M.	5806	Pte.	McNulty, P.
11681	Pte.	Hynes, J.	6021	Pte.	McQuillan, T.
11501	L.-Sgt.	Jenkins, D.	6782	L.-Sgt.	Mehegan, D.
8517	L.-Cpl.	Jenkins, J.	10020	B'dsman	Mills, F.
11956	Pte.	Johnson, S.	7586	L.-Sgt.	Moran, J.
1767	Sgt.	Joyce, P.	12747	Pte.	Morgan, E.
10039	Pte.	Kane, H.	7763	Pte.	Moore, P.
4957	L.-Sgt.	Kearney, P.	1964	Pte.	Morrison, J.
10595	L.-Cpl.	Keenan, E.	10354	L.-Sgt.	Morrissey, M.
8228	Pte.	Keenan, P.	11659	Pte.	Murphy, J.
7871	Pte.	Kelleher, D.	6211	Sgt.	Murphy, M.
11034	L.-Cpl.	Kelly, E.	6892	Sgt.	Murphy, M.
2746	Sgt.	Keniry, T.	4140	Pte.	Murphy, T.
8702	Pte.	Kennedy, M.	8720	Pte.	Naylor, H.
11008	L.-Cpl.	Kennedy, W.	10823	Pte.	Neagle, T.
112	Sgt.	Kenny, M.	6484	Sgt.	Nolan, P.
5939	Pte.	Kenny, M.	4029	Pte.	Nolan, P.
8465	Sgt.	Kenny, T.	11888	Pte.	Nott, P.
2807	Sgt.	Keown, F.	7520	Pte.	Nulty, S.
5319	Pte.	Kilkenny, A.	2727	Pte.	O'Brien, M.
7628	Pte.	King, H.	10437	Pte.	O'Brien, M.
3346	C.S.M.	Langrill, J.	6229	Pte.	O'Brien, W.
12233	Sgt.	Larkin, J.	3261	L.-Sgt.	O'Byrne, J.
6474	Pte.	Lavelle, J.	2289	Pte.	O'Connor, J.
10028	Pte.	Lewis, M.	4256	Sgt.	O'Connor, M.
4319	Sgt.	Linnane, J.F.	10251	L.-Cpl.	O'Dea, T.
3686	Pte.	Looney, D.	11897	Pte.	O'Farrell, J.
3272	Pte.	Looran, J.	11425	Pte.	O'Flaherty, J.
3734	Sgt.	Lowe, D.	8810	Pte.	O'Flynn, W.
5764	L.-Sgt.	Luby, T.	7167	Sgt.	O'Hagan, J.
3948	Pte.	Lydon, J.	6184	Sgt.	O'Neill, J.
7075	Pte.	Madden, P.	8122	Pte.	O'Neill, J.
6648	Pte.	Maguire, J.	5786	Sgt.	O'Reilly, J.
9458	Pte.	Maguire, T.	3969	Sgt.	O'Shea, C.
12681	Pte.	Manning, J.	7541	Pte.	O'Sullivan, T.
6078	Pte.	Martin, J.	9565	Pte.	Patton, T.
2494	L.-Cpl.	Mason, T.	5508	Sgt.	Pennington, J.
6939	Pte.	Matear, H.	3096	Sgt.	Pogue, A.
12856	Sgt.	Matthews, E.	10550	Pte.	Power, G.
10443	L.-Cpl.	McAteer, J.	2596	L.-Cpl.	Purdy, McD.
5237	Pte.	McCabe, J.	9882	Pte.	Quinn, J.
7866	Pte.	McCaffrey, S.	3836	Cpl.	Redmond. J.
5096	Sgt.	McCarthy, G.	7295	L.-Cpl.	Redmond, T.
9754	Pte.	McCarthy, P.	3122	Sgt.	Reid, L.
6258	Sgt.	McCarthy, R.	2506	Sgt.	Reilly, T.
8662	L.-Sgt.	McConnell, R.	10826	Pte.	Richerby, G.
6343	L.-Cpl.	McConnell, W.	5279	Pte.	Rochford, J.
3224	Cpl.	McCullagh, E.	776	Pte.	Roche, P.
1910	Sgt.	McCusker, F.	7400	Cpl.	Rolls, E.
4386	Sgt.	McDonald, J.	3638	Pte.	Rowe, M.
7937	Cpl.	McDonnell, M.	8552	Pte.	Ruth, J.
6643	Pte.	McElroy, J.	4817	Pte.	Ryan, D.
6448	Sgt.	McFarlane, R.	9188	L.-Cpl.	Ryan, M.
5532	Pte.	McGinnis, C.	9783	Pte.	Savage, H.
5728	Pte.	McGowan, T.	12523	Sgt.	Savin, J.
7053	Pte.	McGurrin, W.	8096	Sgt.	Scully, J.
10171	L.-Cpl.	McHale, S.	7327	Pte.	Shanahan, W.
7777	L.-Sgt.	McKiernan, M.	6653	Pte.	Shannon, T.
9230	Pte.	McKinney, I.	8932	Pte.	Sharkey, P.
8078	Pte.	McNulty, J.	4548	L.-Cpl.	Sheehan, P.

215

No.	Rank	Name
6860	Pte.	Sheil, P.
6701	Pte.	Slattery, P.
2640	L.-Sgt.	Smith, J.
8112	Pte.	Somers, L.
12400	Pte.	Southern, N.
5995	Pte.	Styles, A.
7223	Sgt.	Sussex, H.
9084	Pte.	Sweeney, D.
8120	Pte.	Sweeney, J.
5837	Pte.	Taylor, G.
2955	Sgt.	Taylor, R.
1725	C.S.M.	Toher, D

No.	Rank	Name
12339	Pte.	Tomlyn, F
7381	Pte.	Troy, W.
10180	Pte.	Tuffy, P.
2208	L.-Sgt	Tynan, P.
9927	L.-Cpl.	Tyrrell, P.
4133	L.-Cpl.	Vanston, J.
6508	Pte.	Waldron, P.
11765	Pte.	Walsh, E.
2759	Sgt.	Weedon, W.
12691	Sgt.	Westbrook, A.
3494	Pte.	Whearty, J.
2695	Pte.	White, J.

BAR TO MILITARY MEDAL

No.	Rank	Name
11794	L.-Cpl.	Bishop, M.
7967	Pte.	Boyton, R.
1999	Sgt.	Denn, A.
2786	Pte.	Doolan, J.
4993	L.-Cpl.	Fitzgerald, M.

No.	Rank	Name
12958	Sgt.	Hamill, R.
7777	L.-Sgt	McKiernan, M
10354	L.-Sgt.	Morrissey, M.
6484	Sgt.	Nolan, P.
5279	Pte.	Rochford, J.

FOREIGN DECORATIONS

CROIX DE GUERRE

No.	Rank	Name
918	S.M.	Cahill, T
4107	C.S.M.	Farrell, J.
6467	Pte.	Gallagher, J.
6448	Sgt.	Macfarlane, R.

No.	Rank	Name
3006	Sgt.	Murphy, F.
4884	Pte.	O'Brien, D.
1033	C.S.M.	Walsh, J.
3987	Sgt.	Wilkinson, J.

MÉDAILLE MILITAIRE

No.	Rank	Name
6193	Sgt.	Dolan, P.
7708	L.-Sgt.	Moyney, J.

No.	Rank	Name
1800	C.S.M.	Proctor, J.
1073	C.S.M.	Rodgers, J.

MÉDAILLE D'HONNEUR
4751 Pte. Brabston, M.

ITALIAN BRONZE MEDAL
3235 Sgt. Milligan, J.

RUSSIAN DECORATIONS

3556 L.-Cpl. O'Leary, M.   Cross of the Order of St. George, 3rd Class
2303 Sgt. Usher, W.   Medal of the Order of St. George, 2nd Class

MERITORIOUS SERVICE MEDAL

No.	Rank	Name
4874	O.R. Sgt.	Ashton, A.
2900	C.Q.M.S.	Curtis, P.
10374	Sgt.	Donovan, P.
4215	Sgt.	Halpin, G.
4707	Sgt.	Hogan, P.
6631	Pte.	Hurley, J.
1175	Sgt.	King, W.
1134	Q.M.S.	Mathews, P.
3374	Q.M.S.	McCarthy, T.
1699	Cpl.	McFadden, J.

No.	Rank	Name
121	S.C.	McKenna, J.
7525	Pte.	Millett, L.
6892	Sgt.	Murphy, M.
2098	Sgt.	O'Brien, J.
216	O.R.Q.M.S.	O'Gorman, R.
4972	S.M.	Price, G.
1158	Sgt.Dr.	Smith, G.
2087	O.R.Q.M.S.	Smythe, J.
1549	Q.M.S.	Thompson, W.
2103	Sgt.	Walsh, J.

Index

Abbat, Max, 62
Abingley Camp, 144–5
Achiet-le-Grand, 154
Acquin, 19, 21
Air warfare:
  German 'planes in The Salient, 143–4, 145, 146
Aisne, River: (1918) surprise offensive, 184
Aisomont, 189
Albert, King of the Belgians, 123
Alexander, Lieut.-Col. Hon. H. R. L. G., D.S.O.,
  M.C., 22, 25, 30, 40, 44, 53, 67, 83, 91, 93, 94, 96,
  107, 150, 152, 153, 156, 159, 161, 162, 163, 165,
  167, 170, 171, 172, 179, 180, 184, 186, 194, 196,
  197, 198, 199
Alexander, Major Hon. W. S. P., D.S.O., 112, 119,
  136, 137, 142, 144, 159, 196, 197, 199
Ambrines, 154
American troops: baseball match with, 184
Amiens, 162, 163
Anderson, Lieut. E. E., M.C., 149, 198, 200
Anneux, 156
Anstey, Sgt. C., M.M., 36, 213
Antoine, General, 153
Antrobus, Capt. P. H., M.C., 52
Ardee, Brig.-Gen. Lord, C.B., C.B.E. (Grenadier
  Guards), 170, 180, 196, 197
Arleux-en-Gohelle, 165
Arleux Loop, the, 165
Armentières, 38, 171
Armfield, 2nd Lieut. A. S., 139, 195
Armistice, the, 188
Army Line, the, 166
Arques, 126
Arras, 163, 164; prison billets at, 163; battles
  round, (1917), 123, 126; (1918), 163–4
Arrewage, 175, 176
Artillery Wood, 137, 139
Auchonvillers, 90
Aumont, 100
Austen, Sgt., 87
Australian forces in action: the Somme, 105;
  Vieux-Berquin, 172, 176, 177, 179; Villers-
  Bretonneux, 184
Authie, 90
Authies valley, 90
Avesnes, 181
Avroult, 20
Ayette, 170

Bagot, Lieut. C. E., 147, 152, 196
Bailleul–Willerval sector, 165
Bambridge, Capt. G. L. St. C., M.C., 94, 95, 97,
  108, 172, 173, 174, 175, 177, 197, 198, 202
"Bangalore torpedoes," 63
Bapaume, 93, 96, 154
Baring, Colonel G. (Coldstream), 95
Barly, 181, 184
Barry, 2nd Lieut. P. R. J., M.C., 204

Bavincourt, 181, 184
Bayly, 2nd Lieut. N. D., 159, 195, 197
Beaulencourt, 154
Beaumetz-les-Loges, 161, 166
Bedford Camp, 143
Béhagnies, 167
Bellew, Sgt., 179–180
Bellew, 2nd Lieut, R. C., 144, 195
Berguette, 89
Bernafay Corner, 114
Bertincourt, 160
Béthonsart, 166
Béthune, 38
Billon, 115, 123
Bird, Major J. B., 23, 84
Black, Capt. J., M.C., 99, 109, 140, 142, 198, 200
Blacker-Douglass, Lieut. R. St. J., M.C., 199
Bleuet Farm, 128, 129, 130, 131, 142, 143
Boesinghe, 126, 127, 129 sqq., 143, 145
Bois d'Aval, 176, 179, 180
Bois de Hem, 122
Bois de Warnimont, 90
Bois Hugo, 23, 24, 28
Boisleux-au-Mont, 166
Bollezeele, 81, 89
Bombing accidents, 69,115
Bombing School competition won by 2nd
  Battalion, 63
Borré, 179
Bourlon Village, 155, 156
Bourlon Wood, 154, 155, 156–9, 160
Bourre river, 174
Boyd-Rochford, Lieut. (Scots Guards), 94
Brandhoek, 78
Bray-sur-Somme, 165
Brennan, Sgt. J., M.M., 36, 214
Brew, Lieut., C. H., 40, 46, 48, 50, 51, 56, 60, 61,
  89, 91, 97, 195, 196
Briquetterie, the, 144
Broembeek, the, crossing of, 145, 146, 147, 148,
  150–2
Bronfay, 107
"Broody Hens, the," 106
Brophy, Pte., 36
Browne, Capt. Rev. Father F. M., M.C., 152, 196
Bruton, Capt. S. (Coldstream Guards), 131
Bucquoy, 170
Budd, Capt. E., M.C., 89, 199, 200, 201
Bullecourt, 154
Buller, Lieut. N. M., 139, 171, 196
Burbure, 22
Burg, 189
Burke, 2nd Lieut., E. H. R., 181
Butler, Brig.-Gen. Hon. L. J. P., C.M.G., D.S.O., 18,
  24, 25, 28, 40, 43, 62, 64, 78–9, 99, 100, 194, 197
Byng, Gen, Sir Julian, G.C.B., 154
Byng-Hopwood, Col. (Coldstream Guards), 131
Byrne, "Cock," 70

Cahill, Lance-Cpl., 36
Calais, 69–71
Cambrai: (1917) offensive on, 127, 154, 155–61; (1918) 188
Camp A, Trônes Wood, 101
Camp P, near Poperinghe, 88
Camp 108, Bronfay, 107
Canadian forces in action: Ypres, 64, 81, 83
Cannon Trench, 132, 136
Captain's Farm, 139
Cardoen Farm, 127, 128
Cardoen Street, 78
Cariboo Trench, 132, 136
Carnoy, 91, 97, 99, 105
Cary-Elwes, Lieut. W. G., 153, 159, 195
Cassel, 71
Cassidy, 2nd Lieut. M. B., 177, 195, 197
Castlerosse, Capt. Viscount, 89, 197
Caterham, 181
Caudescure, 175
Cavalry, British: on the Somme, 94, 120
Cavan, Major-Gen. the Earl of, K.P., K.C.B., 21, 40, 52
Central Boyau, 29
Chalk-Pit Wood, Loos, 23, 24, 25, 28, 30
Charleroi, 188–9
Chasseur Farm, 129
Chelers, 170–1
Cheshire Regt., 152
Chichester, Major Hon. A.C.S., D.S.O., O.B.E., 71, 73, 78, 197, 198
Christmas celebrations: (1915) 52–3; (1916) 109; (1917) 162
Cinema films taken in front line, 55
Citadel Camp, 97
Clifford, 2nd Lieut. W. F. J., 24, 28, 195
Close, Lieut. B. S., 78. 95, 149, 152, 180, 181, 195, 196
Coldstream Guards
  1st Battalion:
    (1915) Loos, the Hohenzollern trenches, 23, 24, 33, 38, 44; Laventie, 46, 50, 51, 52
    (1916) Laventie, 55, 56, 57, 60, 61, 66; Ypres, 73, 77, 78–9, 83, 88; the Somme: Ginchy, 90, 93, 95, 99, 101
    (1917) the Somme: Rancourt, 112, 118, 119; Yser Canal, 127, 136, 139, 140, 142; the Somme: Bourlon Wood, 156, 158;
    (1918) Eton football played by, 162; Pierrot troupe of, 149
  2nd Battalion:
    (1917), Yser Canal and the Broembeck, 144, 151; the Somme: Gouzeaucourt, 160
  3rd Battalion
    (1915) Laventie, 42, 43
    (1917) Yser Canal and the Broembeek, 132, 133, 142, 145
    (1918) in 4th Guards Brigade, 162n., 164; the Somme: March Push, 166; Vieux-Berquin, 172–3, 174, 175, 179; the advance, 185, 188
Cole, Sgt., 109
Collett, Lieut. H. A. A., M.C., 204
Cologne, advance to and occupation of, 188–90
Colquhoun, Capt. Sir I. (Scots Guards), 96, 119

Combles, 92, 106, 107, 111
Comesky, Lance-Sgt., 34
Commanding Officers, 2nd Battalion Irish Guards, list of, 194
Concrete blockhouses, German, 128, 143
Connaught, Field-Marshal H. R. H. the Duke of, K.G., 100, 152
Conroy, Pte., 145
Convent, the, Ypres, 73
Corbie, 111, 123
Corry, Colonel (Grenadier Guards), 21, 43
Couin, 91
Courcelles, 154, 167
Coxon, Lieut. R. E., 36. 40
Crawford, Lieut. G. L., 99, 139, 196
Crespigny, Gen. C. R. C. de, 95
Criel Plage, 184–8
"Crump, The," 70
Culvert, the, 83
Curlu, 123
Curran, Sgt., 104
Cuthbert, Capt. (Scots Guards), 24

Dagger, Lieut. R. L., 181, 196
Dalton, Lieut. J. W., 144, 167, 196
Dame, 2nd Lieut. J. W. M., 149, 195
Dead End, 55
Decorations awarded to Irish Guards:
  Officers, 197–204
  W.O.'s, N.C.O.'s, and men, 205–16
  2nd Battalion, 48, 99, 144
De Lisle, Gen. Sir H., K.C.B., D.S.O., 149
Delville Wood, 104
De Moleyns, Lieut. A. F. D., 143, 144, 196
Denson, Lieut. P. G., 88, 108, 109, 196
Dent, Capt. E. D., 175, 177, 195
De Wippe Cabaret, 131
Digby, Capt. Hon. K. (Coldstream Guards), 95
Divisional Entrenching Battalion, 49
Dohem, 20, 21
Dollar, Lieut. J. B., 91, 97
Donoghue, Pte., 139
Drouvin, 32
Drums: 1st Irish Guards, 47; 2nd Irish Guards, 44, 47, 149
Duke of Cornwall's Light Infantry, 176
Dulwich Camp, 149, 152
Dummies, use of, in front line, 61–2, 63, 67–8
Dunne, Pte., 88
Durant, Lieut. N. F., 159
Durham Light Infantry, 97

East Lancashire Regt., 170
East Yorkshire Regt., 29
Ecques, 154
Ecurie Camp, 166
Ehrenfeld, 189
Elverdinghe, 84, 127, 128, 142, 144, 152
Elverdinghe Château, 84, 88, 127
Erith Street, 48
Ervillers, 167
Esquelbecq, 89
Essex Regt., 149
Estaires, 53, 172, 173

Eton football match, 162
Etricourt, 161

Fampoux, 163, 165
Faraday, 2nd Lieut. H. V., 203
Farbus, 166
"Fatigues," moral effect of, 75–6, 80
Faulkner, 2nd Lieut. W. D., M.C., 149, 159, 181, 184, 198
Feilding, Maj.-Gen. Sir G., C.M.G., D.S.O., 21, 23, 33, 34, 41, 99, 132
Ferguson, Major R. H., 133, 136, 137, 142, 145, 146, 163, 194, 196
Fergusson, Maj.-Gen. Sir C., K.C.M.G., D.S.O. 162*n*., 165, 171, 189
Ferme Beaulieu, 179, 180
Ferme Gombert, 173, 174, 175
Fins, 161
FitzGerald, Major Lord Desmond, M.C., 52, 69
FitzGerald, Lieut. D. J. B., 143, 144, 147, 197
FitzGerald, Capt. J. S. N. M.B.E., M.C., 29, 40, 44, 69, 84, 88, 90, 95. 107, 198
FitzGerald, Capt. M. R., 97, 174, 175, 177, 196, 197
Flers, 92
Flesquières, 154, 155, 156
Foch, Marshal, 184
Fontaine-Notre-Dame, 155. 156, 158
Foster, Capt. (Coldstream Guards), 175
Fourché Farm, 142
Frégicourt, 111
French forces in action: the Somme, 92, 106; Ypres (1917), 131, 133, 140, 142, 151, 152; 1918 offensive, 184
Fricourt, 89

Gas, first use of, at Ypres, 64
Gauche Wood, 160
George V., H. M. King, 90, 98, 129
Germany, entry into, 189
Gibson, Lieut. T. C., O.B.E., 147, 149, 196, 197
Ginchy, 91, 92–7, 104, 122, 161
Glennon, Sgt., 88, 105
Gloucestershire Regt., 177
Godman, Colonel (Scots Guards), 95, 119
Gomiecourt, 89
Gonnelieu, 154, 160
Gordon, Lieut.-Col. A. F. L., D.S.O., M.C., 180, 184, 194, 197, 198
Gordon Highlanders, 163; advice on pipers' kilts sought from, 145
Gore-Langton, Capt. M. V., M.C., 199
Gort, Lieut.-Col. Viscount, V.C., 21
Gouzeaucourt, 160, 161
Gouzeaucourt Wood, 161
Graincourt, 156, 160
Grayson, Lieut. R. H. S., 28, 196
Green, 2nd Lieutenant (Coldstream Guards), 50, 51
Greer, Lieut.-Col. E. B. M.C., 49, 56, 73, 78, 89, 90, 91, 111, 119, 132, 133, 136, 137*n*., 139, 140, 143, 194, 195, 196, 198
Greer, Lieut. F. St. L., M.C., 87, 94, 99, 115, 195, 198

Grenadier Guards:
  1st Battalion:
    (1915) Laventie, 63
    Drums of, 181
  2nd Battalion:
    (1916) Ypres, 78, 79, 80; the Somme: Ginchy, Lesbœufs, 95, 98
    (1917) the Somme: Sailly-Saillisel, 106, 108; Yser Canal and the Broembeek, 142
  3rd Battalion:
    (1915) Loos, the Hohenzollern, Laventie, 23, 31, 43
    (1916) the Somme: Ginchy, 93, 95, 101
    (1917) Yser Canal, 127, 138, 142; the Somme: Bourlon Wood, 156
    Boxing competitions, 81–2
  4th Battalion:
    (1915) formation, 15
    (1916) Laventie, 55; the Somme, 91
    (1918) in 4th Guards Brigade, 162*n*., 164; Arleux, 165; the Somme: March Push, 166, 167; Vieux-Berquin, 173, 174, 175, 179; the advance, 185, 188
Grimwood, C.S.M., 130
Gruyterzaele Farm, 151
Guards Brigade:
  4th Guards Brigade created, 162, 164; its stand at Vieux-Berquin, 176, 178–9; as a training corps, 181, 185
Guards Division, march through London, 192–3
Gueudecourt, 92, 98, 100
Guildford Street, 34, 35
Guillemont, 93, 97
Gunston, Major D. W., M.C., 107, 133, 136, 137, 142, 198
Gusty Trench, 104

Hague, Ian, 81
Haie Wood, 106, 107, 110
Haig, Field-Marshal Sir Douglas, G.C.B., 69, 153, 162, 178
Haking, Lieut-Gen., Sir R., G.B.E., K.C.B., 20, 21
"Hallam, Basil," 91
Halpin, Sgt., 88
Hamel, 184
Hamelincourt, 166
Hammond, 2nd Lieut. C. E., M.C., 201
Hanbury, Capt. C. E. R., 111, 114, 133, 142, 152, 195
Hannay, Capt. R., 40, 133, 196
Hanoverian Fusiliers, 73rd, 138
"Happy" Battalions, the mystery of, 60, 153, 193
Happy Valley, 91
Haquin, 22
Harmignies–Mons road, 192
Harmsworth, Capt., Hon. H. A. V. St. G., M.C., 153, 159, 195, 196, 198, 201
Harradine, C.S.M., D.C.M., 88, 213
Harrison, 2nd Lieut. S. S., M.C., 201
Hartmannsweillerkopf operations, lecture on, 53
Harvey, Capt. E. M., M.C., 201
Harvey, Capt. F. M., M.C. (R.A.M.C.), 99, 108
Havre, Le, 19
Hazebrouck, 53, 89, 171, 176, 179, 180

Heard, Lieut. R. H. W., M.C., 99, 175, 195, 196, 202
Hébuterne, 89
Hegarty, Capt. D. J., M.C., 203
Hell Fire Corner, 79, 80
Hely-Hutchinson, Capt. M. R., M.C., 92, 108, 133, 154, 198
Herzeele, 128, 149, 150
Hey Wood, 137
Higgins, Pte., 36
Hilley, Pte., 148
Hindenburg Line, the: attacked and broken, 154, 155
Hine, 2nd Lieut, G. V. B., 29, 30, 195
Hohenzollern Redoubt, the, 29 sqq.
Hondeghem, 180, 181
Honnecourt, 110
Honsfeld, 189
Hooge, 81, 82
Hopley, Capt, F. J. (Grenadier Guards), 94
Hordern, Lieut. H. R., 68, 88, 90, 196
Hornoy, 100
Horton, Pte., 34
Houbingham, 145
Houlle Camp, 152, 154
Household Battalion disbanded 166
Houthulst Forest, 143, 144, 145, 150
Hubbard, Capt. G. N., 22, 35, 37, 40, 42, 196
Hudson-Kinahan, Lieut. D. D., 32, 40, 75, 195
Hunter Street, 129, 131
Hutchinson, 2nd Lieut. A. E., M.C., 203
Hyne, Lieut. C. G. H. C., 88, 97, 195, 196

Innes, Lieut. A. G. W., M.C., 199
International Corner, 128
Irish Guards:
  1st Battalion:
    (1914) The Salient and first Battle of Ypres, 71
    (1915) meet 2nd Battalion at St. Pierre, 20; Laventie, 47, 53
    (1916) Merville, 53, 62; Ginchy, 94; Lesbœufs, 98; meet 2nd Battalion at Aumont, 100; Lesbœufs, Sailly-Saillisel, Combles, 106, 109
    (1917) the Somme: Sailly-Saillisel, 120; Gouzeaucourt, Gonnelieu, 160
  2nd Battalion:
    a "happy" Battalion, 60, 153, 193
    Commanding Officers of, 194
    (1915) formation, 15–18; leave England, 19; Havre, 19; Acquin, 19, 21; meet 1st Battalion at St. Pierre, 20; Linghem, Haquin, 22; Le Rutoire, 22–3; Loos, Chalk-Pit Wood, 23–8; Verquigneul, 28; Vermelles, the Hohenzollern, 29–38, 40; Bourecq, 38–41; La Gorgue, 41, 43–44; Laventie, 41–3; Merville, 44; Laventie, 44–7, 48–53; La Gorgue, Merville, 47–8, 53–5
    (1916) Laventie, 55–62, 63–4, 66–8; La Gorgue, 62, 68; Merville, 64–6; Wormhoudt, Poperinghe, 68, 71; Calais, 69–71; Ypres Salient, 71–6, 77–82; Poperinghe, 76; Brandhoek, 78; Proven, Bollezeele, 81–2, 89; Hooge, 82–3; Vlamertinghe, 83–4; Elverdinghe, the Yser Canal, 84–8; Camp P,

88–9; the Somme: Lucheux, Mailly-Maillet, Couin, 90–1; Méricourt l'Abbé, 98–9; Ginchy, 91–2, 93–7; Carnoy, 97; Lesbœufs, 98–9; Trônes Wood, Carnoy, Méricourt-en-Vimeux, 99–100; meet 1st Battalion at Aumont, 100; Méaulte, Trônes Wood, 101; Lesbœufs, Sailly-Saillisel, Combles, Haie Wood, 104–7, 107–10; Bronfay, 107
    (1917) the Somme: Corbie, Maurepas, 111; Rancourt, 111–14, 115–18; Morval, Ville, Priez Farm, Billon, 114–15; St. Pierre Vaast Wood, 119–21; railway and road work, 121–3; Curlu, Méricourt l'Abbé, 123–6; Ypres Salient: Elverdinghe, the Yser Canal, 127–8, 129–36; Herzeele, 128–9; third Battle of Ypres, Boesinghe, 133–40; the Steenbeek, 142–3; Porchester Camp, Paddington Camp, Abingley Camp, 142–5; the Broembeek, Houthulst Forest, 145–9, 150-2; Dulwich Camp, Putney Camp, Herzeele, Houlle Camp, 149–50, 152–4; the Somme: Cambrai offensive, Bourlon Wood, 155–9; Gouzeaucourt, 160–1; Simencourt, 161–2
    (1918) Arras and the Scarpe, 163–4; transferred to 4th Guards Brigade, 164–5; Bray, 165; Arleux, 165; Villers-Brulin, Béthonsart, 166; March Push: Hamelincourt, Moyenneville, Ayette, 166–70; Chelers, 170, 171; Vieux-Berquin, 171–8; Bois d'Aval, Ferme Beaulieu, 179–80; Hondeghem, 180–1; Barly, Bavincourt, 181–4; Criel Plage, 184–6; after the Armistice: Cambrai, Maubeuge, Charleroi, 188–9; the journey to Cologne, 189–90
    (1919) the march through London, 192–3

James, Lieut. G. L. B., 40, 130, 195

Kane, Lieut. J. J., 142, 145, 196
Keenan, Capt. J. B., 41, 69, 95, 131, 171, 196
Kent, 2nd Lieut. G. R., 171, 181
Kerry, Lieut.-Col. the Earl of, M.V.O., D.S.O., 18
King Edward's Horse, 120
King, Pte., 113–14
King's Own Yorkshire Light Infantry, 29, 90; 12th, 179
Kingston, Pte., 34
Kipling, Lieut. J., 7–8, 24, 28, 195, 197
Kitchener, Field-Marshal Earl, K.G., 18
Knapp, Capt. Rev. Father S. S., D.S.O. M.C., 20, 52, 69, 114–15, 132, 138, 139, 143, 195
Koekuit, 151

La Bassée, fighting round, 171
La Couronne, 172, 176
La Flinque Farm, 48, 52
La Justice, 156, 160
Labour Battalions: the "Broody Hens," 106; the Montauban camp, 121
Lancashire Farm, 86
Lancers, 21st, 120
Lane-Fox, Capt. Rev. Father P. J., 69
Laventie, 38, 41 sqq., 44 sqq., 55, 63, 64, 74
Laventie East post, 55

Law, Capt. H. F. D'A. S., M.C., 180, 196, 198
Lawson, Capt. J. I., M.C. (R.A.M.C), 202
Le Cornet Perdu, 173, 175
Lees, Capt. D., D.S.O., M.C. (R.A.M.C.), 139, 144
Leicestershire Regt., 32, 160
L'Epinette Farm, 173
Le Rutoire Farm, 22
Lesbœufs, 100, 122, 161; attack and capture of, 92, 93, 96, 98, 161
Lesves, 189
Le Transloy, 98, 122, 161
Leuze Wood, 92
Levy, Capt. M. B., M.C., 149, 162, 173, 177, 195, 198
Lille, 34
Lillers, 38
Linghem, 21
Little Willie trench, 34–5
Lloyd, Maj-Gen. Sir Francis, K.C.B., D.S.O., 18, 53
Lofting, 2nd Lieut, H. J., 130, 196
London Regt., 3rd, 99
Lone Tree, Loos, 22
Long-Innes, Major P. S., M.C., 170, 196, 198
Loos: preparations for, 21, 22; the battle, 22–8
Lucas, Sgt., 105
Lucheux, 89
Lumbres, 19, 21
Lynch-Blosse, 2nd Lieut. F. C. L., 154, 159, 196
Lys, river, German offensive and defeat on, 178
Lysaght, Lieut. J. L., 90, 94, 144, 147, 153, 198
Lyttelton, Capt. O. (Grenadier Guards), 96

McCalmont, Lieut.-Col. R. C. A., D.S.O., 52
McCarthy, Lance-Sgt. G., 34
Macfarlane, Sgt. R., 153, 216
MacGuinn, Sgt., 73
M'Guinness, Sgt., 147
Mackenzie, Lieut. (Scots Guards), 95
McNally, Sgt., 139
McNeill, Capt. R., 76, 84, 88
Madden, Lieut.-Col. G. H. C., 18, 196
Maher, Lieut. J. C., 162, 177, 195
Mailly-Maillet, 90
Maltz Horn Camp, 110
Manning, Lieut. B. O. D., 143, 146, 149, 197
Mansell Camp, 101
March Push, the, 163, 166–70, 177–8
Marchienne, 188
Marcoing, 155
Marguerite Farm, 131
Maricourt, 89, 108
Marne river: second battle (1918), 184
Marshall, Lieut. J. N., V.C., M.C., 203, 204
Martinpuich, 92
Mathew, 2nd Lieut. T., M.C., 162, 180, 198, 202
Maubeuge: advance on, 188
Maurepas, 111, 113
Maxse, Gen. Sir Ivor, K.C.B., D.S.O., 126
Méaulte, 101
Menin road, the, 74, 79, 82
Méricourt-en-Vimeux, 99–100, 101
Méricourt l'Abbé, 91, 123–6
Merville, 44, 53, 64–6, 171–2, 173
Messines, 126, 153

Middlesex Regt., 21st, 167
Milligan, Sgt., D.C.M., 140, 144, 213
Mining operations: Laventie, 66, 67
Monash, Lieut.-Gen. Sir J., K.C.B., 184
Mondicourt, 181
Monmouthshire Regt., 32
Montauban, 89, 121
Montgomery, Lieut. H., 29, 40, 41, 89, 92, 97, 122, 195
Moodie, Lieut. D. A. B., M.C., 201
Moore, Capt. C. J. O'H., M.C., 40, 53, 62, 70, 171, 175, 177, 179, 197, 198, 202
Morval, 92, 98, 106, 111, 114, 122
Mory, 167, 185
Moyenneville, 167, 170, 185
Moyney, Sgt. J., V.C., 148–9, 213
Murphy, Drill-Sgt., 105, 145
Murphy, Lieut. L. D., M.C., 149, 198, 204
Mylne, Lieut. E. L., M.C., 88, 94, 95, 96, 97, 195, 198

Namur Crossing, 151
Neall, Pte., M.M. (D.C.L.I.), 180
Neuf Berquin, 68, 172
Ney Copse, 146–7, 148
Ney Wood, 146, 151
Nieppe, Forest of, 171–2, 174, 176, 177, 178, 179
Nile Trench, 85, 88
Nœux-les-Mines, 22
Nolan, Lance-Sgt., 104, 105
Norfolk Regt., 28
North Moated Grange Street, 48
Northumberland Avenue, 164
Noyelles, 22, 38, 155
Nugent, Major T. E. G., M.C., 34, 35, 40, 43, 69, 159, 181, 196, 198, 202
Nutting, Capt. A. R. S., M.C., 76, 88, 91, 130, 138, 184, 196, 198, 200

O'Brien, 2nd Lieut. C. S., M.C., 202
O'Brien, Capt. Hon. H. B., M.C., 162, 167, 197, 198, 202
O'Connor, Lieut. A. E., 149, 159
O'Hagan, Sgt., 86
Ogilvy, Capt. Hon. B. A. A., M.C., 204
Ostreville, 154
Ouffey, 189
Ovillers-la-Boisselle, 89
Oxford and Bucks Light Infantry, 81

Paddington Camp, 144
Paget, Capt. A. W. L., M.C., 132, 196, 198, 203
Paget, Capt. R. S. G., 130, 196
Pakenham-Law, 2nd Lieut. T., 24, 28, 195
Paradis, 172
Paris, July 14th celebrations in, 88, 184
Park, Lieut. R. H. M., M.C., 200
Parsons, Lieut. D. C., 40, 97, 195, 196
Pawlett, Lieut.-Col. (Canadian Army), 153
Péronne, 119
Petit Han, 189
Petit Houvain, 89
Picantin post, 55
Pierrots, the Coldstream, 149

Pioneer Barracks, Ehrenfeld, 189
Pipers, Irish Guards, 123, 145, 149, 180
Plateau, 107
Platt, Capt. (Coldstream Guards), 79
Plumer, General Sir H., G.C.B., 180
Ponsonby, Maj.-Gen., C.B., 88, 137, 147, 148
Pont du Hem, 48, 51, 52, 66, 67
Pont Rondin, 172, 173
Pont Rucken, 189
Poperinghe, 68, 69, 71, 76
Porchester Camp, 142–3
Portuguese troops, 154, 171
Power, Cpl., 147
Pradelles, 171
Presles, 189
Priez Farm, 115
Prison billets: Arras, 163; Ypres, 77
Proven, 81, 142, 149, 150
Puits 14 bis, Loos, 23, 24, 25, 30
Purcell, Lieut. C. F., 97, 195
Putney Camp, 149
Pym, Capt. A. R., 34, 35, 40, 44, 78
Pym, Lieut. F. L. M., 78, 79, 84, 85, 86, 195, 197

Quadrilateral, the, 94
Quarry, the, 109
Quinn, Lance-Cpl., D.C.M., 48, 213

Radford, Capt. ("Basil Hallam"), 91
Railway Wood, 79, 80
Rancourt, 111 sqq.
Rankin, Capt. R., 29, 40, 196
Rawlinson, General Sir H., K.C.M.G., 99, 185
Rea, Lieut. W. G., 142, 159
Red House, Laventie, 46, 47, 55, 61, 63, 64, 74
Redmond, John, M.P., 43
Redmond, Capt. W. A., D.S.O., 143, 146, 197, 200
Reford, Capt. R. B. S., M.C., 76, 159, 196, 198
Reid, Sgt., 88
Reid, Lieut.-Col. P. L., O.B.E., 78, 82, 91, 108, 111, 112, 194, 196, 197
Ribecourt, 155, 160
Riencourt, 154
Ritchie, Lieut. (R.E.), 31
Rocke, Lieut.-Col. C, E. A. S., D.S.O., 88, 90, 93, 95, 96, 97, 196, 197
Rocquigny, 121, 122
Roddy, Sgt., 114
Rœux, 163
Ross, Capt. H. (Scots Guards), 123
Rouge Croix, 42
Rowan-Hamilton, Lieut., A. J., 29, 35, 37, 195
Royal Canadian Regt., 83
Royal Engineers, 42, 55, 69, 78, 131
Royal Irish Constabulary (late) in Irish Guards, 43
Royal Welsh Fusiliers, 48
Rue du Bacquerot, 48, 67
Rue Tilleloy, 48
Rugby Road, 67
"Russian saps," 67

Sailly-Labourse, 22, 28
Sailly-Saillisel, 106, 115, 118, 120

St. Julien, 54, 148
St. Léger, 166, 185
St. Patrick's Day, 70, 166
St. Pierre Vaast Wood, 111, 113, 115, 118, 120, 121
St. Pol, 89, 153, 166
St. Pol Fervent, 166
St. Sylvestre, 68
Sanctuary Wood, 83
Sassoon, Capt. R. E., M.C., 25, 28, 136, 137, 142, 144, 145, 153, 156, 159, 161, 196, 198, 200
Savage, Pte., 109
Scarpe river, posts on, 163, 165
Scots Guards,
    1st Batt.: Loos, 23, 24; Ypres, 88; the Somme, 93, 95, 101; Rancourt, 119, 120; Ypres, Boesinghe, the Broembeek, 132, 136–7, 138, 147, 150, 152; Bourlon Wood, 156, 160
    2nd Batt., Laventie, 44; the Broembeek, 150; Bourlon Wood, 156
Sensée river valley, 166, 167
Sentier Farm, 142
Sergison-Brooke, Brig.-Gen., C.M.G., D.S.O., 164
Settrington, Lieut. Lord, 177, 195, 197
Shaftesbury Avenue, 164
Sherwood Foresters, 33
Signal Farm, 142
Simencourt, 161, 162
Skipton Road, Ypres, 84
Smith, Cpl., 82
Smith, Lieut. F. S. L., M.C., 177, 197, 198, 202
Somme, The:
    (1916) the battle, 89 sqq.
    (1917) 154 sqq.
    (1918) March Push and recovery on, 166–70, 180–1, 184
South African Infantry Regt.,1st, 161
South Moated Grange, 41
"Spanish fever," outbreak of, 181
Spectrum Trench, 104
Stavelot, 189
Steenbeck river, 132, 142, 143, 145
Steenvoorde, 83
Stevens, Capt. W. B., 28, 196
Synge, Lieut. A. F., 153, 159, 195
Synge, Capt. F. P. H., M.C., 36, 37, 41, 87, 133, 139, 195, 196, 198

Tallents, Major T. F., M.C., 35, 36, 37, 196, 198
Tanks, the first, 91
Taped assembly lines, 150–1
Tatinghem, 20
Taylor, Miss Laurette, 53
Tennant, Lieut. M. (Scots Guards), 94, 96
Tilleloy road, 48
Timoney, Pte., 184
Tindall, 2nd Lieut. A. A., 177, 197
Tisdall, Lieut. C. R., M.C., 199
Tomkins, 2nd Lieut. A. G., 92, 97, 195
Towland, Pte., 88
Trench: drainage system (1915), 49–50
Trescault, 155, 156
Trônes Wood,97, 98, 99, 101, 104, 107, 121, 161
Troy, Pte., 216

Vaudricourt, 32
Vaughan, 2nd Lieut. K. C., 90, 92, 97, 195
Vaughan-Morgan, Lieut. G. E. C., 139, 196
Verdun, 74, 77
Vermelles, 22, 24, 25, 29, 37
Vernon, Capt. C. A. J., M.C., 204
Verquigneul, 28
Verte Rue, 175, 176
Vesey, Lieut.-Col. Hon, T. E., 18, 24, 28, 196, 198
Vierhoek, 172, 173
Vieux-Berquin, 68, 171–7, 184
Vieux Moulin, 173
Vieux Reng, 188
Ville-sous-Corbie, 114, 115
Villers-au-Bois, 165
Villers-Bretonneux, 184
Villers-Brulin, 166
Villers-Cotterêts, 89, 184
Vimy Ridge, 164
Vlamertinghe, 76, 83, 84

Walkrantz trench, 129
Walshe, Pte., 85
Walters, Lieut. G. Y. L., 97
Wanquetin, 162
Ward, Major H. F., 143, 147
Warley, 15, 60
Watson, Capt. B. B., O.B.E., 40, 197
Welsh Guards, 48, 142, 152, 159, 164
Welsh Regt., 9th, 68
West Face trench, 34, 35, 36
West Lane trench, 81
West Riding Regt., 158

West Yorkshire Regt., 166
Whittaker, Lieut. (Brigade Bombing Officer), 109
Wieltje, 78
Wieltje trench, 78
Willerval–Bailleul sector, 165
Wilson, C.S.M. J. B. (13th East Yorks), 109
Wilson, 2nd Lieut. T. B., 130, 195
Winchester Farm, 49
Winchester House, 51, 66
Winchester Road (Street), 41, 49, 61
Wismes, 20
Wisques, 20
Witts, Capt. F. H., D.S.O., M.C., 40, 91, 196, 197, 198
Woodhouse, Major P. R., D.S.O., M.C. (R.A.M.C.), 199
Wordley, Lieut. S. S., 159, 196
Wormhoudt, 68, 81
Würtembergers, raid by the, 146, 148, 152
Wynter, Lieut. C. D., 23, 28

Yorkshire Regt., 167
Young, Major (R.A.), 50
Young, Major G. E. S., 107, 109, 196
Ypres
  (1914) First Battle, 41, 64
  (1916) 71–3, 74 *sqq.*, 83, 84–8
  (1917) 126–7, 128–9, 130 *sqq.*
Yser Canal, fighting on, 84, 87, 88, 127, 130, 132, 133 *sqq.*

Zigomala, Lieut. J. C. M.B.E., 91, 195, 196
Zouave Wood, 83

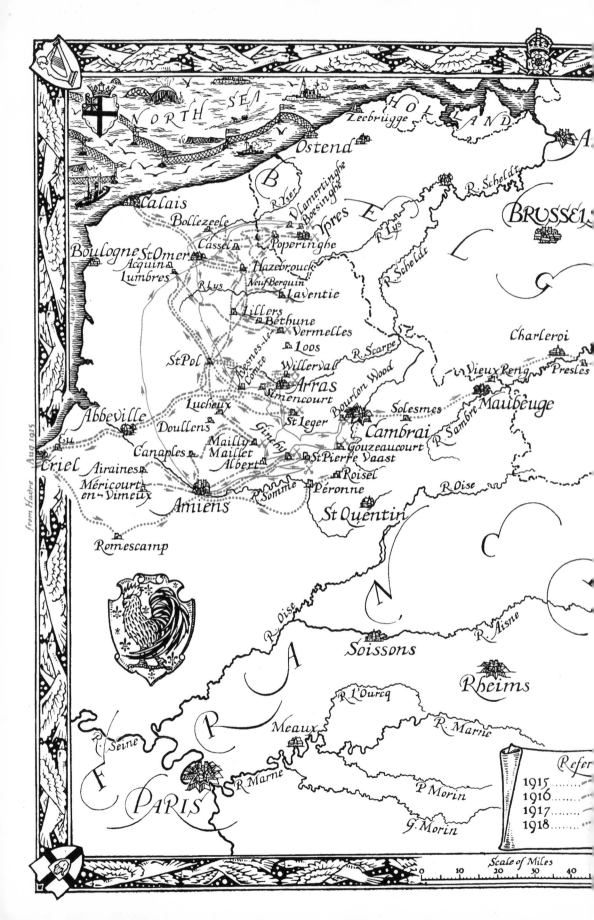

NORTH SEA

HOLLAND

Zeebrügge

Ostend

BRUSSELS

Calais

Bollezeele

Ypres

Poperinghe

R. Yser

Vlamertinghe
Boesinghe

R. Lys

R. Scheldt

Boulogne

St Omer

Cassel

Hazebrouck

Neuf Berquin

Laventie

Acquin
Lumbres

R. Lys

R. Scheldt

Charleroi

Lillers

Béthune

Vermelles

Loos

R. Scarpe

Vieux Reng

Presles

St Pol

Willerval

Arras

Simencourt

Bourlon Wood

Solesmes

Maubeuge

Abbeville

Lucheux

Doullens

St Leger

Cambrai

R. Sambre

Eu

Canaples

Mailly
Maillet

Ginchy

Gouzeaucourt

Criel

Airaines

Albert

St Pierre Vaast

Roisel

Méricourt
en-Vimeux

R. Somme

Péronne

R. Oise

Amiens

St Quentin

Romescamp

R. Oise

R. Aisne

Soissons

Rheims

R. l'Ourcq

Meaux

R. Marne

R. Seine

R. Marne

P. Morin

PARIS

G. Morin

Refer

1915 ....
1916 ....
1917 ....
1918 ....

Kesnes-le-Comte

from Hadre   Aug 1915

Scale of Miles

0   10   20   30   40